Productivity Strategies

Bruce McAfee is an assistant professor of Management at Old Dominion University, Norfolk, Virginia, and holds a Ph.D. in Organizational/Industrial Psychology from Wayne State University. An accomplished author, he currently teaches Organizational Behavior and Personnel Management.

William Poffenberger, Ph.D., is a Management and Marketing consultant in Detroit, a former Associate Professor of Marketing and Psychology, and currently an Adjunct Professor of Management at Wayne State University and Central Michigan University. He teaches Organizational Behavior and Industrial Psychology, and he specializes in statistics and applied research as a management function. His consulting practice currently concentrates on the integration of microcomputer technology into the health care industry and related organizational development.

Productivity Strategies

Enhancing Employee Job Performance

R. BRUCE McAFEE
WILLIAM POFFENBERGER

A SPECTRUM BOOK

PRENTICE-HALL, INC., Englewood Cliffs, New Jersey 07632

Library of Congress Cataloging in Publication Data

McAfee, R. Bruce.
   Productivity strategies.

  "A Spectrum Book."
  Includes bibliographies and index.
  1. Personnel management. 2. Labor productivity.
I. Poffenberger, William. II. Title.
HF5549.M3395   658.3'14   81-17701
                          AACR2

ISBN 0-13-725093-2

ISBN 0-13-725085-1 {PBK.}

Editorial/production supervision and interior design
  by Louise M. Marcewicz
Cover design by Peggy Brier
Manufacturing buyer: Barbara A. Frick

10 9 8 7 6 5 4 3 2 1

Prentice-Hall International, Inc., *London*
Prentice-Hall of Australia Pty. Limited, *Sydney*
Prentice-Hall of Canada, Ltd., *Toronto*
Prentice-Hall of India Private Limited, *New Delhi*
Prentice-Hall of Japan, Inc., *Tokyo*
Prentice-Hall of Southeast Asia Pte. Ltd., *Singapore*
Whitehall Books Limited, *Wellington, New Zealand*

Contents

Productivity
Strategies

1

Introduction
and Orientation

INTRODUCTION

This book focuses on an issue of critical importance to every manager: improving employee productivity. This issue is critical because unlike most other supervisory responsibilities, this one cannot be ignored, swept under the rug, or delayed until next week. There are two reasons for this: First, managers are typically assigned the responsibility for maintaining a highly productive work force and are evaluated in terms of how successfully they accomplish this objective. Second, every action a manager takes affects the productivity of subordinates even though the manager may not have intended it or be aware of it. Every time a supervisor gives instructions, provides the employee with feedback on job performance, or asks the employee questions, it affects the employee's job performance in some way. Even saying or not saying "Good morning" to employees may affect productivity in some large or small way. In general, every time a supervisor interacts with an employee, that employee's performance is affected. One could argue that even noninteraction with employees affects job-related behavior. Imagine what would happen to employee productivity if a typical supervisor went into the office for several days in a row, shut the door, and never looked out to see what any of the employees were doing.

Productivity is Not a Simple Issue

With the number of computer-oriented people in the world these days the terms *input* and *output* are fairly familiar to nearly everyone. Output is what you get out of a system, a task, or an employee. Input consists of those things you need to put into the system, task, or employee before the output will occur.

The productivity of employees is a question of output. Recent publications frequently describe employee productivity in terms of both *efficiency* and *effectiveness*. Both terms are approaches to judging the level of output of an employee.

When we use the term "efficiency" we are judging the output of an employee against the inputs necessary to obtain that output. The term "effectiveness" refers to the obtained output compared to potential output. Both ways of looking at productivity have strengths and weaknesses. Managers can select whichever definition they prefer, or they may use both. Regardless of which definition is selected, if we intend to increase the productivity of our employees, we need some way to determine whether an increase in the initial levels of productivity has occurred. Without a way to determine this, we can never know if the strategies we brought to bear on the problem were or were not effective.

Measuring Changes

Anytime you want to know if productivity has improved you must evaluate the level of productivity *before* using a strategy you hope will work, and then you must evaluate once again *after* the strategy has been implemented. (How long after is another issue.)

You must also use the same set of inputs for estimating efficiency and the same potential level of output for estimating effectiveness in the "before" and the "after" evaluations. If you do this, changes in employee productivity may be evaluated with relative ease. Any changes you make in using the strategy may then be interpreted. You must remember, however, that whatever you find out about changes in the productivity of your employees is inescapably tied to the particular sets of inputs and estimates of potential output with which you began. If you alter your definitions and then find a positive effect, you will not know whether it is the altered definition of productivity or the strategy you used which produced the effect you wanted.

Improving Productivity

Before proceeding to a discussion of the contingency approach to improving employee productivity, let us briefly look at the strategies currently available for solving productivity problems. These form an integral part of the contingency appoach.

Over the years, theorists have observed that employee productivity, regardless of whether it is defined in terms of efficiency or effectiveness, is a function of both the employee's ability and motivation to perform. Mathematically, ability times motivation equals job performance.

Ability × Motivation = Job Performance

Ability refers to the employee's prior training, experience, and education, whereas motivation is typically thought of as an employee's desire to perform a job well. Our focus in this book is on the motivational component of the formula for it is here that the most difficult challenges facing a manager are found. Managers cannot change an employee's prior job experience, education, or training. They can, however, increase (or decrease) an employee's motivation quite quickly.

One of the most perplexing aspects of improving employee motivation is that there appear to be literally hundreds of actions available to managers to accomplish this task. With so many options available, it is not surprising that many managers simply do not know where to begin. We do not deny that there are many alternatives available for improving employee motivation. For practical purposes, however, all of them fall into one or more of the following seven basic strategies. We will describe each of these strategies briefly now. Chapters Two through Eight discuss these strategies comprehensively. One chapter is allocated to each strategy.

DESCRIPTION
OF THE STRATEGIES

Using Positive Reinforcement
and Shaping

One way to improve an employee's job performance is to reward desired behavior but not undesired behavior. When, how, and how frequently an employee should be rewarded is an integral part of this approach.

Using Effective Discipline and Punishment

This approach to improving employee productivity stresses the importance of having and utilizing effective disciplinary procedures. How and when to discipline an employee so as to actually improve job performance while avoiding undesirable side-effects is the goal of this approach.

Treating People Fairly

This strategy for improving employee productivity recommends that managers treat their employees fairly or convince employees they are in fact receiving fair treatment. What is meant by treating people fairly and how employees determine if they are being treated fairly are important components of this strategy.

Satisfying Employee Needs

One of the oldest and best known productivity enhancing strategies is to determine what an employee's needs are and to make need-satisfiers available. This approach requires an understanding of basic human needs and the ways people differ in the strength of their needs.

Setting Work - Related Goals

This approach argues that setting difficult and measurable goals for employees or allowing employees to set goals for themselves can result in higher employee productivity.

Restructuring Jobs

This approach recommends that jobs be designed or structured in such a way that they provide employees with feelings of accomplishment, achievement, and responsibility.

Basing Rewards on Job Performance

A supervisor who uses this approach rewards employees based on the quality and quantity of their work. The higher the subordinate's productivity, the greater the reward. Managers using this approach realize that seniority and education *per se* are not proper criteria upon which to base rewards.

THE CONTINGENCY APPROACH TO IMPROVING EMPLOYEE PRODUCTIVITY

The contingency approach consists of a set of assumptions regarding employee behavior, a set of strategies for increasing productivity, and a recommended framework or set of steps a manager can follow when attempting to improve employee productivity. Each will now be discussed.

Basic Principles

There are three basic assumptions or principles which are an integral part of the contingency approach. These are:

1. No single approach for increasing employee productivity will be effective under all conditions.
2. Most approaches currently available to improve employee productivity will be effective under certain conditions.
3. Under certain conditions two or more approaches to improving employee productivity will be just as effective.

Let us consider each of these briefly.

No Single Approach Is Always Effective.   For years managers have been attempting to find some basic and powerful strategy (we will call this "Strategy X") that will solve all of their employee problems once and for all. They search for a strategy that will improve every employee's job performance not only now, but forever. Unhappily there never has been such a strategy and we feel quite confident in stating that there never will be!

Certainly if there was such a management strategy you would have heard about it by now. No one could possibly keep such a discovery a secret-- the temptation for the certain Nobel prize alone would be too much. The reason there never will be such a strategy for management stems from employee differences in terms of values, beliefs, attitudes, basic personality, and probably some other things we missed. Since no two people are identical, the strategy which improves one employee's job productivity may or may not improve another's. Also, what worked at one time for a particular employee may not work at another time. For the sake of argument, however, let us assume that someone did find an employee productivity strategy ("Strategy X") which always worked. What would happen? Eventually, everyone would know that Strategy X was effective in improving employee productivity. However, undoubtedly when some employees realized this, they would conclude that Strategy X was being used to manipulate them. They would then decide, in their infinite perversity, to rebel against the use of Strategy X by not letting it affect them or their productivity. All experienced managers and supervisors know only too well that this can happen. The result? Strategy X would no longer be an effective tool for improving employee productivity.

The implication of the above scenario is that instead of searching for Strategy X, supervisors and managers would be wise to focus on becoming familiar with the strategies for improving employee productivity which were just described and to learn when each is appropriate.

Many Approaches Are Effective. Over the years many books and articles have appeared which have suggested that if managers want to improve the productivity of their employees they need only use the particular approach advocated in these books or articles. Each of these typically begins with an analysis of why previous approaches have been unsuccessful and why the new approach will work effectively. Then, a few months later, yet another approach appears which in turn explains why the previous approach did not work and why the newer one will. This cycle repeats itself year after year. Management by objectives, flexitime, rewards based on performance, wage incentives, job enrichment, and discipline, to name a few, have all been recommended as cure-alls at one time or another only to have been criticized at a later date.

Is one to conclude that all of these approaches should be discarded because they are ineffective? Certainly not. One could surmise that each of these approaches will probably be successful under certain conditions. The critical questions then are not whether a given strategy will be effective, but under what conditions it will be successful and how successful it will be.

Some Approaches Work Equally Well. The contingency approach suggests that under certain conditions two or more approaches to increasing employee productivity will be equally effective. The popular management literature on employee productivity has led managers to believe (and continues to do so) that, given a specific situation, there is only one approach which will be successful in improving employee job performance. Unfortunately many managers have spent untold hours needlessly searching for the "one best way" to manage. We believe that there is often no one best way to improve employee productivity. In fact, under certain conditions, a number of strategies may be equally effective. The moral of the story is this: A manager should not search for the sharpest needle in the haystack when any needle will do perfectly well.

SPECIFIC STEPS IN THE CONTINGENCY APPROACH

Now that three major principles regarding employees and the strategies for improving their productivity have been described, let us look at the specific steps the contingency approach recommends a manager follow when attempting to solve an employee productivity problem. To do so we have organized our discussion around a "Strategy Guide," or flow chart (Figure 1-1). We have found over the years that such flow charts are often very helpful to supervisors because they allow them to visualize the material being discussed. They also encourage logical, structured thinking about problems.

In studying this and other flow charts presented throughout the book, the reader is reminded that these charts are akin to a roadmap. They suggest alternative routes to follow and they pinpoint critical decisions which must be made. Maps and flow charts, however, should not be confused in your thinking with the actual territory one is traversing. Neither maps nor flow charts are totally accurate depictions of reality. Hence, both should be considered as general guides to action, not as sets of mechanical steps to follow regardless of circumstances. Keep in mind that no driver would steer his car around a detour sign and attempt to drive across a partially completed bridge just because the map showed that this was the road to take across the Mississippi River.

Actual Behavior
Versus Desired Behavior

Desired/Actual. The Contingency Approach begins with the assumption that an employee's actual job behavior does not match (is

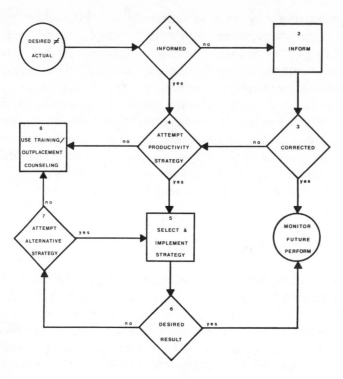

Figure 1-1. The Contingency Approach: Strategy Guide

not equal to) the behavior desired by the manager. In order for any manager to legitimately claim that an employee's behavior is undesirable, it is necessary to specify what the desired behavior is or would be. A complaint frequently encountered is that the employee "isn't doing the job properly." Such a general statement is not very enlightening to either the employee or to other managers who might be involved in the problem unless there is a definition of what is meant by "properly." To say the employee is "not working fast enough" is somewhat better, but not much. To make the statement ("not fast enough") specific enough to be useful, the manager must specify how fast is "fast enough."

> A requirement is "specific enough" when the manager and others (including the employee) can tell whether or not the requirement has been met.

In order to determine what an employee is actually doing on the job, a manager must be able to recognize, conceptualize, or identify the behavior of people within an organization. A football coach, for example, must be able to identify the actions a quarterback is taking on the field. He must be able to recognize when the quarterback is passing the ball, when he is handing the ball off to the fullback, and when he is fumbling the ball. While this step sounds incredibly simple, it frequently is not.

Want a demonstration? Assume that the coach is a manager, the quarterback is one of the manager's subordinates, and for "passing the ball" read "writing a report," for "handing the ball off" read "delegating," and for "fumbling" read any undesirable behavior you have recently witnessed.

Often, for either a manager or a football coach, it requires considerable knowledge about the activity being observed before recognition of relevant behaviors becomes accurate. For example, if you knew nothing about football would you know when the quarterback fumbled the ball? Certainly not! You would not know what the word "fumble" meant. (You would not even know the meanings of the words "quarterback" or "football.")

Keeping Employees Informed

Step 1   Informed?   One of the easiest interventions the manager can perform whenever an employee's actual behavior is not the same as the desired behavior is to *inform the employee* of the performance deficit and to specify the desired behavior. This strategy costs next to nothing and can have very rapid results.

Far more frequently than one might expect employees are not performing the behaviors desired by managers simply because they do not know either what the desired behavior is or that a discrepancy exists between what they are doing and what is wanted. Therefore, the manager is always wise to check immediately to see whether or not the employees are informed about the discrepancy between the actual behavior and the desired behavior. However, it is clearly necessary that the manager be able to specify the desired behavior before this approach will work.

Giving Information Effectively

Steps 2 and 3   Inform ... Corrected?   If it is found that the desired behavior can be obtained by simply informing the employee of the nature of the desired behavior, then the manager need only proceed to the final step, the monitoring of future behavior. If, however, the giving of information does not produce the desired behavior, the more complicated course of action must be followed, that is, the implementation of an employee productivity strategy.

Two precautions should be observed when making a judgment about the effectiveness of giving information. First, new behaviors require some time to be acquired, and time must be allowed for the employee to integrate the new information into the previous working style. The other precaution is to make certain that information is given to the right employee. Many employees have interdependent jobs. It is entirely possible that the performance deficit observed is more a function of inappropriate work behavior of another employee whose work output is interdependent with the first employee's work. For example, frequently employees who use machinery in their work, such as lathe operators, may exhibit an apparent performance deficit because of excessive setup time caused by the work behavior of an employee on the previous shift. In such a case, the employee on the previous shift is the more appropriate target for the management intervention. Since that employee may report to another manager, this illustration also demonstrates a case in which an explicitly defined desired behavior is needed to communicate to the manager of the previous shift the need for cooperative management action.

Selecting and Implementing an Employee Productivity Strategy

Step 4 Attempt Productivity Strategy?   In this step you must decide whether to utilize one of the seven productivity strategies or to refer the problem to others by using Step 8. If the problem you are facing is one of motivation or leadership then proceed to Step 5 and select an appropriate strategy. If, however, the employee does not have sufficient capabilities to perform as you wish consider training. If personal or emotional problems seem to be interfering with productivity consider a counseling referral. If you can conceive of no way to continue working with this employee consider outplacement.

Step 5 Select & Implement Strategy.   This step requires that the manager decide which strategy should be implemented in order to improve the employee's productivity. In order to make this decision, managers must understand why employees act the way they do and know the different strategies that can be used to improve employee productivity.

A football coach needs to know why a quarterback passed the ball, why he handed the ball off to the fullback, and why the ball was fumbled. Without understanding why a subordinate took certain actions, a manager cannot determine what managerial actions should be taken in response. Chapter Nine discusses this issue more fully.

In addition to being able to identify and understand a subordinate's actions, a successful manager must also know the actions that can be taken to improve the subordinate's job performance. A teacher, for example, must know a number of different strategies for quieting a student who is boisterous in class. A coach must know different techniques a quarterback can use so as not to fumble the ball. A riding instructor will tell a student who complains of too much bouncing in the saddle that the solution is to sit back firmly in the saddle with ''heels down and toes in'' putting almost no pressure on the stirrups. This is the last thing the student rider would try independently, yet the technique works perfectly. It works because of the facts of human and horse anatomy. A few riding instructors know these anatomical facts but all riding instructors know the technique works and have a basic understanding of how it works. A football coach must know that holding a football in a certain way is likely to reduce fumbles. It is not necessary for the coach to have a full grasp of the details of human anatomy or biomechanics, as long as he has a basic understanding of why holding a football in a certain way will reduce fumbles. The basic understanding will suffice, the details may be safely left to technical specialists.

The distinction between basic understanding and precise mastery of technical details can stand some elaboration. Managers need not and should not be concerned with technical details, yet in the absence of a basic understanding of the reasons behind their actions, managers become simply robots following a set of pre-programmed steps. This is a very important distinction.

As an illustration, consider the manager of a computer systems department who is asked by the organization's purchasing agent to recommend an appropriate compiler acquisition. The manager will rightly ask what use the compiler will be put to and by whom. Suppose that the answer is that the compiler has been requested by programmers in accounting for converting object code to source code. In a simple world where the only programming languages are BASIC, COBOL, and FORTRAN, the manager will unhesitatingly respond that what is most likely wanted is a COBOL compiler. The most common programming language used in accounting is COBOL because, of the three available languages, it provides the most efficient control over accounting report formats. Here is an excellent example of what was called "basic understanding" above. This same manager probably could not distinguish between a FORTRAN and a BASIC "do-loop" and should not be expected to be able to make this distinction. This is a technical detail rarely, if ever, needed in management decision making. The manager knows that there are subordinates who can provide this information should it ever be needed.

By the same token, a car driver does not need to know every aspect of a car's functioning in order to successfully operate a car. It is helpful, though, for the driver to know enough about a car's operation to successfully operate a new or different car and to do occasional troubleshooting. At minimum, it is helpful to know where the gasoline filler cap and oil "dip" stick are located if the service station attendant cannot find them.

Chapters Two through Eight present seven different strategies a manager can utilize in order to improve employee productivity (see Figure 1-2).

By way of preview, we should mention that a similar format is followed in presenting each strategy. We begin each chapter with a description of the managerial action a leader can take to improve the employee's productivity. To provide greater clarity and practical relevance we cite examples of organizations which have taken the action. Next, we explain the logic or rationale which underlies the action, so users will know why a given action may be successful. We then provide a basic diagram of the implementation of the strategy which serves as a "roadmap" for the use of the action in practice. We discuss the action in terms of the diagram by pointing out which decisions need to be made, the information necessary for making each decision, the problems to expect, and the consequences to consider at each stage of the implementation.

Chapter Nine presents a synthesis of the preceding material and centers on a method for choosing among the strategies in actual practice.

Determining Your Success

Step 6 Desired Result?   After a manager has implemented a given strategy for improving employee job performance, the next procedure must be to determine if the strategy was successful. This step entails evaluating the employee's job performance and comparing

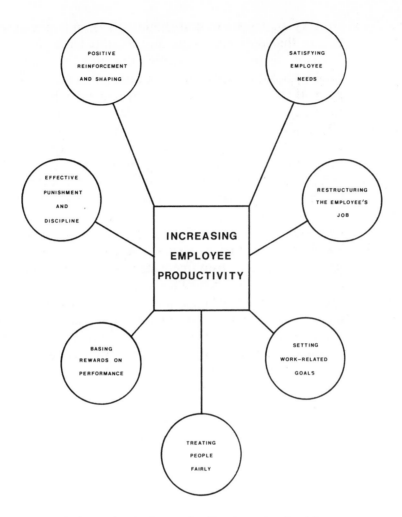

Figure 1-2. Strategies for Improving Employee Productivity

actual performance to desired performance. Since this comparison was discussed on page 7 it will not be repeated here.

Trying an Alternative Strategy

Step 7 Attempt Alternative Strategy. Managers cannot expect to be infallible in selecting a strategy for improving employee productivity. The strategy they think will most likely succeed may, in fact, fail. The fact that a manager is not infallible should in no way discourage a manager from trying to improve employee job performance. Instead, we believe it is critical for a manager to adopt a strategy analogous to that used in diagnostic medicine. Physicians realize that they must give medications based on the information available to them. They realize that this information may not be totally comprehensive, let alone accurate. Nonetheless, they give patients the medication which they believe will most likely improve the patient's health. After the patient takes the medication, the physician will evaluate how effective it has been in restoring the patient's health. If they judge a medication to be ineffective, they then prescribe a different one. This trial and error process typically continues until an effective medication is found. On some occasions, however, the physician may realize that he does not have the necessary knowledge to deal with the patient's problem. The normal procedure in such cases is to seek consultation from an appropriate specialist. On other occasions the physician may realize that the patient's illness is truly incurable, and nothing can be done.

In a sense, one role of a supervisor is that of being an employee productivity diagnostician. Managers typically have the responsibility for curing employee productivity ills. Just like physicians, supervisors typically do not have comprehensive or completely accurate information about their employees. They cannot read the minds of their subordinates to see why productivity is not at an optimum level. Nonetheless, if employee productivity is to increase, a supervisor must prescribe a strategy (medication) which is likely to be effective. Just like a physician, if the first strategy is not effective, supervisors need to select another strategy and try it, continuing the process until an effective strategy is found. A supervisor is also like a physician in that on some occasions seeking the advice of specialists is necessary and advisable. A supervisor may ask his direct superior in the organization for assistance in solving an employee productivity problem or perhaps some specialist in a staff position (for example personnel department staff). On some occasions, a manager may want to solicit the opinions of outside consultants.

Step 8   Use Training/Outplacement/Counseling   Finally, just like the physician, a manager may realize that the patient is terminally ill-- that the employee productivity problem has no workable solution. This typically occurs in situations where managers have no authority to implement the needed strategy. For example, foremen on assembly lines in large unionized organizations frequently encounter this problem. In addition, managers may not be able to solve an employee productivity problem due to the unique nature of an individual employee's personality or ability. Employees may be stubborn, insolent, have an "I don't care" attitude, and refuse to improve their job performance out of sheer "cussedness." An employee may not have the mental or physical ability to increase productivity, or he may be experiencing long-term personal stress which makes him dysfunctional. Under any of these conditions, the manager may want to consider using a counseling or outplacement strategy, such as termination, transfer, demotion, and so on.

Monitoring Future Employee Performance

Monitor Future Performance   When the manager reaches this step, the employee productivity problem has been remedied-- for the moment. Since the conditions of both business and personal lives of employees change, nothing can be expected to work forever. Management is a continuous process of creatively dealing with employee performances which deviate from the desired performance. Each instance constitutes an opportunity both to refine management skills and to produce a more viable organization.

It is always wise for the manager to initiate some procedure for the monitoring of future employee performance. This may be accomplished by normal managerial information systems as required by the particular management application. It may also be accomplished by using an employee-maintained feedback system as an adjunct monitoring system. (An example of such a system used by Emery Air Freight is given in Chapter Two.)

When performance becomes unsatisfactory in the future, it is once again time to consider the behaviors that are desired versus the actual behaviors, consult the procedures recommended,and begin again.

SUMMARY

In this chapter we have treated the issue of productivity at length, including its definition, its measurement, and its improvement. Productivity is a major issue of central concern to effective managers.

The contingency approach to increasing employee productivity is introduced. It is based on the idea that what is appropriate depends on the contingencies of the manager's situation.

The contingency approach consists of:

Three basic principles about the effectiveness of strategies for improving the productivity of employees.

A grouping of motivational approaches into seven core strategies each of which will be discussed in subsequent chapters.

A series of steps to use when one is faced with the question of how to increase employee productivity.

In Chapter Nine the reader will find the contingency approach reviewed once again, from the perspective of familiarity with the seven core motivation strategies. Guidelines for choosing the appropriate strategy for the manager's particular situation will also be given in the final chapter.

RECOMMENDED READINGS

Blum, M. L. and Naylor, J. C. *Industrial Psychology: Its Theoretical and Social Foundations*. New York: Harper & Row, Pub., 1968.

Likert, R. *The Human Organization*. New York: McGraw-Hill, 1967.

Likert, R. *New Patterns of Management*. New York: McGraw-Hill, 1961.

McClelland, D. C., et al. *The Achievement Motive*. New York: Appleton-Century-Crofts, 1953.

McClelland, D. C. *The Achieving Society*. Princeton, N. J.: D. Van Nostrand, 1961.

Massie, J. L. and Douglas, J. *Managing: A Contemporary Introduction*. Englewood Cliffs, N. J.: Prentice-Hall, 1977.

Mayo, E. *The Human Problems of an Industrial Civilization*. New York: Macmillian, 1933.

Taylor, F. W. *The Principles of Scientific Management*. New York: Harper Bros., 1911.

Trewatha, R. L. and Newport, M. G. *Management: Functions and Behavior*. Dallas, Texas: B.P.I. Inc., 1976.

2

Positive Reinforcement and Shaping

INTRODUCTION

Sally is a secretary for the Harmon Corporation, a small manufacturer of model toys. She has worked for the company for six years and her job performance, until recently, has been satisfactory. She has maintained her typing of correspondence at a reasonable speed, but during the last three months, she has been making an increasing number of typing errors. Sally's boss, Ellen, has tried to improve Sally's typing by using encouragement and several other standard techniques. None of these techniques have been successful.

One day, however, just before Ellen was about ready to transfer Sally to a job requiring less typing, she heard about a new approach to improving employee productivity. She decided to try it.

The new approach utilized two steps. Before taking any actions with regard to the employee, the manager first measures the level of the employee's productivity. Ellen chose to measure both the speed and the error rate in Sally's case. Ellen checked over the correspondence typed by Sally during the past week. Together with Sally she determined that the typical letter contained an average of three errors before any corrections were made. Ellen showed Sally how to make a chart that would record the error rate for each day using a simple bar-graph system. Sally agreed that, while perfect typing would be impossible, certainly one error in each five letters was a realistic goal. That would mean an average error rate of 1-5 (.2) errors per letter. Sally agreed to try lowering her error rate and to keep a chart of her progress in her desk drawer.

At the end of the next day Ellen noticed two charts posted on the wall next to Sally's desk. One chart showed the error rate with provisions for recording all of the days in the month. Sally had noted her error rate for the previous day with a red bar indicating an average error rate of three. Next to this was a second red bar indicating an average of two errors. As Sally was covering her typewriter and preparing to leave Ellen approached her. Following the advice of the new approach, Ellen immediately praised Sally for the improvement shown. Sally replied, "Well, two errors is still too much.", and at the same time a grin of pleasure crossed her face. Ellen asked about the second chart and was informed by Sally that she had decided, on her own, to chart her typing speed as well. Sally told Ellen that her intent was to first get her error rate down and then work on raising her typing speed. The next day, again about quitting time, Ellen again visited Sally's desk and saw an error rate of 1½ errors indicated on the first chart. The second chart showed that over the three days recorded thus far, Sally's typing speed had not diminished. Ellen again complimented Sally on her progress and for the initiative in working on typing speed as well. By the end of the week, Sally's error rate was almost to the target level of one error in five letters. Ellen maintained the praise during the week for each instance of progress.

Sally's error rate slowly decreased over the next week until only one error was made in every five letters, the rate which had been the goal. During the next two weeks, Ellen discontinued the daily quitting time visits and slowly adopted the practice of praising Ellen less often and at less predictable times. The new approach advised a "tapering off" method in which the regular, predictable, and frequent praise of the first phases of the program was to be gradually replaced by less and less frequent praise given at less and less predictable times. As the new approach suggested, Sally maintained her newly improved typing skills at about the same levels even with the reduced frequency of praise.

Ellen had dreaded replacing Sally and supervising the training of her replacement. She was very happy with the results of the new technique.

The preceding example demonstrates one use of a motivational technique known as "positive reinforcement." Its basic premise is that behavior is controlled by its immediate consequences. Behaviors can be made more or less frequent by what happens immediately after they occur. In the example, Sally's behavior was changed by giving her positive reinforcement each day as she reduced the number of typing errors she made. Positive reinforcement was also used to maintain Sally's productivity at a high level.

The concepts "shaping" and "reinforcement schedules" are closely associated with the concept of positive reinforcement. Since all of these terms may not be familiar to the reader, we will begin by defining and giving a brief explanation of each. Even for those readers already familiar with these terms a reading of the following material will probably be helpful. We describe each of the terms using examples from business and using a point of view that may help to clarify and deepen the reader's understanding.

Positive Reinforcement

A positive reinforcer is "anything which strengthens the behavior it follows and makes the behavior more likely." If an employee is given a bonus for completing a particularly important project on time and, as a result, the employee completes other important projects on time in the future, the bonus would be said to be a positive reinforcer.

It is a positive reinforcer because it has these effects, not just because the manager thinks a bonus is a reward. In effect, a positive reinforcer could be considered any reward that works, that is, any reward which changes the employee's behavior in the desired direction.

It should be stressed that what may serve as a positive reinforcer for one individual may not work the same way for another. As was mentioned in previous chapters, one individual may be motivated by a bonus or raise whereas another may not. Also, it is important to remember that something which serves as a positive reinforcer at one point in time for a given individual may not at another point in time.

In the example cited at the beginning of the chapter, praise was a positive reinforcer for Sally; it decreased her typing error rate. Although praise was effective with this particular secretary, it might not be with another.

Now a word about groups versus individuals. Managers should be especially careful when attempting to reinforce a group as opposed to an individual. The "group reinforcer" will work only if most or all of the individuals in the group experience the reward given as a positive reinforcer.

Shaping

"Shaping" is one way in which positive reinforcement can be used. In this technique, behavior is gradually changed by selectively reinforcing behaviors that are successively more similar to the kind of behavior desired. A manager cannot expect that a subordinate's performance will instantly change from totally unacceptable to totally acceptable. Therefore, the manager should *reward the employee for progress* made towards goals, not for perfection in performance. Since progress toward the goal is what is wanted, each instance of progress is rewarded. Since successive approximations to the goal are being reinforced, the term "principle of successive approximation" is occasionally cited instead of the term "shaping."

In the secretary example, Sally was reinforced successively for the progress she made toward improving her typing skills. Since Ellen was rewarding Sally's improvements toward the goal, she was using the technique of shaping.

Reinforcement Schedules

The concept of reinforcement schedules refers to the *pattern* in which desirable behavior should be reinforced. Two major reinforcement schedules are often discussed: continuous reinforcement and intermittent reinforcement.

Using continuous reinforcement, individuals receive positive reinforcement each and every time their behavior improves or changes in the desired direction. Such was the case with Sally at the beginning of the chapter. With intermittent reinforcement, not every desired behavior is reinforced. Instead, behavior is reinforced either randomly or according to a predetermined ratio, such as reinforcing the employee for every five instances of desired performance, or administering reinforcement (wages) every Friday. Generally speaking, continuous positive reinforcement would be used when a manager is first trying to change an employee's behavior.

Intermittent reinforcement, on the other hand, is indicated when the manager wants to maintain the employee's behavior at a desirable level. More will be said about both continuous and intermittent reinforcement later in this chapter. At this point our purpose is only to introduce the idea of reinforcement schedules.

EXAMPLES

The use of positive reinforcement is widespread in industry. Indeed, no organization can change or even maintain the behavior of its employees without using positive reinforcement to some degree. However, although all organizations use positive reinforcement, only a few implement it using the shaping technique and/or carefully planned reinforcement schedules. How several organizations have utilized "Behavior Modification" (the name often given to these concepts) will be described below.

Emery Air Freight

Perhaps the most well known application of reinforcement—based strategies to industry are Feeney's studies at Emery Air Freight. The basic procedure used by Feeney was to:

1. conduct a performance audit
2. provide employees with feedback regarding job performance
3. use positive reinforcement

The performance audit is a technique for identifying problems and determining specific, workable solutions. It is also used to determine the worth of any performance improvement program to the organization. It is an essential part of behavior modification in that it includes a description of "base rates," the status of employee behavior before any systematic behavior change plans are implemented. After all, we can not tell if anything has improved if we do not know where we started.

The second step, providing feedback, is designed to let employees know the company's performance standards and how they are currently performing according to those standards. In addition, the feedback reportedly serves as a reinforcer in its own right. Based on the performance audit, Feeney set standards or goals for each job in various departments. He then required that all workers measure their own performance in relation to this goal as they progressed. At the end of the day, the performance report was given to the supervisor. In some departments, charts showing both the company goals and employee performance were conspicuously placed on the wall of the workplace.

The third procedure was to administer positive reinforcement to employees for anything they were presently doing on the job which was desirable or any improvement in their job performance. At no time was the supervisor to criticize or threaten the employee. To illustrate, the Emery Air Freight studies cite the case of John, a cargo handler whose attendance was unsatisfactory. In order to improve his attendance the supervisor utilized positive reinforcement and feedback in the following way:

> 1st Day—"John, you came to work nineteen times out of twenty-two last month. When you are here we make more flights. Try to shoot for twenty-one or twenty-two days."

> 2nd Day—"Appreciate your coming to work today, John. Keep that up and you'll be here twenty-one or twenty-two days out of twenty-two."

> 3rd Day—"You've been here three days in a row now. Look at the percentage of flights we've made in the last three days. Keep shooting for twenty-one or twenty-two days."

> 5th Day—"You've been here all week. Thank you, John. Only seventeen days to go for a perfect record this month."

In each case above, the manager followed the procedure of rewarding the employee and at the same time giving a reminder of the company goals.

When training managers to use positive reinforcement, Emery's training staff asks them to discard the way managers typically view employee performance (Figure 2-1).

Instead, managers are to think of performance as it is shown in Figure 2-2.

In order to help managers determine which rewards should be used as reinforcers, Emery gives each manager two elaborate instruction workbooks prepared "in-house" and geared to the specific work situation of the company. One of these is entitled "Feedback" and the

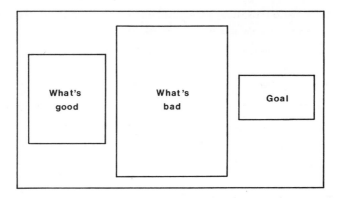

Figure 2-1. Typical View of Performance

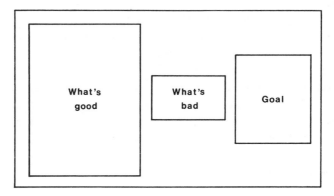

Figure 2-2. Preferred View of Performance

other "Positive Reinforcement." The latter workbook enumerates more than 150 different types of rewards a manager can use. Most of these are quite inexpensive. They include interacting with the employee, approving of employee requests, reducing or eliminating employee constraints, giving employees recognition, and inviting an individual to participate in a discussion.

When administering positive reinforcement, managers are told to follow a number of rules:

1. Find and reward any good performance, however slight, setting goals for what is not done rather than calling attention to what is bad.

2. Shape behavior gradually toward the goal.

3. Use the many nonfinancial rewards available to you.

4. To establish or strengthen desired behavior you utilize schedules of reinforcement.

5. **A high frequency of reinforcement is ne** ____ .o get performance started toward a desired goal. ____

6. _____ reinforcements are

_____ per week after the initial

_____ uire one or more per day, at

_____ ..ain performance.

_____ .ciniorcement should be determined by fluctuations in performance.

How successful has Emery Air Freight's approach been? When the company first implemented behavior modification, they concentrated on two departments: Customer Service and Containerized Shipping. Before behavior modification was introduced in the Customer Service department, company standards were met only 30% to 40% of the time. After behavior modification was introduced, the corresponding figures were 90% to 95%. Remarkably, most of this improvement occurred within just a few days, which suggests the importance of feedback. After using behavior modification as an overt company policy for four years, performance in the vast majority of Emery's Customer Service offices still averaged 90% to 95%.

In the Containerized Shipping operation, the results were similar. Container usage rose from 45% to 95% and remained at that level.

From a financial viewpoint, behavior modification was a resounding success. Emery reportedly saved over three million dollars over a three year period. The costs of implementing the program including staff time and extra costs of rewards averaged $5,150 per year.

A Manufacturing/Distribution Company

In the Journal of Applied Psychology, Pedalino and Gamboa (1974) report an experiment they conducted at an unnamed manufacturing/distribution company which wanted to reduce absenteeism among its production workers. Their solution consisted of using positive reinforcement to encourage workers to come to work each day.

Simply stated, the authors devised a system in which workers who came to work on time each day were allowed to draw a card from a deck. At the end of a week, those who were present all five days possessed a five-card stud poker hand. The company paid the high hand twenty dollars. In the words of the authors:

> Each day an employee comes to work and is on time, he is allowed to choose a card from a deck of playing cards. At the end of the five-day week he will have five cards or a normal poker hand. The highest hand wins $20.00. There will be eight winners, one for approximately each department. (Pedalino and Gamboa, 1974)

The critical question, of course, is, "Did it work?." The experiment ran for about four months. During that time an 18.27 percent decrease in absenteeism was attained as an average. Since the initial rate of absence (3.01 percent) was rather low in comparison to many other firms, the degree of possible decrease was severely limited. The fact that a marked decrease was found under these conditions is quite impressive.

This experiment points out two of the critical aspects of positive reinforcement. One is that it must be continued. A follow-up study conducted twenty-two weeks after the experiment was terminated indicated that the absence rate had returned to about its original level. Secondly, the study points out that positive reinforcement need not be continuous to be effective. When the experimenters had the poker game played on an every-other-week basis (rather than weekly) they found that absenteeism remained low.

An elaboration on this strategy was not reported but could have been used. Suppose that the company needed workers for overtime on weekends. It would be possible to give one or two additional cards to those who came in on time for the Saturday work day. In this case, it is possible to project that workers desiring overtime on Saturday would become more plentiful if they could then select their best five cards from a hand of six or seven.

Safety in a Bakery

In the opening example of this chapter the typing error rate of a secretary was improved by the systematic use of reinforcement. While an increasing error rate for a secretary poses a real problem in efficiency, an increasing injury rate may pose a problem of life and death.

The reinforcement techniques of behavior modification are potentially effective in modifying the frequency of any work behavior, regardless of the seriousness of the problem. In the bakery industry the average injury rate is less than twenty injuries per million hours worked. To place this in some perspective, two other industry injury rates are given below:

Underground Mining = less than 35/1,000,000

Automobile, Steel = less than 5/1,000,000

The bakery in question experienced an increasing injury rate which had reached 53.8 per million hours worked. In addition, the company's insurance firm had raised their workers' compensation insurance rates and sent their own investigators to inspect the bakery. These investigaators concluded that the safety problem was not due to defects in machinery or mechanical safeguards. Instead, they concluded that the increased injury rate was due primarily to unsafe employee work practices.

The intervention in this setting followed a procedure similar to that used by Feeney at Emery Air Freight. First, the employee work behaviors were surveyed and base lines were recorded. All applications have some unique aspects and in this situation it was necessary to devise a set of observational codes which could be used to identify and record safe and unsafe work behaviors. Next, employees were given training consisting of pairs of slides which showed both the safe and an unsafe method of performing various bakery tasks. The supervisors were given special training in identifying safe procedures and were instructed to compliment the employee whenever a safely performed work procedure was witnessed.

Following training—again using a technique similar to one used at Emery—a chart was posted in a public area which depicted the percentage of work behaviors safely performed by time periods. Thus, employees could readily see the current level of safety and the trends.

The result of this effort was that a stable rate of 10 injuries per million hours worked was attained. Readers wishing to consult the original source for this case should obtain Komaki, Barwick, and Scott (1978), listed in the recommended readings at the end of this chapter.

Absentee Hospital Employees

In our lectures, someone in the audience invariably questions the idea that "tapering off" reinforcements after initial training and introducing a more or less random reinforcement schedule will maintain performance at an acceptable level. The hospital-based experiment reported here pairs a variant of the "gambling" incentive used above in the manufacturing example with a test of the relative efficiency of continuous versus less frequent, random reinforcement. Since predictable employee availablity is critical to appropriate health care in a hospital, this example, too, is one where reinforcement techniques were used to correct an employee problem of potential seriousness.

Six nursing units in a hospital were randomly assigned to either Group A or Group B, so that three nursing units were in each group. The nursing units consisted of nurses, ward clerks, and nursing assistants.

In both groups the employees became eligible for a twenty dollar cash prize drawing. In Group A an employee was eligible for the drawing if he was never absent during a three-week period. In Group B eligibility for the drawing required that an employee not be absent on any one of eight days during the same three-week period. The eight days were randomly selected from the three weeks. To summarize, Group A employees had to be present every day while Group B employees had to be present only eight days in order to qualify for the twenty dollar drawing.

The investigators found that under both types of reward a significant decrease in absenteeism was obtained. Further, and this is meaningful for the question of continuous versus random intermittent reinforcement, no significant differences were found in the results of the two systems.

These results are not suprising if you assume the employee's point of view for a moment. The only strategy which will always work in either system is to come to work every day. This demonstrates the practical power of the random reward schedule. Since an employee can never tell before coming to work whether or not this particular day is one on which a reinforcement depends, there are no alternatives but to come to work or to risk losing the reward. This logic applies to either the continuous or the intermittent system.

REASONS

The rationale behind the use of administering rewards may be grouped into two subsections. These are:

1. Thorndike's "Law of Effect" and Reinforcement
2. Skinner's Contributions.

These subsections will be covered next.

Please note that in presenting the underlying rationale for this and subsequent strategies, our purpose is to provide the reader with a sufficiently detailed understanding of what is to be done and why it is done so that unique situations may be dealt with. An analogy may help here. Most motor vehicle laws require that the driver act in a "safe and prudent manner" when operating a motor vehicle. The same states also specify a maximum speed limit. In certain unusual situations, such as when portions of a load keep dropping from a truck in front of your car and another car is close behind you, it is necessary to exceed the speed limit and pass the truck in order to drive in a safe and prudent manner. The first priority is to protect yourself, not to follow the "letter of the law."

Just as the purpose of a motor vehicle code is to preserve public safety, the purpose of the strategies we present is to increase employee productivity. If, in an unusual situation, a portion of a recommended strategy is not meeting the goal of increasing productivity, but is having the opposite effect, then that portion should be omitted or altered. While we have included provision for ceasing a strategy when it is not working as anticipated in each of the strategy guides, the same notion may be applied to any step or element within any given strategy.

The underlying rationale for each strategy must be quite well understood in order to make intelligent choices. We do not maintain that practical managers must become accomplished theoreticians. Neither do we advocate the opposite extreme. Managers cannot afford to act like robots simply following a set of prescribed steps.

Thorndike's "Law of Effect" and Reinforcement

The actions of positive reinforcement, shaping, and reinforcement schedules all rest in part on Thorndike's "Law of Effect" (originally published in 1913):

When a modifiable connection between a situation and a response is made and is accompanied or followed by a satisfying state of affairs, that connection's strength is increased; when made and accompanied by an annoying state of affairs, its strength is decreased. (from Hilgard and Bowers, 1966)

This law states that if a person is rewarded for performing a given action, the probability that the action will be repeated in the future is increased. By the same token, if a person is punished for performing a given action, the probability of that action being repeated is decreased. The law of effect suggests that people seek pleasure and want to avoid pain. It stresses that a lawful relationship exists between actions and the consequences which follow the actions.

Although poorly defined in its operations (Just what does a "satisfying state of affairs" mean?) this law is one of the most powerful discoveries in the history of the behavioral sciences. In his review of the motivational literature, Vroom (1964) concluded:

Without a doubt the law of effect or principle of reinforcement must be included among the most substantiated findings of experimental psychology and is at the same time among the most useful findings for an applied psychology concerned with the control of human behavior.

Skinner's Contributions

Although in the mind of the general public, B. F. Skinner is usually regarded as the founder of behavior modification, this impression is not altogether accurate. Skinner, however, has undoubtedly emerged as the most consistently eloquent proselytizer for this approach. His extensive personal contributions, his stature as a scientist, and his great skill as a writer contribute in no small part to the general impression that Skinner invented behavior modification.

Actually, nobody knows who first invented behavior modification. Skinner's *Science and Human Behavior* (1953) was probably the first major work to describe human personality as sets of operants (that is Skinner-talk for a piece of behavior) and to suggest methods for their change and control. Among nonscientists, animal trainers, parents, and managers have been using portions of behavior modification technology with success throughout human history. Prior to the destruction of Pompei, Pliny the Younger describes the operant conditioning of fish by the tapping of his father's staff (of course, he did not call it operant conditioning). Much earlier, the first domestication of the horse about 2150 B.C. must have taken considerable sophistication in the practical aspects of behavior modification. Even today the Moscow Circus regularly features trained bears, a traditional Russian entertainment dating back millenia. Clearly, a bear trainer who survives his trade must be a master of behavior modification.

Not all of the contributions of Skinner and his colleagues will be reviewed here. Instead, we present three topics critical to the manager's understanding of behavior modification and required for its implementation. The topics are:

1. recording base line performance
2. major types of reinforcement schedules
3. considerations in delivering reinforcement

Recording Baseline Performance. With just a little thought it is evident that we have to know how often a behavior occurs before the behavior modification program begins. Without this information there is no way to judge progress. Our recommendation is brief and simple. Record the initial level of performance and then record the level of performance at equal time intervals throughout the behavior modification effort. Use the same method of measuring for the duration since different measures usually give different results.

If a sales agent typically makes ten calls on clients a day, record a ten for the baseline figure and then the number made on each subsequent day of the program. If the program is working as expected, the number of calls should increase to some number above ten and increase more or less steadily until some reasonable maximum is reached. Make a graph of the number of calls for ready reference. Better yet, have the sales agents keep records and make daily entries on a graph so that any improvement or lack of improvement is readily apparent to everyone.

Major Types of Reinforcement Schedules. The discovery that it is the schedule of reinforcement rather than the simple occurrence of a reinforcement that exerts a powerful influence on behavior may have been Skinner's most profound contribution. People don't just respond to stimuli, they respond to patterns of stimuli. A reinforcement schedule is just a pattern extended over time.

The chart below shows the basic types of reinforcement schedules. Understand these and the less common types will be easy to master.

	RATIO of Behaviors to Reinforcements	Time INTERVALS when Reinforcement Occurs
FIXED	Fixed Ratio (FR)	Fixed Interval (FI)
VARIABLE	Variable Ratio (VR)	Variable Interval (VI)

Figure 2-3. Reinforcement Schedules

Fixed ratio schedules (FR) are used in shaping a new behavior. More specifically, the schedule would be "FR-1"—which means that for every desired behavior one unit of reinforcement is given. Thus, the manager will begin with FR-1 for shaping and then proceed to larger ratios (like FR-10 or FR-50) after the behavior has become established. The FR schedules are the best way to bring about a new behavior but a poor way to maintain a new behavior. It simply takes too much of the manager's or trainer's time. One solution to this problem is to use a different schedule than FR.

Variable ratio (VR) schedules are one alternative to the disadvantages of the FR schedule. Suppose an employee has been reinforced on an FR-10 schedule. The manager can shift this employee gradually to a VR-10 schedule. Unlike the FR-10 schedule which involves giving one reinforcement after every ten desired behaviors, the VR-10 schedule requires that a reinforcement follow after ten behaviors *as an average*. The employee may be reinforced for six behaviors, then twelve, then ten, then eleven, then eight, and so on. The exact number of behaviors required for a reinforcement will vary at random. What is meant by VR-10 is that the average number required will be ten, but sometimes more will be required and sometimes less. This tends to eliminate rigid expectations by the employee and is more realistically similar to actual working conditions.

Fixed interval (FI) schedules and variable interval (VI) schedules are fixed or variable in exactly the same sense that the ratio schedules discussed above were fixed or variable. The difference with interval schedules is that the reinforcements are dependent on the time at which the desired behavior occurred rather than just the number of behaviors. These schedules may be used to produce consistency in behaviors which are already being performed at a satisfactory rate. In VR-10 scheduling, the employee's behavior is observed every ten units of time (minutes, hours, days, and so on) and if a desired behavior is occurring then a reinforcement is delivered. Note that this schedule reinforces the employee for performance which is relatively consistent over time. Of course, if employees know that their work will be checked every ten minutes, they may watch the clock and perform only every ten minutes. They will know when to look busy and act accordingly.

One solution to this drawback of the VR schedules is to use a variable interval (VI) schedule. Under this schedule (assuming VI-10 for comparison purposes), the employee's job performance will be observed every ten minutes on the average (just like VR). Thus the random sequence for observing (in minutes) might be something like 6,14,12,8,10,13,7,9,11 or any other set of numbers with an average of 10. Performance is observed every ten minutes on the average but there is never any certainty about just when the observation will occur. The only strategy to maximize reinforcements under this set of rules is to work at a relatively high rate and to work steadily.

Additional Considerations in Delivering Reinforcement. The word to remember here is *contiguity*—two things or events have contiguity if they are close to each other. Contiguity may be in terms of physical distance where the less distance there is the more contiguity exists. Contiguity may also exist in terms of time. The less time between two events the more contiguous they are. The ultimate in temporal contiguity is two events that happen at the same time!

Reinforcement has its greatest effect when it is contiguous with the behavior reinforced. This means that employees should be reinforced as soon after the desired behavior as possible.

Managers should make sure that an undesirable behavior has not occurred between the time the desired behavior occurred and the time the reinforcement is given. If this happens the reinforcement will have its strongest effect on the undesirable behavior, which is exactly what you do not want.

Survey of Research Results

The actions of positive reinforcement, shaping, and reinforcement schedules and their underlying theories have been studied intensively, particularly in laboratory settings using animals. Most organizational studies, however, have been in mental health and educational settings. Although the actions themselves are used, often unknowingly, by many companies, controlled experiments in industry examining the effects of these actions on employee behavior are relatively limited. Thus, remarkably little is known regarding many aspects of these actions. This lack of a solid research base, however, should not discourage the manager from using the actions described. One should keep in mind that many of the other actions discussed in this text do not have a firm research base either! However, it does suggest that a manager must exercise caution in utilizing the actions and pay particular attention to the effects of these actions on employee behavior.

Just how can we be so rash as to recommend managerial actions which are not firmly grounded in research? Most of the day-to-day behavior of managers is founded far more on custom and intuition than on hard-nosed research results. This is not a state of affairs we applaud. We strongly recommend that all managers, when faced with the need for research in order to optimize their outcomes, become their own researchers. Limited applied research is just as much a management skill as any other.

Ethical Criticisms of Behavior Modification

The actions included in behavior modification as well as their underlying theories have undoubtedly received more ethical criticism than any other single approach to improving employee productivity. Because of the nature of some of these criticisms, it is important for a manager who may wish to use behavior modification to be familiar with them. We assume that most readers will not want to undertake activities which are immoral or unethical.

In reviewing these criticisms, no overt attempt will be made to judge their legitimacy. We intentionally state that no "overt" attempt will be made. It would be less than honest for us not to note that we think most of these criticisms are inappropriate. There is no sense in pretending we are dispassionate and aloof on this issue and we do not pretend (even to ourselves) that our opinions will not come through in the following in various subtle ways. It is far better for the reader to know where we stand. Armed with this knowledge, readers must make their own judgments in the light of their own values and beliefs. It should be further noted that at least two articles cited at the end of this chapter, one by Schneier and another by Babb & Kopp, also discuss the criticisms.

Manipulative? One of the major criticisms directed at behavior modification is that it is manipulative. In using the shaping technique, for example, people are rewarded for making progress toward a goal and undesired behaviors are ignored. Since the manager is deliberately trying to change the employee's behavior and does not tell the employee what is being done, is not that manipulative and therefore unethical? Behaviorists have countered that every action a manager takes has its effects on the employee's behavior in some way. Even taking no action at all has effects on behavior. Thus, there is no way the manager can avoid affecting the subordinate's behavior, so why not do it systematically?

Dehumanizing? Behavior modification has also been criticized for being mechanical, dictatorial, and above all, dehumanizing. It amounts to treating people as if they were ordinary animals such as pigeons, rats, or dogs. Behaviorists argue that it is not at all dehumanizing. Behavior modification simply recognizes that the behavior of people, like that of the other animals, is a function of its consequences.

Bribery? A common criticism directed at behavior modification is that positive reinforcement is just another way of describing bribery. If every time a person improves his or her performance you give that person a reward, such as money or praise, is that not bribery? Is bribery not immoral? Shouldn't people learn to perform effectively just for the enjoyment work itself brings rather than for what they can get out of it? Behaviorists counter that behavior modification is not bribery any more than any other motivational strategy and, therefore, if it works, why not use it?

IMPLEMENTATION

The strategy guide or flow-diagram shown in Figure 2-4 consists of thirteen steps. When you use behavior modification in your organization the actual sequence of steps you will use will include those represented in the diagram.

Let us "walk through" the Strategy Guide, step by step, and examine both the process of behavior modification and the considerations unique to using this process.

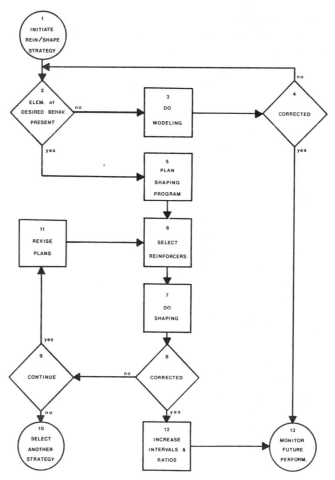

Figure 2-4. Positive Reinforcement and Shaping: Strategy Guide

Knowing Your Goal

Step 1   Initiate   Reinforcement/Shaping   Strategy.   Before taking overt action, this is the time to briefly review what you are about to do, making certain that you understand each of the steps to follow. Before beginning, answer the following questions for yourself:

1. What is the employee doing now that is desirable—or, what behavior is lacking?
2. What is your goal, that is, what will the employee be doing after your behavior modification program reaches a successful conclusion?

Now write down your answers.

What happens if you do not answer these two questions? You will not know what you are doing; either give up or go back to the beginning. Anything you do without knowing the answers to these questions will just be wasted effort.

Recognizing the Desired Behaviors

Step 2 Elements Of Desired Behavior Present?   Here is the first of the four decisions you will have to make during implementation of this action. Look back to the answer you gave to the second question above. Consider what it is you want the employee to do. Now, compare this with your answer to the first question. Is the employee now doing something of what you desire? If the answer is yes, go on to Step 5 and begin to plan the strengthening of the behavioral elements already present while building in those elements which are still lacking. If the answer is no, proceed to Step 3 and begin "modeling."

Step 3 Do Modeling.   "Modeling" consists of just showing the employee what is wanted, but with some subtle refinements. Unless you have only one subordinate, you should not personally show the employee what to do. Another employee should demonstrate the desired behavior. There are two things you can do to make "modeling" different from just "showing." First, select a model who is as much like the employee as possible. Second, reinforce the model in the presence of the employee immediately after the action is performed. A simple verbal compliment will usually do. When the model is reinforced the employee will experience vicarious reinforcement; it will be as if the employee had been reinforced. The more similar the model is to the employee, the more effective this strategy will be.

Step 4 Corrected?   This is the second of the four decisions in the process. After modeling, wait for several occasions when the desired behavior could have been performed. At this point check to see if the employee is performing the desired activity or behavior. Clearly, you must wait at least until the beginning of the following work day to find out if an employee is coming to work on time. You should realize that modeling is a suprisingly powerful technique and that modeling alone may be sufficient to produce the desired behavioral change. If the behavioral deficit has been corrected you are almost done. Proceed to the last section in this chapter, on motitoring future performance (Step 13). If the desired behavior is still not occuring return to the section on modeling (Step 2). By now at least some elements of the desired behavior should be present and you may proceed to the next step. In the unlikely event that this is not so do more modeling.

Planning a Shaping Program

Step 5 Plan Shaping Program. Now comes a bit of planning. Remember, the strategy now becomes one of giving reinforcement for all progress toward the desired behavior. Normal variation in the employee's behavior will produce some movement toward the goal you specified and each desired movement must be reinforced. This should go rather quickly since you have already told the employee what is expected and perhaps you have had the behavior modeled by another employee. The plan consists of setting up circumstances in which the employee can perform the desired behavior, and paying attention to the behavior by the direct supervisor. If you are not the direct supervisor, then this person should plan the shaping program with you.

Step 6 Select Reinforcers. The reinforcements which you select must be appropriate for the employee. Just because you think a certain reward is what the employee wants does not mean that this is actually true. The choice of appropriate rewards is a major management skill and one for which we can only provide guidelines. What is possible in any organization is unique to that setting. One suggestion, however, always seems to be helpful. Try using praise. Praise costs nothing and is severely lacking in the experience of many employees. Don't fake it. Praise must be genuine. This is not difficult since any employees who improve their work performance are making your life easier and if you let them know, the praise can be both genuine and effective.

Implement Your Plans

Step 7 Do Shaping. Now implement the shaping plan you just devised. The main thing to remember here is to be very attentive to the employee's behavior. The rewards you will be using work best if they are given as soon after the desired behavior as possible. Experimental evidence indicates that the best results are obtained if the interval between the behavior and reinforcement is .5 seconds. This is impossible in practice, but the point is "faster is better."

Evaluating Results and Further Options

Step 8 Corrected?   As discussed earlier (p. 25) check for the desired result. We all know that in the "real world" nothing ever works correctly the first time so expect to cycle through this step at least once more. In this step you must also decide if the employee is making some progress in the program. If progress is occuring, then clearly you should continue with the program. If there is no apparent progress you have one last decision to make--whether to continue.

Step 9 Continue?   Let us consider briefly the reasons why there might be no progress to this point. First, remember that acquiring a new set of work behaviors will always require some time. Have you waited long enough for the new behavioral elements to become a part of the employee's work patterns? If you have waited long enough, check to see if more powerful reinforcers have interfered. The most likely source of more powerful reinforcers is the peer group. Will a revision in the shaping plan be likely to bring results? If you have reason to believe that behavior modification is not working in this case it is entirely appropriate to select some other action. Managers are free to make mistakes but not to perpetuate them forever.

Step 10 Select Another Strategy.   The selection of another strategy at this point is entirely appropriate. It is done in the same way that you first selected this action. If you have not already used the Contingency Approach as presented in the final chapter we encourage you to explore it as one way to search for alternate approaches. If you had selected the reinforcement and shaping strategy using this approach, return and select the next most likely solution.

DO NOT CONTINUE THIS ACTION IF IT IS NOT WORKING

If necessary, let it be known that you are not personally committed to the solutions you attempt. Remember, you are not running for political office and do not need to doggedly pursue courses of action when it becomes apparent that they are no longer advisable. You do not need to show your determination by being inflexible.

Step 11 Revise Plans.   When deciding how to correct or whether to continue a plan of action you may have found good reasons to expect that the strategy will be successful if more time is allowed or if you make some revisions in your implementation plans. This is the point at which such revisions should be made before going back to the process of shaping.

*What To Do When the Strategy Is
Successful*

Step 12 Increase Intervals & Ratios.   On the other hand, things may very well have worked out just as expected; they usually do after a few revisions. As we pointed out earlier, during the shaping process you were using FR-1 as the reinforcement schedule; that is, almost every single appropriate response was quickly reinforced. While this is a fine way to do shaping, it is very wasteful of time as a method of maintaining either new behaviors or desirable old behaviors. Also, it will not work very long because it rapidly "adapts out," that is, the employee becomes used to it. The solution is to increase the behavior/reinforcement ratios and to begin using increased interval reinforcement as well.

Step 13 Monitor Future Performance.   There is far more to this step than meets the eye as most readers will know already. Here we enter the fascinating and insidious world of performance appraisal. It is worth a book by itself.

In accordance with our recommendations about the manager as a generalist we will assume that you have the appropriate staff specialists to deal with this issue. Think of performance appraisal as your "early warning" system. Used correctly you will be able to forestall many of the major human resource problems before they reach serious proportions.

SUMMARY

In this chapter we have considered the use of systematic reinforcement and shaping in increasing employee productivity. We began with a classic case of the aided self-modification of work behavior using a secretary's job as the example.

The action of behavior modification in general and the systematic use of reinforcement in particular were related to the practical problems of a manager attempting to modify the work behavior of an employee.

Four examples of the use of reward systems in addition to the opening example were offered to demonstrate some of the variety possible in both problems which may be solved and in types of applications when using this technique.

The theoretical reasons underlying behavior modification and reward systems were presented in order to clarify and promote a deeper understanding of the operative mechanisms and assumptions used to derive this recommended technique. For those readers who wish to consult original sources and related materials a list of recommended readings is provided.

A strategy guide in flow-chart form was presented which outlined the steps, sequence, and various branching decisions necessary for the implementation of the technique. A discussion of the potential problems a manager may expect as well as a discussion of the subtle distinctions which may have to be made was presented.

This strategy, while powerful when used alone, is also a fine adjunct strategy. It may be combined profitably with any of the other strategies, even punishment—once the punished actions have ceased.

One of the most-used reinforcers is praise. Praise has many advantages which mere financial rewards do not. Praise costs nothing. It improves the employee's image of the leader, serves to satisfy employee needs for recognition, makes employees think more highly of the leader, and, generally serves to increase the leader's ability to influence while at the same time directly improving employee productivity.

Praise has a cumulative effect and is almost impossible to do incorrectly. A major advantage of praise is that it works nearly every time with almost everybody. A manager who is unsure of where to begin and who has not yet developed the requisite skills for the more complex and demanding strategies we present may safely use praise as the first step in increasing productivity. Even praise poorly given can be effective.

The comments about praise apply to other reinforcements as well, with the exception that they may take more time and cost the organization more. The planning of involved shaping programs to build new skills and as a part of employee training takes a good basic understanding of the principles of behavior modification. Praise, however, may be used immediately and without fear of negative consequences except with the most emotionally disturbed employees. Employees who respond to praise with inappropriate emotions (like anger or withdrawal) should be considered as candidates for a counseling referral.

RECOMMENDED READINGS

Adam, E.E. "Behavior Modification in Quality Control." *Academy of Management Journal* 18 (1975), 662-79.

Argyris, C. "Beyond Freedom and Dignity by B. F. Skinner." (an essay review). Harvard Educational Review 41(4) (1971): 550-67.

Babb, H.W. and Kopp, D.G. "Applications of Behavior Modification in Organizations: A Review and Critique." *Academy of Management Review* 21(4) (1978): 281-92.

Business Week "New Tool: ' Reinforcement ' for Good Work." 18 December 1971, pp. 76-77.

Business Week,, 'Where Skinner's Theories Work." 2 December 1972, pp. 64-65.

Fry, F.L. "Operant Conditioning in Organizational Settings: Of Mice or Men?" *Personnel* (1974): 17-24.

Gagne, R.M. "Military Training and Principles of Learning." *American Psychologist* 17, (1962): 83-91.

Goldstein, A.P. and Sorcher, M. *Changing Supervisory Behavior.* Elmsford, N. Y.: Pergamon Press, 1974.

Hamner, W.C. "Reinforcement Theory and Contingency Management in Organizational Settings." From *Motivation and Work Behavior,* edited by R.M. Steers and L.W. Porter. New York: McGraw-Hill, 1975.

Hamner, W.C. and Hamner, E.P. "Behavior Modification on the Bottom Line." From *Organizational Dynamics*, (American Management Association), Spring 1976: pp. 2-21.

Jablonsky, S.F. and DeVries, D.L. "Operant Conditioning Principles Extrapolated to the Theory of Management." *Organizational Behavior and Human Performamce* 7 (1972): 340-58.

Komaki, J.; Barwick, K.D.; and Scott, L.R. "A Behavioral Approach to Occupational Safety: Pinpointing and Reinforcing Safe Performance in a Food Manufacturing Plant." *Journal of Applied Psychology* 63(4) (1978): 434-45.

Locke, E.A. "Critical Analysis of the Concept of Causality in Behavioristic Psychology." *Psychological Reports* 31 (1973): 175-98.

Locke, E.A. "The Myths of Behavior Mod in Organizations." *Academy of Management Review*, October 1977,pp. 543-53.

Nord, W. R. "Improving Attendance Through Rewards." *Personnel Administration* 33(6) (1970): 37-41.

Organizational Dynamics, "At Emery Air Freight: Positive Reinforcement Boosts Performance." 1(3) (1973): 41-50.

Pedalino, E. and Gamboa, V.U. "Behavior Modification and Absenteeism: Intervention in One Industrial Setting," *Journal of Applied Psychology* 59, (1974) 694-98.

Schneier, C.E. "Behavior Modification in Management: A Review and Critique." *Academy of Management Journal* 17 (1974): 528-48.

Skinner, B.F. *Beyond Freedom and Dignity*. New York: Alfred A. Knopf, 1971.

Stevens, T.A. and Burroughs, W.A. "An Application of Operant Conditioning to Absenteeism in a Hospital Setting." *Journal of Applied Psychology* 63(4) (1978).518-21.

Thorndike, E.H. *Human Learning*. Cambridge, Mass.: Massachusetts Institute of Technology Press, 1966.

Yukl, G.A. and Latham, G.P. "Consequences of Reinforcement Schedules and Incentive Magnitudes for Employee Performance: Problems Encountered in an Industrial Setting." *Journal of Applied Psychology* 60 (1975): 294-98.

3

Discipline
and Punishment

INTRODUCTION

*Photocopying Backside Gets
Secretary Canned*

MOLINE, Ill. (AP)-- Jodi Stutz says she had no idea that when she put her bare bottom on the Xerox machine, she was putting her job on the line.

"I can't believe I got fired over this," she said Tuesday. "I just can't believe it."

Miss Stutz, a 21-year-old secretary, said that one night after work last month at Deere & Co. she decided to christen the new copying machine on the floor by sneaking into the Xerox room and making a picture of her bottom.

"A lot of people were taking pictures of their hands and their faces and fooling around," she said. "So I decided I would take a picture of my bottom, thinking it would be kind of fun just to see what it would look like."

While another secretary stood watch at the door, Miss Stutz pulled down her pants, hopped up on the machine, and pushed the "Print" button.

"It was very, very funny," she said, giggling. "It borderlined on crude, maybe, but it was funny."

43

Her superiors, however, didn't think so. Word got around after Miss Stutz showed friends in the office her copy.

She said that her boss, Jack Fritts, asked her about rumors that she had thrown a big party in the Xerox room, that three men had helped her get undressed and then guarded the door, that she had sent copies of her rear as an invitation to a birthday party.

She said she told him all those rumors were false, but when he asked if she had, in a moment of indiscretion, copied her bottom, she lied.

Jim Coogan, Deere director of advertising, then reportedly got the secretary who had stood watch to confess and Miss Stutz was called on the carpet.

"They said something like it wasn't in the company's best interest to make a copy of my bottom," she said. "Of course, they never came right out and said it. They were too embarrassed to say what the incident was, but we all knew."

She said she expected a reprimand, but instead she was given two options—quit or be fired.

"I talked to them a long time to get them to change their mind or at least put me on probation," said Miss Stutz, who is now working as a waitress. "My work record was excellent, and they even admitted it was. I told them I was really sorry about it and everything."

A Deere spokesman declined comment Tuesday.

ACTION

In the previous chapter we discussed how organizations can use rewards to improve employee job performance. In this chapter, we will focus on the use of discipline, punishment, and penalties.

The preceding Associated Press (1980) example demonstrates the operation of an organization's disciplinary procedure which incorporates the use of penalties. Jodi Stutz apparently broke a company rule which prohibits the improper use of a Xerox machine. More importantly, she also lied about using the machine and hence presumably broke the organization's rule regarding honesty. As a result of her actions she was penalized in the most severe or strictest manner available to an organization—she was fired.

It is important at the onset to distinguish between *discipline*, *punishment*, and *penalties* and to spell out the relationship between them. We will begin with the concept of discipline.

Traditionally, discipline has been viewed in numerous ways. Some conceptualize it broadly, as the act of behaving and working in an orderly way. This definition suggests that if an organization is to function effectively, it is essential that each employee work for the interests of the organization and not transgress the rights of others. Discipline can also be viewed as simply a form of training which is designed to change or regulate employee behavior. In this text, we will define discipline as the molding of employee behavior through punishment. What, then, is punishment?

Punishment is typically defined as "the presentation of an aversive event or the removal of a positive event following a response which decreases the frequency of that response." (Kazadin, 1975). Simply put, punishment encompasses two basic actions: 1) taking action against an employee (for example, verbal warning, written warning, suspension, stern glances) which has the effect of reducing or eliminating an unwanted behavior, or 2) withholding a reward from an employee in an attempt to reduce or eliminate an undesirable behavior (for example "You are not going to get a raise because you were absent from work twenty days last year.")

There are three aspects of this definition that deserve further discussion. First, the definition of punishment presented above incorporates two distinct actions, not just one. People often lose sight of the fact that withholding a reward in an attempt to reduce or eliminate a behavior is just as much a part of punishment as is the more visual and aggressive action of administering a punitive action.

Secondly, this definition makes no *a priori* judgment as to what specific actions an individual either will or will not find punishing. Instead, it simply states that if an action reduces the frequency of a given response, it is punishment. If an action does not, in retrospect, reduce the response frequency, it is not punishment. For example, if a manager rebukes a machine operator for not wearing protective goggles, and the worker wears them from then on, the rebuke is defined as punishment. If the rebuke did not result in the employee wearing protective goggles more frequently, then it was not punishment. In the chapter on positive reinforcement we noted that positive reinforcement was conceived of as any reward that works, that is, any reward that increases the frequency of a given behavior. By way of comparison, punishment is also described as any aversive action which works, that is, any action which reduces the frequency of a given behavior.

Defining punishment in a retrospective manner has one serious drawback. It does not make clear in advance those actions which will reduce or eliminate an employee's undesirable behavior and those which will not. Managers, quite understandably, would like to have this information. Stated differently, they would like to know in advance, and with complete certainty, which actions constitute punishment to employees and which do not. It is important to realize that such a list does not exist now and never will. The reason for this was partially explained in Chapter One. People differ significantly in terms of what they find punishing. As evidence, remember that while many employees find it punishing to be fired, others actually find it rewarding because they can then collect unemployment compensation.

The third aspect of this definition which deserves further elaboration is that withholding a reward is only punishment if the purpose of this action is to decrease the frequency of a response. Withholding a reward for other reasons, then, is not punishment. Consider the following situation. Four employees are being considered for a promotion. One of them is selected based strictly on a superior work record and managerial potential. Since the other three were not promoted, could one argue that they were punished? No, not if one defines punishment as it is typically defined (unless, of course, the expressed purpose of not promoting the other employees is to reduce or eliminate an undesirable behavior on their part). Why is this seemingly minute distinction important? The authors have found that both employees and students occasionally label as punishment actions taken by managers which, in fact, are not punishments. On occasion, these mislabels can create employee dissatisfaction toward a manager and, if communicated to the manager, can lead to feelings of guilt. When faced with this situation, a manager should point out to the particular employees that the withholding of a reward is punishment only if the intent is to decrease the frequency of a particular response.

Thus far we have defined discipline and punishment and pointed out the interrelationships between them. What remains is a definition of the term "penalty."

A penalty is an action taken by a manager which the manager believes (and hopes) will be punishing to an employee, that is, will change the employee's behavior in the desired direction. Penalties take many forms within an organization but the most common are verbal warnings and written warnings, suspensions, and discharge. It is important to understand that penalties do not always favorably change an employee's behavior. For example, giving an employee a written warning may not affect his job performance at all. Managers, of course, attempt to select penalties which will be effective but there is no guarantee that a given action will have the desired effect.

In practice, punishment is often thought of as a penalty that worked. Using the retrospective definition, the employee's job behavior was changed in the desired direction. The reader can now see that this notion is indeed true.

EXAMPLES

Discipline is undoubtedly the most common approach to improving employee productivity used in organizations at the present time. Almost all medium- and large-sized organizations use penalties within a set of formalized disciplinary procedures which they follow. Smaller companies also utilize penalties considerably even though they may not have formalized systems.

Examples of specific punishments (for example, "chewing out" of employees, cross glances, finger pointing, rebukes, and suspensions) used in organizations abound. We realize that the reader is already aware of many of these and, hence, no worthwhile purpose would be served by listing or describing all of them here. Instead, therefore, we will first describe and present a typical progressive penalty system so that the reader will become knowledgeable about how typical disciplinary systems operate. We will then describe a novel approach to discipline which attempts to not use punishment, called "discipline without punishment." Finally, we will present two studies which have been conducted on the effects of penalties on employee behavior.

The Progressive Penalty System

Undoubtedly the most common form of disciplinary-punishment procedures utilized in industry is the progressive penalty system. Note that the term "penalty" is used rather than "punishment." This reflects the distinction made earlier between the two terms. A penalty given to a worker may or may not be experienced as punishing.

Considerable variation exists among organizations in terms of the mechanics of their progressive penalty systems. However, most distinguish between very serious and less serious offenses and almost all systems contain a series of four or more disciplinary steps which supervisors follow when a rule violation occurs. Successively greater penalties are associated with each step. Hence the name Progressive Penalty System. An example of this system follows. It is interesting to observe that this organization has a review procedure built into the disciplinary system, a feature which is not contained in all systems.

Progressive Penalty System
Example

1) PURPOSE—The purpose of this disciplinary policy is to set forth principles and guidelines designed to achieve fair and consistent treatment of employees in disciplinary matters. In all but serious offenses, the organization will follow a progressive disciplinary policy designed to correct behavior or attitudes which are not acceptable in a work environment.

2) TYPES OF OFFENSES—Offenses by employees are of two general classes:

A. SERIOUS OFFENSES—Serious offenses are offenses which justify a termination or suspension without prior verbal or written warnings or other attempts to correct the conduct of the employee involved. Serious offenses are of the type set forth in paragraph three below.

B. LESS SERIOUS OFFENSES—Less serious offenses are offenses which do not call for termination of an employee for the first offense but for milder forms of discipline aimed at correcting the improper conduct of employees. Less serious offenses are of the type set forth in paragraph four below.

3) SERIOUS OFFENSES—The following offenses are of the type which are considered serious offenses which justify termination for the first offense. The following are for purposes of illustration and are not considered to be all-inclusive: theft or mishandling of monies, deliberate falsification of records, refusal to follow a direct order, use of drugs or intoxicants on company property, immoral conduct, assault, dishonesty, insubordination, and gross negligence.

4) LESS SERIOUS OFFENSES—The following offenses are of the type which are considered less serious offenses. In disciplining employees for less serious offenses, progressive disciplinary procedures set forth in paragraph 5 are to be followed. The following are for purposes of illustration and are not to be considered all-inclusive: absenteeism, leaving the work site without permission, failure to be physically present at the work site, failure to notify the supervisor of an absence, tardiness, horseplay, and failure to turn in required reports on time.

5) PROGRESSIVE DISCIPLINARY PROCEDURE—In disciplining an employee for less serious offenses, the following

sequence will take place: a) First offense, Verbal warning; b) Second offense, Written warning; c) Third offense, Suspension; and d) Fourth offense, Termination.

No two cases are ever alike and the progressive disciplinary path will vary from case to case. The steps set forth above are a suggested norm.

6) REVIEW PROCEDURE—Any employee who wishes to contest any disciplinary action must comply with the following procedure:

STEP ONE—The employee first must discuss the matter with the immediate supervisor.

STEP TWO—If the matter is not resolved under Step One, the employee may file a written grievance with the immediate supervisor within five (5) working days of the date of the event or the occurrence giving rise to the grievance. Such written grievance shall be on forms provided by the supervisor and shall describe the facts surrounding the grievance and set forth the relief desired. The supervisor shall answer the grievance in writing.

STEP THREE—If the matter is not resolved under Step Two, the employee may, within three (3) working days after receipt of the supervisor's written answer, request that the matter be appealed to the President. The decision of the President will be final and binding on all concerned.

Discipline Without Punishment

In an article entitled "Discipline Without Punishment," Huberman (1965) describes a disciplinary procedure instituted at a Douglas fir plywood mill which had a work force of 550 unionized employees. The most unique feature of the procedure was the company's attempt to establish a disciplinary procedure which did not utilize "punishment." The procedure itself consisted of a series of steps which supervisors follow when an employee breaks a rule:

Step 1: Foreman offers the worker a casual and friendly reminder on the job that a work rule was broken.

Step 2: Upon a second rule violation, the foreman will again correct the violation, usually on the job and, in addition, will call the employee into his or her office for a friendly discussion. During the discussion the supervisor explains the need for the rule and makes sure the worker understands the explanation.

Step 3: In the event of another violation, Step 2 is repeated with a few modifications. The shift foreman is also present during the discussion. The employee is told that if he finds the work or work rules distasteful then perhaps he should seek another job. The employee is told that vocational counseling is available through the Personnel Office. The conversation is confirmed in a letter to the employee's home.

Step 4: Following the next rule violation within 6-8 weeks of Step 3, the supervisor and shift foreman meet again with the employee. The employee is directed to go home for the rest of the day and consider seriously whether he does or does not wish to abide by the company rules. He is paid for the time he is at home and is told that another violation will lead to termination.

Step 5: If a further incident occurs within 6-8 weeks, the employee is terminated.

If several incidents occur within a short span of time, the company may skip Steps 2 and 3. By the same token if criminal behavior or fighting occurs within the plant, the employee is terminated immediately.

The company reports that one question which is frequently asked about the plan is whether the organization is not eliminating minor forms of punishment (warnings and suspensions) while retaining the most severe form-discharge. In response the company argues that discharge should be construed as punishment "only if it is done out of a desire to achieve retribution," that is, "to pay the employee back." Since this is not the company's motive, Huberman argues that discharge is not punishment.

How successful has this approach to discipline been? After the plan had been in operation for two years, Huberman reported that it has been very successful. The plan has the full support of the supervisory staff; morale, work habits and the level of discipline are reported as satisfactory. Huberman reported that eighty-seven letters were sent to a total of sixty-two employees during the two-year period. These letters resulted in eleven voluntary terminations (no discharges) while the remaining fifty-one employees improved their job behavior to a satisfactory level.

Several aspects of this study deserve comment. First, the reader will undoubtedly realize that Huberman has defined both discipline and punishment differently than we have in this chapter. Huberman appears to be using the broad definition of the term "discipline," which excludes the concept of punishment. He also appears to be using the word "punishment" to mean what we have called "penalties." Secondly, and more importantly in practice, one must wonder whether the company's actions (Steps 1 through 5) are perceived by the workers as penalties or not. Presumably, the supervisor does not intend to penalize the worker when taking these steps. The critical question, however, is how the employees perceive and react to the manager's action. If the employee improves the work behavior in question as a result of the manager's actions, which is clearly the intent of the entire system, we would regard those actions as punishment based on our definition of the term.

Cashier Study

While examples demonstrating the use of discipline and penalties in industry are plentiful, remarkably few studies have been conducted regarding the effects of penalties on employee behavior. One notable exception is a study on theft prevention conducted by Marholin and Gray (1976).

In that study, the authors examined the effects of fining six cashiers of a small twelve-hour-a-day, seven-day-a-week restaurant, for cash register shortages. The procedure followed was this: if any single day's cash shortage equaled or exceeded one percent of that day's sales receipts, the total shortage, divided by the number of cashiers working that day, was subtracted from each cashier's salary for that particular day. The investigation ran for forty-one days and was divided into four periods. During the first period, which lasted five days, the investigators found that the cash register was short on all five days for a total of 4.02 percent of sales. In the remaining three periods, the fine procedure was instituted for twelve days (Period 2), rescinded for three days (Period 3), and reinstituted for twenty-one days (Period 4). The effects of fines on cash register shortages are reported in Table 3-1.

Table 3-1: Effects of Fines on Cash Register Shortages

	Period 1 No Fine	Period 2 1% Fine	Period 3 No Fine	Period 4 1% Fine
Average Shortage	4.02%	0.43%	4.16%	0.04%
Days in Period	5	12	3	21
Shortage Days	5	2	3	0

The results are quite dramatic. They show a drastic reduction in shortages during days the penalty was in effect. It is particularly interesting to note that during Period 3 when the fines were removed, shortages occurred on all three days and averaged 4.16 percent of sales.

While this study could be criticized for its small sample size and short duration, it is important because it demonstrates one of the benefits that penalties can potentially have over other strategies for improving employee productivity, namely, that it can result in rapid behavior change if administered properly. None of the other strategies discussed in this book typically have this important attribute.

Three Methods of Reducing Absenteeism

Another study on employee discipline compared three methods of treating absenteeism. It was conducted by A. L. Gary (1971). In conducting the study, Gary analyzed the personnel records of 150 employees: fifty employees had been penalized progressively and the penalty remained a permanent part of their record; fifty had been penalized but in a manner not consistent with the normal progression and/or subsequently had the penalty removed from their record; and fifty had broken the organizational rule regarding absenteeism but had not received any penalty. Gary found that absenteeism over a twenty-month period was lower for the group of employees who had been penalized progressively (the first group) than for either of the other two groups.

The study is important because it demonstrates that consistent application of the penalties called for by a progressive penalty system is more effective in changing employee behavior than is the haphazard application of penalties. This study also demonstrates that penalties can change employee behavior, specifically absenteeism.

REASONS

The reasons for using penalties may be grouped into two sections: 1) Thorndike's "Law of Effect" and 2) the "Hot Stove Rules." We will now discuss each of these.

Thorndike's Law of Effect

In the previous chapter on the use of reinforcement and shaping we cited the Law of Effect as one underlying rationale for the use of reinforcement. Concurrently, this powerful concept also serves as an underlying theory for the use of penalties.

At the risk of being repetitive, Thorndike's Law of Effect states:

> When a modifiable connection between a situation and a response is made and is accompanied or followed by a satisfying state of affairs, that connection's strength is increased; when made and accompanied by an annoying state of affairs, its strength is decreased. (from Hilgard and Bowers, 1966)

As this law relates to discipline, it states that if a person is disciplined for performing an action, the action is less likely to occur again. As we mentioned previously, this law assumes that people want to avoid pain. It stresses that a lawful relationship exists between actions and the consequences which follow the actions.

The "Hot Stove Rules"

The "Hot Stove Rules" of discipline can be attributed to Douglas McGregor (1967). This notion is one of the most useful analogies we have encountered since it is amusing, familiar, and very much to the point. It is simple to understand and very easy to remember. It is a universal part of the human experience.

A stove is one of the most cherished and useful possessions of any family. It is a source of hot apple pie, turkey at Thanksgiving, and chocolate cake. Its heat helps remove the chill on a frosty November morning. There is one simple rule: "Don't touch."

In spite of our favorable attitude toward the stove, it will burn us if we touch it accidentally. The stove is a powerful teacher because it takes only one touch to teach us that when it is hot it can hurt us. It causes us to change our behavior immediately and permanently. The stove is a consistent teacher, too. It will deliver its lesson to anybody at any time. It does not discriminate.

The stove accomplishes all of this without causing us any damaging emotional reactions. We do not even harbor any resentment or hatred toward the stove even though it punished us. Why is it that the stove can change our behavior so effectively and yet not create any resentment, anger, or hostility? Contained in the answer to this question are the principles of an effective disciplinary policy and of the effective use of penalties.

The penalty is immediate.   When a person touches a hot stove, the pain is immediate. Therefore, persons who touch the stove can easily associate their behavior with the consequence. There is no doubt about where the pain came from. They know that touching a hot stove causes pain. The hot stove does not wait until a person has touched it several times before it burns them. It responds instantly on the very first occasion.

The Penalty is Directed Toward One's Actions, Not One's Personality.   The hot stove directs its penalty towards one's actions. It does not degrade the personality of the individual who touches it. It does not condemn the person's behavior or attempt to shame the individual. It does not try to ''get even'' with the offender. It deals only with the behavior of touching it when it is hot. It has no concern with shame or guilt. It does not care that you did not mean to touch it or that you may be ''sorry'' that you did. A hot stove simply and directly burns.

The Penalty Is Consistent Across Time and People.   The hot stove burns anyone and everyone who touches it. It does not grant any exceptions. The person's age, sex, minority status, physical appearance, prior work experience, or social status are irrelevant. Even seniority will not help. The son or daughter of the president gets no special favors. A hot stove is a true equal opportunity employer.

The hot stove is also entirely consistent from one time to another. Regardless of when someone touches the hot stove, it burns him. The stove does not become more lenient on some days and less lenient on others for no apparent reason. It does not abruptly decide to administer its punishment to someone so as to ''set an example for others.''

The Penalty Is Moderately Severe in Intensity.   When anybody touches a hot stove a moderately severe penalty is administered the very first time. The hot stove does not begin with a penalty of low intensity at first and then gradually increase its severity. (In the light of the Gary study (1971) discussed above, we are not sure this is an advantage.)

The Penalty Provides Important Information.   When a person touches a hot stove, it provides him directly with important information regarding his past behavior. It provides him with knowledge of why the behavior was inappropriate. Since the rule violated was simple, it lets him know clearly how the behavior can be changed to avoid future punishment. He knows the consequences if the behavior does not change.

The Penalty Occurs in a Warm, Supportive Setting. Most people have positive feelings toward a hot stove. It provides warmth and food. The fact that a hot stove has a simple inflexible rule ("Don't touch") does not change one's favorable feelings toward it.

The Rule is Realistic. The "Don't touch" rule is realistic and practical. It is not the result of a whim or fancy of the moment. It is not a symptom of a pathological need to demonstrate power. It is not an issue of control. It is very real and necessary.

In summary, the hot stove is a most effective teacher. Its punishment is immediate, consistent, equitable, and only moderately severe. The hot stove provides important information and its penalties are delivered in a warm and friendly context. It is more realistic than punitive.

POTENTIAL SIDE EFFECTS OF DISCIPLINE

All of the approaches to increasing employee productivity can backfire, particularly if they are handled improperly. It is possible for each of them to result in negative consequences for the organization. In recent years, educators, psychologists, sociologists, and behavioral scientists have been quick to point out the negative consequences of discipline—particularly punishment. They have cited case studies in child-rearing and in organizational settings.

It is our belief that most, if not all, of these negative side effects can be avoided if the manager is able to follow the "hot stove rules." However, since it is not always possible to follow these rules (because of internal policy, union contracts, and so on) some negative side effects will undoubtedly occur. The potential occurrences of such effects should not lead managers to conclude that discipline or punishment should never be used. All approaches to improving employee productivity can potentially lead to undesirable consequences. This is an aspect of the manager's job. It goes with the territory.

We believe that managers should be aware of these potential negative consequences so that they can take steps to minimize the likelihood of their occurence and reduce their impact, if they do indeed occur.

There are several potential side effects which deserve special consideration. Each will now be reviewed.

Suppression Versus Elimination

Punishment may only suppress undesirable behavior rather than eliminate it. When the threat of punishment is removed, the formerly suppressed behavior may reappear.

It is important to observe that even if discipline or punishment only suppresses behavior, this is not necessarily a negative consequence of its use. After all, eliminating a behavior entirely may not be necessary for an organization to function effectively. For example, if two employees stop fighting with each other for fear of being fired, does it really matter that their desire to fight has only been suppressed? Probably not. On the other hand, suppression of behavior, rather than elimination of it, may prove disadvantageous if the costs of supervision become excessive. Consider two supervisors who must constantly monitor the behavior of two employees to keep them from fighting with each other. The mere suppression of the behavior in such a case truely becomes a disadvantage.

Extreme Emotional Reactions
May Result

Discipline/punishment may produce fear, anxiety, hatred, hostility, and other energy-consuming, dysfunctional emotional behavior.

Discipline, if improperly administered, can cause anxiety in the person disciplined. For that matter, it can even cause anxiety in the person delivering the discipline. The former's anxiety can manifest itself in numerous ways. It can result in hostility toward the person administering the discipline (the supervisor) which in turn can lead to attempts to "get even" with the supervisor. Employee sabotage or output restriction are examples of some ways employees "get even" with a supervisor. In addition, the hostility may cause employees to use their creative abilities to figure out ways to break the rules without incurring discipline.

The fear that is associated with discipline/punishment may lead the disciplined employee to avoid the supervisor. This, in turn, may make it more difficult for the supervisor to monitor the employee's job performance and improve it. Fear of being punished may also encourage employees to hide any errors that they make. To illustrate, factory workers may put a small damaged tool into their lunch box or throw it into a trash receptacle rather than report the damage to management out of a fear of punishment. It is important to observe that when employees hide errors rather than report them it may have very dysfunctional effects on the organization. The attempts of Richard M. Nixon and his aides to hide the Watergate scandal from their employers (*we* are their employers) was quite dysfunctional for the nation. If all employees hide broken tools rather than report them, it is difficult for management to determine whether a specific tool is working satisfactorily. Expensive and nonproductive close supervision is necessary in such cases in order to preserve effectiveness.

Because fear of being punished may result in lying by employee, managers face a dilemma. How does one convince employees to tell the truth about errors they have made? If the manager penalizes employees for making errors they are almost certain to lie about

Figure 3-1. Punishment and Discipline: Strategy Guide

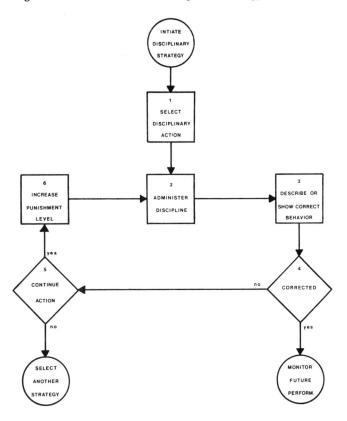

future errors. By the same token, if employees make errors and the supervisor does nothing about it, what incentive is there for them to change their behavior? One possible solution to the dilemma is for managers to develop a tolerance for some level of employee error. If employees understand they will not be penalized for only a reasonable number of errors, they would be more likely to tell the truth. The knowledge that excessive errors would result in certain penalties should provide some incentive for employees to improve their subsequent performance.

Finally, fear of punishment may cause rigidity in employee behavior. Employees may become afraid to do anything without first obtaining the supervisor's approval. While this may be beneficial to an organization, it is more likely to result in reduced initiative and creativity on the employee's part. This, in turn, may make it nearly impossible for the organization to function effectively.

IMPLEMENTATION

Many of the basic principles of the effective use of discipline and punishment have already been presented. What remains is to organize and integrate these principles into a meaningful framework for action.

The preceding page presents a strategy guide showing five steps. The reader is reminded that this strategy guide is meant to serve as a basic "roadmap" for action. Since each situation encountered by a manager is somewhat unique, some modification to the basic approach may be required. Nonetheless, the fundamentals presented here are applicable in virtually all situations.

Please note that in this and subsequent strategy guides the "Initiate...Strategy," "Select Another Strategy," and, "Monitor Future Performance" steps in the guide are standard beginning and end points. Accordingly, they will not be numbered or discussed with other than a brief reference.

Step 1 Select Disciplinary Action. We begin our analysis by assuming that an employee has been informed, either orally or in written form (direct orders, posted rules, employee handbooks, and so on), of what is expected in terms of desired or acceptable behavior. We assume further that the employee's recent behavior is inappropriate, that is, it is not what is desired by the supervisor and specified by the relevant rules. Finally, we assume that the supervisor has selected discipline as the appropriate action for changing the employee's behavior, based on an analysis of the situation (Chapter Nine).

How severe should the penalty be? Theoretically, a manager should select that level of severity which is just sufficient to insure that the employee changes the behavior to the desired level. For some employees, only a minimal penalty level, such as a verbal statement or rebuke, may be all that is necessary. For others, a suspension or other form of severe penalty may be required. It is important to remember in this regard that one of the "Hot Stove Rules" suggests that a moderately severe punishment will probably be required to be effective. Undoubtedly, this is true for the average employee. Clearly, a manager must exercise good judgment in determining the appropriate level of discipline to be used. In selecting the appropriate level of severity, it is important for a manager to remember that the purpose of the discipline is to change the employee's behavior. Unfortunately, managers often lose sight of this fact and the results are then usually counterproductive. Discipline should never be used to "get even" with an employee or to "set an example" or to "show the employee who is the boss."

Many organizations have formalized policies which leave little discretion to the supervisor regarding the level of discipline which is to be used. Under these conditions, the supervisor typically has little choice but to comply with the company rules or policies.

One of the major advantages of having formalized and mandatory penalty levels is that it helps to insure consistency of treatment for rule offenders. This is extremely important as we shall soon see. On the negative side, it can result in an employee receiving a penalty greater than the optimal level necessary to change behavior or in a penalty which may lack the intensity necessary to elicit the desired change.

One alternative which a supervisor may wish to consider using when selecting a penalty level is to follow the "discipline without punishment" approach described earlier. This approach makes no attempt to overtly penalize employees although the effect may be to do so. It involves the employee in the disciplinary process as an active rather than a passive participant. It should be apparent to the reader that the "discipline without punishment" approach is fully consistent with the idea that supervisors should administer only the minimum effective level of discipline—that which is sufficient to change the employee's behavior. It recognizes the fact that discipline alone, without overt penalties, may be sufficient for behavioral change.

Step 2 Administer Discipline. In administering discipline to an employee, four of the "Hot Stove Rules" are particularly relevant. First, the penalty or disciplinary action should be used immediately after the employee has engaged in an inappropriate behavior. Why is this necessary? Remember that the goal of using penalties is to change the employee's behavior. Studies on the use of penalties indicate that if employees are to change their behavior they must be able to clearly associate the disciplinary stimulus with the inappropriate behavior. They must connect their behavior with the consequences of that behavior. The longer the time span between the unacceptable behavior and its consequences, the less likely the employee will associate the two.

There is yet another and perhaps more important reason why the discipline should be immediate. Employees do not typically work in isolation. Instead they work in groups and, hence, the behavior of one employee is observed by many others. If one employee engages in an inappropriate behavior (for example, fails to wear safety glasses, smokes in unauthorized places, arrives to work late, and so on) and the supervisor appears to be taking no action, other employees may erroneously conclude that the behavior is acceptable or that the organization is not consistent in its rule enforcement. No worthwhile organizational purpose is served by allowing employees to reach these conclusions. It is far more likely that the observing employees will respond by "testing the limits" of the rules.

Yet another risk associated with the use of delayed rather than immediate discipline is that rule violators may engage in subsequent rule violations. For example, a construction worker who works without a hard hat once may try to get away with not wearing it in the future. The employee's continued rule violations can be quite detrimental to the organization even if the other workers do not follow suit, particularly if the offense is a serious one, such as stealing or selling narcotics on company property.

Thus far, we have suggested that penalties should be administered immediately after an inappropriate behavior has occurred. Equally important is the principle that to be most effective, penalties should be consistent at all times and for all people. Why is this true? Briefly, the underlying rationale for consistency in discipline rests on "Expectancy Theory" (Chapter Eight: Basing Rewards on Performance) and "Equity Theory" (Chapter Four: Treating Employees Fairly). The former suggests that people's actions are based in part on their perceptions of the likelihood or probability that engaging in a given behavior will result in rewards or penalties. The logical extension of this theory to the use of penalties is that if a person knows with complete certainty (100 percent probability) that a given action will be penalized, he will be less apt to take that action than if he is uncertain about whether that action will be penalized. Using the "Hot Stove" analogy, a person is less likely or willing to touch a stove known to be hot (100 percent certain) than a stove with an unknown probability of being hot. How does a worker determine how likely it is that penalties will follow if a specific action is taken? He makes this judgment based on his past experience. He observes whether or not the organization administers penalties consistently at all times and for all people.

Equity theory (treated fully in the next chapter) stresses the need for organizations to treat people fairly. It states that people determine if they are being treated fairly by comparing themselves with how others are treated. Furthermore, it argues that if people are not treated fairly, their morale will suffer and they may take actions designed to "get even" with the organization or some individual. "You put me down so if I put you down we're even." Let us now extend this theory to the administration of discipline. If an organization penalizes one employee for an action but not another for the same action or disciplines a person for an action which occurred last week but not for the same act this week, the disciplinary actions taken will probably be viewed as unfair not only by the person disciplined but by other employees as well. Hence, morale may suffer and employees may engage in retaliation against the company or some particular manager. It is common for competent union organizers to utilize the perceived inequities within an organization as a recruiting tool.

One issue that frequently surfaces regarding consistency of penalties is whether or not extenuating circumstances should be taken into account when administering them. For example, suppose two workers are both seen working without wearing hard hats in an area where hard hats are required. Suppose further that one of the workers has thirty years seniority and a spotless record, and is perhaps the best employee in the company. The second worker is a new employee and is seen as a marginal worker at best. If the company has a policy which requires that workers who fail to wear hard hats in designated areas are to receive a three-day suspension, should both employees receive equal penalties? Should not the superior worker be given special consideration because of an outstanding work record?

Some have argued that if an organization considers any extenuating circumstances when administering penalties it runs counter to the idea of consistency. They argue that the concepts of consistency and extenuating circumstances are mutually contradictory. We disagree. It is entirely possible and, in terms of equity, it is sometimes advisable to consider extenuating circumstances. To do so, however, requires that the organization inform employees that extenuating circumstances will be considered in all, or some specific, disciplinary cases. It should also spell out what specific factors (for example, length of service, performance record, age, type of violation) will be considered.

If an organization then always considers these factors when disciplining employees and does it uniformly at all times and for all people, it would not necessarily be violating the consistency principle. Given a set of extenuating circumstances, the organization could then be potentially consistent.

Unfortunately, many managers discipline some employees without first informing all employees that extenuating circumstances will be considered. Or, they fail to define what extenuating factors will be considered. In either case, the consistency principle is definitely violated. As a result, employees may feel that the organization, or at least the manager, is not treating them fairly.

In addition to the notions of immediacy and consistency, discipline should also be administered in an impersonal manner. This does not mean that it should never be done orally or on a one-to-one basis. It does not mean the manager should attempt to emulate a robot and not express any personal feelings when talking with the employee regarding the behavior for which the discipline is given. What "impersonal" means in this context is that a manager should discipline the employee in private when possible and focus the discussion on the employee's behavior and the consequences of that behavior, rather than on the employee's personality. When an employee engages in an inappropriate action, managers occasionally feel like saying, "Joe, you were a complete idiot for doing that!", or, "Mary, you are irresponsible." While these statements may, indeed, be true, derogatory statements about the employee's whole personality are just plain "overkill" and are never ultimately helpful. The purpose of administering discipline is to change behavior, not to vent pent-up feelings. The cost of losing sight of this principle is anger and defensiveness on the part of the employee—conditions that are not conducive to either rational understanding or effective behavioral change.

If managers focus on the employee's behavior or the consequences of the behavior, the chances that the employee will actually change the behavior are increased. This is true because discussions of a specific behavior are considerably less threatening and more specific in terms of the changes expected than are personality accusations. Two examples will illustrate:

POOR: Joe, you are a complete idiot for not completing your sales reports accurately.

BETTER: Joe, when you don't complete your sales reports accurately, shipments of your orders are delayed. This costs us money and it costs you money.

POOR: Mary, you are irresponsible. I must give you a written warning.

BETTER: Mary, you were late to work again. That delays others from completing their work. I am going to give you a written warning.

There is yet another important factor which the "Hot Stove" analogy suggests and which is important in implementing disciplinary actions. Penalties should ideally be delivered within the context of a warm and friendly relationship between the supervisor and subordinate. This is so because subordinates are much more apt to accept a penalty and change their behavior if their supervisor helped them to develop their skills and abilities and has rewarded them frequently in some way. The supervisor who has not been a source of rewards and praise is less likely to be successful. Observe that in everyday relationships with others, people are much more willing to change their behavior when criticized by their friends than when strangers or enemies criticize them. The same phenomenon occurs in industrial relationships. If an employee values your good opinion of him and the praise and rewards you have previously given, then he must also take your criticisms seriously.

In some organizations, managers and employees have developed such animosity between them over the years that this rule is repeatedly violated out of necessity. Ideally, managers in these situations would attempt to improve these relationships over a period of time. In the meantime, however, they still will need to administer penalties in a less than ideal atmosphere. The only advice we can offer to managers trapped in this situation is to prepare themselves for one or more of the negative side effects of discipline which were discussed previously. With knowledge of what can happen the effects may sometimes be minimized.

Step 3 Describe or Show Correct Behavior. Earlier in the chapter we suggested that if the use of penalties is to be effective in changing behavior it must have informational value. The employee should know what behavior is expected, why it is expected, and what will happen if an inappropriate behavior is repeated. Administering discipline immediately, consistently, and impersonally all have information value but they typically fail to provide an employee with information about why the behavior was inappropriate. Supervisors, too, frequently fail to provide this information to employees. They are prone to say simply "Don't do this or that" without any explanation. Numerous studies have demonstrated that explaining why something should not be done can lead to permanent behavioral change while simply giving orders without an explanation often leads only to a repression of the forbidden act. In one of these studies (Walters and Cheyne, 1966), a group of eighty-four first grade boys were given toys to play with. Some of the boys were told beforehand, without any explanation, that they were not to touch certain toys. Others were given the same instructions accompanied by an explanation of why the proscribed toys were not to be touched. It was found that punishment given for touching the toys was far more effective for the second (explanation) group than for the first group (orders only).

On occasion, simply explaining to an employee why his behavior is inappropriate may not be sufficient. The supervisor may need to actually show or demonstrate to the employee why this is so. A carpenter, for example, may not understand why wearing protective goggles is essential when driving cut nails. A demonstration by the supervisor showing how cut nails can shatter may convincingly demonstrate this point and save the supervisor from needing to discuss this issue with the carpenter at a future date.

Step 4 Corrected? If the correct level of punishment has been used, the response to the punished act was relatively immediate, and the correct behavior was shown or explained, then the strategy is frequently effective. If you judge that the punishment goals have been reached, the proper course of action is to discontinue punishment, exit the strategy guide at "Monitor Future Performance," and give consideration to proceeding to a reinforcement strategy. The reason for moving on to the use of reinforcement is, as was shown in the previous chapter, that now you have a desired behavior and steps to maintain that behavior are now appropriate. If you choose to do this, however, be careful that the undesirable behavior has completely vanished! If it has not, the reinforcements used with the intent of maintaining the new behavior may inadvertently strengthen leftover elements of the undesirable behavior as well.

If the situation has not been corrected go on to Step 5.

Step 5 Continue Action?   The opening of Step 4 suggested three conditions which typically lead to success with this strategy. If you find that one or more of these conditions are absent, then you may wish to try the strategy again. Do not neglect the "Hot Stove Rules"--check that you have followed them. Since the most usual lack is the correct level of punishment, an element of these rules, Step 6 suggests raising the punishment level.

Why should you decide to not continue with this strategy? If all three conditions for success were present (correct level, immediacy, and feedback about what is correct) and, in addition, it is inadvisable, for whatever reason, to increase the punishment level, then the strategy should be terminated. You may then consider another strategy—either one of the six remaining core strategies or an appropriate outplacement strategy as covered in Chapter One.

Step 6 Increase Punishment Level.   This step, of course, only occurs if previous steps were unsuccessful in changing the employee's behavior.

Earlier in this chapter, we suggested that a manager ideally should select and deliver that penalty level which is just sufficient to bring about the desired change in employee behavior. Accurately estimating this optimal level is quite difficult. Errors in judgment will undoubtedly occur and should be expected. When the initial level of a penalty is found to be insufficient, the manager must try again using the next level of severity. If this is not successful, yet a higher level may be necessary. Keep in mind that the alternatives of terminating the employee or selecting a different strategy are always available to the manager should the use of penalties prove ineffective.

SUMMARY

In this chapter we have examined the effective use of discipline. We have defined "discipline" and "punishment" and "penalty" and shown their interrelationships. We have compared a progressive penalty system with the "discipline without punishment" approach.

We have described two studies which demonstrate the effects of penalties on employee behavior. Both of these studies indicate that penalties, if administered properly, can be an effective management tool for changing employee behavior.

The theory or rationale underlying the use of discipline was described in terms of Thorndike's Law of Effect and, by analogy, using McGregor's "Hot Stove" rules. We noted that if these rules are not followed when delivering penalties, one or more negative side effects frequently result. Finally, we presented a step-by-step strategy guide for use when planning and executing disciplinary actions.

Unlike some of the other motivational strategies presented in this book, the use of penalties has the potential for changing an employee's behavior quickly. The emphasis here is on the word "potential," for penalties are not always effective. When employees are engaging in intolerable behaviors such as violating important safety rules, damaging company property, or fighting, quick behavioral change is often necessary. Some disciplinary action is probably the only strategy that has the potential for being effective in these situations.

In addition to being relatively quick, penalties are usually financially inexpensive to use. It costs little or nothing to give an employee an oral or written warning. Even suspensions are usually quite inexpensive, since employees are typically not paid for the period of their suspension. It is important to add that setting up a disciplinary system and communicating it to all employees does involve some initial expense. However, even this one-time expense is not usually very high.

Another important attribute of the use of discipline is that employees are accustomed to the presence of rules. Throughout their lives, such as in school, at home, or in various social or sports activities, people are asked to abide by certain rules. As a result of this pattern, employees have come to expect rules and constraints, and some even feel uneasy if they are not provided. Disciplinary rules serve to reduce employee uncertainty about acceptable and unacceptable behavior. Thus, in a very real sense, managers are meeting a cultural norm when they establish rules. They are satisfying the desires and meeting the expectations of employees. Establishing equitable rules and enforcing them often serves, then, to improve employee-manager relations. It may simultaneously improve employee perceptions of the manager as one who is competent, fair, and firm (not harsh).

It is important to observe that administering penalties has certain drawbacks. It may result in dysfunctional emotional employee behavior, as we have observed earlier. This is particularly true if the "Hot Stove" rules are not followed. In addition, administering discipline to a violent individual may only provide him with an excuse to retaliate. Drug addicts, alcoholics, mentally ill employees, and senile workers are not likely to respond to penalties either. Counseling referrals or one of the outplacement strategies is usually more likely to succeed in these situations.

RECOMMENDED READINGS

Arvey, R. O. and Ivancevich, J. M. "Punishment in Organizations: A Review, Propositions, and Research Suggestions." *Academy of Management Review* 5(1) (1980): 123-32.

Belohlav, J.A. and Popp, P.O. "Making Employee Discipline Work." *The Personnel Administrator* 23(3) (1978): 22-nn.

Bocarosky, L.D. "Guidelines to Corrective Discipline." *Personnel Journal* 58(10) (1979): 698-702.

Booker, G. S. "Behavioral Aspects of Disciplinary Action." *Personnel Journal* July 1969, pp. 525-29.

Bureau of National Affairs. "Employee Conduct and Discipline." *Personnel Policies Forum Survey 102. August 1973.*

Donahue, A.L. "Disciplinary Actions in New York State Service: A Radical Change." *Public Personnel Management* 4(2) (1975): 110-12.

Gary, A. L. "Industrial Absenteeism: An Evaluation of Three Methods of Treatment." *Personnel Journal* May 1971, pp. 352-53.

Hamblin, R. L. "Punative and Non-Punative Supervision." *Social Problems* 11 (1964) 345-59.

Hamner, W.C. and Organ, D.W. *Organizational Behavior: An Applied Psychological Approach.* Dallas, Texas: Business Publications Inc., 1978.

Huberman, J. "Discipline Without Punishment." *Harvard Business Review* 42 (1965): 62-68.

Huberman, J. "Discipline Without Punishment Lives." *Harvard Business Review* 53(4) (1975): 6-8.

Huberman, J. "From the Thoughtful Businessman." *Harvard Business Review* 43 (1965): 182-86.

Jennings, K. "Verbal and Physical Abuse Toward Supervision." *The Arbitration Journal* 29(4) (1974): 258-71.

Kazadin, E. *Behavior Modification in Applied Settings.* Homewood, Ill.: Dorsey Press, 1975.

Maier, N. R. F. and Danielson, L. E. "An Evolution of Two Approaches to Discipline in Industry." *Journal of Applied Psychology* 40(5), (1956): 319-23.

Marholin, D. and Gray, D. "Efforts of Group Response-Cost Procedures on Cash Shortages in a Small Business." *Journal of Applied Behavior Analysis* 9 (1976): 25-30.

Martin, R.G. "Five Principles of Corrective Disciplinary Action." *Supervisory Management* 23(1) (1978): 24-28.

McDermot, T.J. and Newhams, T.H. "Discharge-Reinstatement: What Happens Thereafter." *Industrial and Labor Relations Review* 24 (1971): 526-40.

McGregor, D. "Hot Stove Rule of Discipline." From *Personnel: The Human Problems of Management,* edited by G. Strauss and L. Sayles. Englewood Cliffs, N.J.: Prentice-Hall, 1967.

Mulder, F. "Characteristics of Violators of Formal Company Rules," *Journal of Applied Psychology* 55(5) (1971): 500-502.

Provost, G.J.; Smolensky, W.R.; Stephens, R.C.; and Freedman, Y.F. "Alcohol or Drug Use on the Job: A Study of Arbitration Cases." *Employee Relations Law Journal* 5(2) (1979): 245-57.

Rosen, B. and Jerdee, T.H. "Factors Influencing Disciplinary Judgments." *Journal of Applied Psychology* 59(3) (1974): 327-31.

Shershin, M.J. and Boxx, W.R. "Due Process in Discipline and Dismissal." *Supervisory Management* 21(11) (1976): 2-9.

Shull, F.A. and Cummings, L.L. "Enforcing the Rules: How Do Managers Differ?" *Personnel* March & April 1966, pp.33-39.

Sims, H.P. "Further Thoughts on Punishment in Organizations." *Academy of Management Review* 5(1) (1980): 133-38.

Sims, H.P. "Tips and Troubles with Employee Reprimand." *Personnel Administrator* January 1979, pp. 57-60.

Sullivan, D.M. "Employee Discipline: Beware the Company Position." *Industrial Relations* 17(3), (1978): 692-95.

Unterberger, I. and Unterberger, S.H. "Disciplining Professional Employees." *Industrial Relations* 17(3), (1978): 353-59.

Walters, R.H. and Cheyne, J.A. "Some Parameters Influencing the Efforts of Punishment on Social Behavior." Paper presented at the Annual Meeting of the American Psychological Association, New York, 1966.

Welch, B. "Keeping the Discipliners in Line." *Personnel Management* 10(8) (1978): 21-24.

Wohlking, W. "Effective Discipline in Employee Relations." *Personnel Journal* 54 (1975): 489-93.

Wollenberger, J.B. "Acceptable Work Rules and Penalties: A Company Guide." *Personnel* July-August 1963, pp. 23-29.

4

Treating
Employees Fairly

INTRODUCTION

> NEP-O-TISM n. (F nepotisme, fn It nepotismo, fr, nepote   nephew,
> fr. L. nepot-, nepos   grandson, nephew-- more at NEPHEW):
> favoritism shown to a relative (as by giving an appointive job) on the
> basis of relationship.

"Time was," reminisced the old man, "the way to get ahead around
here was to marry the boss's daughter." He looked at the ceiling and
pulled thoughtfully on his pipe once more. "Of course in my time it
was easier... only had to look out for the new son-in-law." He
walked over to the loading dock and carefully peered into his pipe
bowl by the fading light of afternoon. "Nowadays it's the daughter
who wants' to be a manager, too."

Ed backed his hi-lo away from the loading area. It sure was true.
It is who you know or who you are related to, not how hard you
work. With the boss's daughter running the shipping department
now, things sure were not what they used to be.

Angrily, he thought again, "The old man was right, a guy can't
get a fair shake any more." Almost without thinking, but with just a
hint of malice and satisfaction, Ed rammed the hoist lever forward,
slamming the crate to the floor, splintering the wooden skid it rested
on.

Ed's supervisor, Oliver, was worried about Ed. He had been
acting strangely for several weeks now. Crates were damaged fre-

quently, either dropped or sideswiped, and Ed frequently forgot to plug his hi-lo into the recharger at night.

"Hey, Ed, come on over here. I want to talk to you."

"What do you want?" Ed answered moodily.

"What's going on?"

Ed looked uncomfortable. Avoiding Oliver's glance he muttered, "Nothin'-- everything's just fine."

"Oh, sure," Oliver shot back, but with a supportive smile. "I saw you bust that skid and that's not like you."

A little more friendly probing, and it all came out. As Oliver already knew, Ed had expected to be promoted to supervisor when Oliver became the department manager. When Judy came back to the plant and began her training stint as manager Oliver had known that the expected promotions would be delayed for a couple of months while the training took place. Didn't Ed understand that?

"Understand what?" Ed replied with real suprise on his face, "Why doesn't somebody tell me these things? I thought the old man cracked up and decided to let his kids play with the company."

"So," Oliver thought to himself, "Ed's still angry and I guess I don't blame him."

Ed and Oliver finally were able to talk. Once the delay was explained, Ed agreed that nothing fishy was going on. It even seemed like the most reasonable way to handle training a new manager. Ed had a legitimate gripe about not being told what was going on. Oliver really thought that Ed had known all along and the discussion moved on to the department's memo system ending with an agreement from Oliver to make certain that plans were actually communicated.

Oliver's work returned to normal very quickly. In fact, he seemed extra careful and resumed the training of some new employees which had been interrupted earlier.

At the time clock, the old man carefully put his pipe into the top pocket of his coveralls and punched out. "Nothing ever happens around here." he sighed.

ACTION

Equitable Treatment Defined

The preceding case demonstrates the importance of treating employees fairly. We see that Ed's performance was adversely affected because he felt he should have been promoted but was not. In addition, we see that Ed's performance improved once he realized he was being treated fairly. Finally, we can see that by talking with Ed, the supervisor was able to effectively change Ed's performance. To do this, he had to know that Ed felt angry and hurt. He had to know why this was so and not mistake the effects of disappointment for incompetence.

In this chapter, we want to focus on two managerial techniques which can be classified under the action of treating people fairly. One of these is opening up the lines of communication and convincing the employee that treatment is actually fair. The second is to admit that the employee is right (that is that the employee is in fact being treated unfairly) when that is the case and to make appropriate changes when possible. For example, if an employee is upset because he was told he would be paid extra for working on a Saturday, and then was erroneously not paid extra, the manager should admit to the employee that an error was made and then correct the error.

The concept of treating people fairly is one with which virtually everyone is familiar because nearly everyone utilizes this principle when dealing with others in their everyday relationships. When someone drives you to work or school, you feel you should drive them the next time. If a neighbor mows your lawn while you are out of town, you probably feel that it is only right for you to reciprocate.

Managers in organizations have the same beliefs about fairness. The top management often sets up policies that attempt to insure that all employees are treated fairly. In addition, managers of departments often establish their own procedures or guidelines, attempting to establish equity among their employees. In the following sections we show why these attempts to treat others fairly do not always succeed. We also show what the manager can do about these problems.

The Role of Perception in Equity

In your relationships with others, you have undoubtedly observed that you do not always agree with others regarding what is fair. Fairness is related to a person's value system and expectations. As a result, what is seen as fair by one person may be seen as unfair by another.

THERE IS NO OBJECTIVE STANDARD WHICH CAN BE USED TO DETERMINE WHAT WILL BE SEEN AS FAIR.

Fairness is a perception by an individual not a group. Fairness (for the employee) is not based on reality as perceived by the manager or by other employees. A manager may establish a policy or procedure with the best intentions of producing a situation of fairness. The mistake in this approach is the presumption that what is obviously fair to the manager will also be seen as fair by the employees involved.

To demonstrate the importance of perception in determining what is fair, let us consider the case of Ed from two different points of view, Ed's viewpoint, and his manager's viewpoint.

Ed's Viewpoint (the employee).

Ed was counting on making first level supervision this year and all the feedback he had received from his boss encouraged this expectation. When the company owner's daughter and her husband moved back into town and joined the company, Ed experienced some anxiety and resentment. The company generally promoted from within, and now it looked like outsiders would take over. Ed felt angry and sometimes the impulse to smash something got out of control. Ed knew he was angry. What he would not admit to himself was that he was also scared about his future in the company.

Ed's Manager's Viewpoint.

Ed was always a good employee, in fact, one of the best. In spite of his recent episode of sloppy work and puzzling behavior, he was probably still at the top of the promotional list and would be promoted into the supervisor's position as soon as the boss' daughter heads back to Virginia. Why did Ed not understand that Judy was very good and only in training? She had worked for the company for a number of years before beginning her M.B.A. and this position was simply an additional management experience so the company could put her talents to better use. Oliver could not understand what had gotten into Ed. In fact, if Ed did not improve soon, he may have to discipline him. That might push Ed into quitting. Although good workers are hard to find, if this problem continued there would be no choice but to take the chance of losing Ed.

Conclusion

Clearly in this case, Ed and Oliver viewed Ed's situation from different perspectives. While Ed believed he was not being treated fairly, his supervisor believed he was. These perceptual differences are based primarily on the different information each possesses. They are also based on different values and expectations. Fortunately, in this case, Ed's supervisor realized that something was bothering Ed and that he should talk to him.

Oliver's action probably saved an excellent employee for the company and it certainly would make his job a lot easier in the future.

EXAMPLES

As suggested earlier, the vast majority of organizations and the managers who work for them believe that they should treat their employees fairly. They also believe that they do treat their employees fairly. Many organizations state this belief in their personnel policy manuals and employee handbooks. While many organizations could be cited as examples, we will cite four of the prominent ones. Undoubtedly, the reader is aware of other examples as well. Before describing these examples, we should stress that it is doubtless also true that many employees who work for these organizations do not view the policies we shall describe as fair. Indeed, the reader may share this view. This only reinforces what we said earlier: "Fairness is related to a person's values and expectations. As a result, what is seen as fair by one person may be seen as unfair by another."

Allocation of Office Space and Furnishings

The management of a major automobile manufacturing organization has set a policy regarding the sizes of their executives' offices and related matters. The policy states that all executives of equal rank in the company will have offices of equal size. The higher the rank of the executive, the larger the office will be. Thus, when employees are promoted in the company, they receive a larger office. In addition to the size of the executive's office, the size of the secretary's offices increases as the boss's rank in the company increases. Finally, the furnishings in each office are standardized for both the executive and the secretary. The higher one's rank in the organization, the more furnishings of increasing size, luxury, and quality one receives. To facilitate this process, an extensive book of specifications exists, complete with sample swatches of the appropriate carpeting, draperies, upholstery, nameplate dimensions, type and wall placement of paintings, and so on.

Many people, particularly students without industrial experience, find this policy quite amusing when they first learn of it. They believe the company is making far too much of a simple matter. They wonder what difference it makes how large an office is and they question if anybody really cares about how the furnishings in one office compare with the furnishings in another.

The important point is that these policies were established so that employees would feel that they were being treated fairly. It was thought that if one executive received a large office and attractive furnishings and another, of the same organizational rank, received a smaller office with unattractive furnishings, dissension would result among the executives. Management established the policy in order to avoid the possible dissension. The policy is functional as long as the policy is accepted and the visible signs of organizational status are expected by all.

Wage Structure of the United States Civil Service

In an attempt to pay its employees fairly, at least in relationship to one another, each civil service job is evaluated in terms of difficulty, responsibility, and the qualifications required to perform the job. Based on these evaluations, each job is placed into one of eighteen categories or 'GS' ratings. Figure 4-1 relates the three job factors to each GS level. All employees who hold a similar GS rating are paid within the same pay range (Figure 4-2). The specific pay one receives depends on one's GS rating and the 'step' within the rating pay range.

The point here is that government pay policies have been established in this way to reduce pay disagreements among the employees which may result when someone feels they are not being paid fairly. It is thought that people who perform jobs equally in terms of difficulty, responsibility, and qualifications should receive equal pay. From the standpoint of equity, this is a difficult position to argue against. Furthermore, the policy provides that the higher one's job ranks according to these factors, the higher the pay rate should be.

General Schedule Job Classification No.	JOB FACTORS AND THEIR VARYING REQUIREMENTS		
	DIFFICULTY	RESPONSIBILITY	QUALIFICATIONS
1.	simplest routine work		
2.	routine work		some training or experience
3.	somewhat difficult	somewhat responsible	working knowledge
4.	moderately difficult work	moderately responsible work	moderate training, good working knowledge
5.	difficult work	responsible work	considerable training, broad working knowledge, college graduate
6.	difficult work	responsible work	broad working knowledge, special and complex subject
7.	considerable difficulty	considerable responsibility	comprehensive and thorough working knowledge
8.	very difficult	very responsible	comprehensive and thorough working knowledge
9.	very difficult	very responsible	administrative experience, sound capacity for independent work
10.	highly difficult	highly responsible	somewhat extended administrative experience
11.	marked difficulty	marked responsibility	marked capacity for independent work
12.	very high order of difficulty	very high order of responsibility	leadership and attainments of a high order
13.	work of unusual difficulty	work of unusual responsibility	leadership and marked attainments
14.	exceptional difficulty	exceptional responsibility	leadership and unusual attainments
15.	outstanding difficulty	outstanding responsiblity	leadership and exceptional attainments
16.	unusual difficulty and national significance	unusual responsibility and national significance	leadership and exceptional attainments involving national significance
17.	exceptional difficulty	exceptional responsibility	exceptional leadership and attainments
18.	outstanding difficulty	outstanding responsibility	outstanding leadership

Figure 4-1. Job Difficulty Factors

	1	2	3	4	5	6	7	8	9	10
GS-1	$ 7,960	$ 8,225	$ 8,490	$ 8,755	$ 9,020	$ 9,069	$ 9,189	$ 9, 444	$ 9,699	$ 9,954
2	8,951	9,069	9,242	9,531	9,820	10,109	10,398	10,687	10,976	11,265
3	9,766	10,092	10,418	10,744	11,070	11,396	11,722	12,048	12,374	12,700
4	10,963	11,328	11,693	12,058	12,423	12,788	13,153	13,518	13,883	14,248
5	12,266	12,675	13,084	13,493	13,902	14,311	14,720	15,129	15,538	15,947
6	13,672	14,128	14,584	15,040	15,496	15,952	16,408	16,864	17,320	17,776
7	15,193	15,699	16,205	16,711	17,217	17,723	18,229	18,735	19,241	19,747
8	16,826	17,387	17,948	18,509	19,070	19,631	20,192	20,753	21,314	21,875
9	18,585	19,205	19,825	20,445	21,065	21,685	22,305	22,925	23,545	24,165
10	20,467	21,149	21,831	22,513	23,195	23,877	24,559	25,241	25,923	26,605
11	22,486	23,236	23,986	24,736	25,486	26,236	26,986	27,736	28,486	29,236
12	26,951	27,849	28,747	29,645	30,543	31,441	32,339	33,237	34,135	35,033
13	32,048	33,116	34,184	35,252	36,320	37,388	38,456	39,524	40,592	41,660
14	37,871	39,133	40,395	41,657	42,919	44,181	45,443	46,705	47,967	49,229
15	44,547	46,032	47,517	49,002	50,487	*51,972	*53,457	*54,942	*56,427	*57,912
16	49,198	50,838	*52,478	*54,118	*55,758	*57,398	*58,500	*58,500	*58,500	
17	53,849	*55,644	*57,439	*58,500	*58,500					
18	58,500									

*The rate of basic pay payable for employees at these rates is limited to the rate payable for Level V of the Executive Schedule which is expected to remain at $50,112.

Figure 4-2. General Schedule Pay Rates by Step (1981)

Grievance Procedures of Two Organizations

Some form of a grievance procedure is common in most organizations. While grievance procedures serve a number of different purposes, one of their prime objectives is to assure the employee that fair treatment will prevail, that arbitrary discipline by an unjust supervisor will not occur, and that if it does occur, the employee has recourse to regaining equity.

A large number of grievance procedures are quite informal such as the one given below:

> **Example 1: A Less Formal Procedure—"Our Open Door Policy."** In an organization of this size, questions and employee problems which can't be resolved by referring to a handbook are bound to arise. That is why we, over the years, have developed an open door policy under which you can expect immediate, fair, considerate treatment of your problems.

> Your supervisor holds his present position not only because he is proficient in your department's operation, but because he has demonstrated his ability to deal with people. We have found that a frank talk with the supervisor is usually the easiest way to handle specific problems. This is true because your supervisor is responsible for seeing that you get treated fairly and he is generally in the best position to help you.

> A talk with your supervisor will normally be the only step necessary to get a problem straightened out. However, after talking to your supervisor, you should not hesitate to take your problem to any other member of management if you believe it is desirable to do so.

On the other hand, some grievance procedures are quite formal. Perhaps the most elaborate grievance procedures of all are those contained in union-management labor contracts. Below we present a brief example of a formal procedure from a midwestern hospital:

> **Example 2: A More Formal Procedure—Grievance Procedure.** Generally there is ample opportunity for you to discuss with your supervisor any job-related problems. A formal grievance procedure is available to you, however, in the event that normal communication channels fail. It is your responsibility to pursue your grievance to whatever step you deem necessary. Each step must be taken within the allotted time, or the right to use the grievance procedure is

forfeited. You are urged to use this mechanism if the usual means are unsuccessful.

First: If your problem has not been resolved to your satisfaction by your supervisor, whether or not your supervisor is a department head, present it in writing to your department head within five (5) working days (Saturday, Sunday, and holidays excluded) of its occurence. Your department head will meet with you within five (5) working days of the receipt of your grievance in an attempt to resolve it.

Second: If, after your meeting, you feel that the problem has not been resolved, you may appeal directly to the Hospital Administratior within five (5) working days of the meeting with your department head by submitting it to him in writing. The Hospital Administrator, or in his absence his designate, will grant you a hearing within five (5) working days.

No employee will be reprimanded or made to suffer undue harassment or punishment from anyone (supervisor, other. employees, and so on) as a result of initiating a grievance.

Third: If, after the hearing, you feel that the problem remains unresolved, you may appeal, in writing within five (5) working days to the Grievance Committee of the Hospital. Such Grievance Committee will consist of members of the Board of Directors of the Hospital, and the decision of the Committee will be final.

It is important to realize that the steps in grievance procedures themselves are also based on the idea of equity. All employees who have a grievance must follow a prescribed set of steps. Supposedly, no exceptions are made. Thus, employees with identical grievances should receive identical treatment regardless of whether they are a despised troublemaker or the president's daughter or son. In addition, some organizations require that grievances be put before a grievance council which is composed primarily of employees or utilizes impartial arbitrators to settle grievances. Both of these actions are designed to make the grievant feel that the grievance procedure is a fair one.

The prevalence of grievance procedures in industry demonstrates that organizations realize employees sometimes do not feel they are being treated fairly and that they need a means for voicing their concerns. Furthermore, it suggests that organizations believe that it is important for employees to feel they are being treated fairly.

Vacation Scheduling

One problem which many organizations face is that of scheduling employee vacations. This problem is often made more complex by the fact that several employees may want to take vacations at the same time. This may not be feasible. In an attempt to resolve the problem, some organizations have developed a set of procedures for allocating vacation time among employees. One of the major purposes of these procedures is to give employees the feeling that they are being treated fairly. Note that these procedures frequently differ from one company to another which suggests that there are differences in what management and/or employees perceive as being fair. This also indicates the wide range of practices which people will accept as 'fair.'

One photographic products company has the following policy:

> When there is a conflict of vacation time between two or more employees, the employee with the longest seniority shall have preference. Any employee, however, who makes his request after May 15, will not be given seniority recognition and vacation times will be alloted on a first come first served basis.

> Vacation time cannot be carried over from year to year. Unused vacation will be paid for at the end of the year. The company may, however, require the employee to take his unused vacation in lieu of pay.

> An employee who takes his vacation during the period from November 1, thru April 30 will receive one extra vacation day with pay for each vacation week taken. The employee has the option to take the day off with pay or work the extra day with extra pay if the company requests it.

Sometimes, local customs and traditions make special vacation policies necessary. One large automotive plant in "deer-hunting country" has the following policy regarding the scheduling of vacations during deer hunting season in their local collective bargaining agreement.

> **Vacation Time Off for Deer Hunting.** The parties recognize that a large number of Maintenance employees desire vacation time off for deer hunting, and that there is a general preference for the early part

of the season among deer hunters. At the same time, the need to maintain the efficiency of plant operations is an overall controlling factor. In an effort to accommodate as many Maintenance employees as possible in their desires regarding vacation time off for deer hunting, the following procedure will apply in that Department:

1. Employees may make application to their supervisor, during the regular vacation application period, for vacation time off during the approaching deer hunting season.

2. Applicants with unused vacation time remaining available to them shall be granted time off during the deer hunting season, as herein provided, up to the amount of vacation time to which they are still entitled, but not to exceed one (1) full week.

3. The parties recognize the principle that all applicants cannot always be allowed time off during the early part of the season; accordingly, the following shall apply: a) Where 25% or less of the total employees in a classification apply for time off during the early part of the season, all applicants will be allowed such time off. b) Where the total applicants in a classification exceed 25% but are less than 50% of the total employees in a classification, the excess over 25% shall be granted time off during the second week of the season. c) In the event 50% or more of the employees in a classification apply for time off during the early part of the season, the applicants will be divided into two (2) groups, one group being granted the time off during the first week of the season and the other group being granted the requested time off during the second week.

4. The order of preference for the above time off shall be based on date-of-entry seniority in their respective classification.

Clearly, if management can realistically expect that over 50 percent of the work force may be absent during deer hunting season, deer hunting is a local phenomenon of considerable importance and any inequities which interfere with this activity may be expected to have undesirable consequences for the company. In an effort to avoid such consequences by making an attempt to treat deer hunters fairly, the company has agreed to having between 25 percent and 50 percent of their employees absent from work during the deer hunting season.

REASONS

The action of treating people fairly—what many people would regard as plain "common sense"—was formalized by J. Stacey

Adams. While the idea of equity may be as old as the human race, the formal theory is relatively new (1963). The theory specifically attempts to answer two basic questions which are of relevance to managers:

1. How do people determine if they are being treated fairly?
2. Why should managers treat employees fairly?

The answers to each of these questions will now be discussed.

Determination of Fair Treatment

In order to understand how people determine if they are being treated fairly, think of a situation in which you were not treated fairly. How did you determine fairness? You probably said something to yourself like, "Bob got a raise, but I didn't."; "Mary got promoted, but I didn't."; "I had to work overtime, but Stan didn't." or, "I got the same exam scores in the course that Sue did, but she got a higher grade." The main point is that people usually compare themselves with others in order to determine if they are being fairly treated.

What information do people consider in making these comparison judgments? According to "Equity Theory," all of the information people consider can be divided into four categories:

1. Your Outcomes—This refers to all the rewards such as pay, job status, and feeling of responsibility you receive for performing your job.
2. Your Inputs—This refers to all that you contribute and bring to the job, such as your time, physical effort, and education.
3. A Comparison Person's Outcomes—This refers to all the rewards such as pay, job status, and feeling of responsibility which a comparison person receives for performing their job.
4. A Comparison Person's Inputs—This refers to all that a comparison person brings to and contributes to his or her job, such as time, physical effort, and education.

Equity theory states that people consider the above four pieces of information in terms of the following ratio (see Figure 4-3).

Specifically, the theory suggests that people consider their own "outcome/input" in relation to the "outcome/input" of some other person. Based on this comparison, people determine if they are

YOU		COMPARISON PERSON
$\dfrac{\text{Outcomes}}{\text{Inputs}}$	$=$	$\dfrac{\text{Outcomes}}{\text{Inputs}}$

Figure 4-3. Equity Expressed as Ratios

being treated fairly. Thus, if the ratio of your own outcomes to inputs is not equal to the corresponding ratio of the comparison person you will feel that you are being treated unfairly.

Perhaps some illustrations would help clarify the theory. Assume you and one of your coworkers both make "widgets" where you work. Assume further that you produce 100 widgets a day but your coworker, who is extremely industrious and efficient, produces 200 widgets a day. You are paid $50 per day. If your coworker receives twice the pay you do ($100), would you consider this unfair? Probably not, since your production is only half that of your coworker. Other factors being equal (like quality of widgets, amount of scrap produced, and so on), the ratio of your outcomes to inputs is equal to the ratio of your coworker's outcomes to inputs. Both the theory and "common sense" would indicate that you were being fairly treated. Figure 4-4 shows how this situation would be represented.

Now, let's assume that instead of producing only 100 widgets per day you also produce 200. However, you still receive only $50 pay. How would you feel then? Assuming the same other factors are equal, you most likely would feel that you were not treated fairly. You would realize that although you produce as many widgets as your coworker, you only receive one-half the pay. The ratio of your outcomes to inputs would not be equal to the corresponding ratio for your coworker. Figure 4-5 presents this situation. Compare Figure 4-4 with Figure 4-5. What adjustments to your outcomes can you make?

Figure 4-4. A "Fair" Ratio = Equity

	YOU	COWORKER
Outcomes	$ 50	$ 100
Inputs	100 widgets	200 widgets

	YOU	*COWORKER*
Outcomes	$ 50	$ 100
Inputs	200 widgets	200 widgets

Figure 4-5. An "Unfair" Ratio =Inequity

What adjustments to your inputs can you make? How would these adjustments affect the ratio of your outcomes to your inputs?

Why Treat People Fairly?

Now that we have explained how people determine if they are being treated fairly, we can answer the second of the two questions originally posed: Why should managers treat employees fairly?

The answer to this is quite simple and pragmatic: If you do not treat people fairly, they are certain to take actions to reduce inequity. These efforts of employees to reduce inequity may be harmful to the organization or, for that matter, to you personally.

According to equity theory, the underlying dynamics of why and when people take actions to reduce inequity are the following:

1. Tension is created when inequity is felt.
2. The greater the inequity the more tension.
3. Sufficiently great tension leads to action.

Most employee attempts to regain equity are destructive to productivity. Consider the example with which we began this chapter. Ed felt angry because he did not receive either the expected promotion or the reason why (tension caused by felt inequity). Since he was quite angry (sufficient tension for action), he smashed a number of wooden skids. He also took other actions which curtailed or negated to some degree his productivity. Let us look at the four potential groups of actions available to those who attempt to regain equity (Figure 4-6).

As Figure 4-6 shows, one way employees can achieve equity is to reduce their "inputs"—which means productivity. In business settings, this often takes the form of directly restricting work production, that is, producing less. A typist, for example, may restrict

		YOU		COMPARISON PERSON
Outcomes	:	Increase	:	Decrease
Inputs	:	Decrease	:	Increase

Figure 4-6. Four Ways to Regain Equity

output by typing forty words per minute rather than seventy words per minute. The negative effects of these actions on an organization are obvious, particularly if these actions are initiated by a large number of employees (known as a "work slowdown"). It should be stressed that people can be expected to decrease their production levels until inequity, as they perceive it, is eliminated. Thus, in our earlier example in which you were asked to imagine that you were a worker producing 200 widgets and receiving only $50 for this effort, while a coworker also produced 200 widgets but was paid $100, you would probably curtail your production. In fact, you would cut back your production to 100 widgets in order to achieve equity since 50/100 is equal to 100/200.

Another way of achieving equity is to attempt to increase your outcomes. This can take several forms. One would be to simply ask your boss for a raise. A second would be to make your job more rewarding in non financial ways such as socializing more with co-workers, taking longer coffee breaks, or only doing those assignments you enjoy. Some have speculated that "white collar crime" and "blue collar crime" are such equity regaining strategies since they serve to increase outcomes. Many other examples could be cited, but most, as the ones cited above, are specific to a given work situation. The negative effects of people taking such actions vary from one setting to another.

A third way of achieving equity is to decrease the outcomes of others until the ratio of the other person's outcomes to inputs equals the same ratio for you. This can be accomplished in a number of ways, but the effect is to "make life miserable" for the comparison other. This action can be carried out with intensities ranging from mild to severe. Sabotaging another's work is probably one of the most vivid examples of the severe action.

An individual can also achieve equity by increasing the inputs of others. This, too, can be accomplished in many ways but often takes the form of applying individual or group pressure to the comparison other until the other person increases his or her work production sufficiently. Unlike the other employee actions to decrease inequity, this action may have some positive consequences for an organization since productivity by the comparison other may increase. This case is the only exception we know of to the principle stated earlier—that attempts by employees to regain equity are destructive to productivity. Consider that if employees are sufficiently motivated to put pressure on coworkers for more production, they will also be sufficiently motivated to organize a union or perform some other group action.

The four ways of achieving equity just described are not the only ways people can react toward situations in which they feel they are being treated unfairly. Obviously, one could employ a combination of the four actions. In fact the use of a combination is commonplace. Also one can simply withdraw from the situation entirely, that is, leave the organization and seek employment elsewhere. The intermediate position between curtailment of production and leaving the company is to work at a level just barely sufficient to prevent discharge. We might call this "on-the-job-turnover," an expensive matter for the company since it is almost like losing an employee but still paying wages.

Finally, an employee could simply distort what is happening or utilize any of a number of classic defense mechanisms and, in effect, "live with" the inequity.

Figure 4-7 shows some possible actions an employee might take under various levels of perceived unfairness. If employees feel only a small amount of inequity, they typically resort to a small amount of "griping" among themselves. As the degree of *perceived unfairness* increases, the employee typically takes stronger actions such as applying group pressure to fellow workers, restricting productivity, and engaging in mild forms of sabotage. Note that while some of this pressure might be for increase in production, it is far more likely to consist of attempts to organize unions, initiate grievances, start work slowdowns, and so on. When perceived inequity is extremely

Figure 4-7. Levels of Unfairness and Possible Responses

	DEGREE OF PERCEIVED UNFAIRNESS	EXAMPLES OF POSSIBLE EMPLOYEE ACTIONS
T	Very High	Utilization of physical force
E	High	Restricting Output
N		
S	Medium	Doing only selected parts of job
I		
O	Low	Minor griping
N	None	(this probably doesn't exist)

high, employees may engage in more effective forms of sabotage and resort to physical violence. While we do not suggest that all "very high" levels of perceived inequity will necessarily result in the utilization of physical force, the manager must expect that whatever action is taken by the employees, its extremity will also be "very high."

*Summary of Research Results on
Equity*

The action of treating people fairly and its underlying theory, equity theory, have been studied in a number of laboratory experiments. Over fifty studies were conducted between 1963 and 1971. Some studies are still being done, but the number of studies published has dropped off sharply in recent years.

A common research design used in these studies of equity theory went something like this:

An experimenter, posing as an employer, advertizes that a part-time job is available. When the subject arrives for the job, the experimenter "hires" him or her. The experimenter then makes the subjects feel unfairly treated by paying more or less than the going rate and also by telling subjects that their qualifications for the job are lower or higher than a comparison person who is receiving the same pay. The pay itself is either on a piece-rate or hourly basis. After some initial job training, the subjects perform a task for a designated period of time, complete a questionnaire, and are paid. The subject's quantity and quality of work together with their questionnaire responses are then evaluated to determine how the subjects respond to unfair treatment.

In general, most studies are quite supportive of the predictions which equity theory makes. The prediction that equity ratio discrepancies are a source of perceived inequity is well-supported by these studies. It is also found consistently that inequity is a source of tension and that the greater the inequity, the greater the drive to reduce it. Support for these major predictions adds considerable credence to the validity of the theory. The interested reader will find some reviews of equity theory listed at the end of the chapter.

IMPLEMENTATION

The things an employee can find unfair are certainly not limited to the examples given thus far in this chapter. Employees can be very creative in finding newer and more "unheard of" things that trouble them. Regardless of whether the manager thinks these questions make sense, they must be dealt with on some level. Here are a few we have encountered. Most readers will be able to add more.

1. Why do salaried employees keep getting their paychecks when they are sick but hourly employees do not?
2. Why is physical labor not paid as much as mental labor?
3. Why does the boss's secretary come in late half the time and nothing is ever said. But if I do...
4. Why do men have to do all the lifting and other heavy work while women do not do anything hard but get the same rate of pay?
5. Why do some employees have a company car and others do not?

All of these questions and more are heard every day by managers in every line of business. In the strategy guide (Figure 4-8) we present an outline, in flow-chart form, of an approach the manager can use for all such questions, voiced openly or not, justified or not, indicating serious or only annoying problems.

Equity, or fair treatment, is a matter of individual perception. An individual you think is being treated fairly may or may not agree with you. Another person you think is being treated unfairly also may or may not agree with you. The manager must realize that it is the employee's perception of equity or inequity that is important. Employees act based on their own perceptions, not the manager's perceptions.

The manager's decision to implement an equity action must be preceded by information gathering. The information required is necessarily possessed only by the employee since it is the employee's perception which is the required information. The equity action assumes that the employee's perception was one of inequity.

After the decision to utilize an equity action as a management technique has been made the following steps should be initiated:

Step 1 Perception of Inequity Accurate?   Once the employee's perception is known, the manager must determine if the employee's perception of inequity is based on accurate information. The manager may not think that the perception is accurate. The reasons for differing perceptions about the same situation usually are that the situation is not viewed in the same way by the manager and the

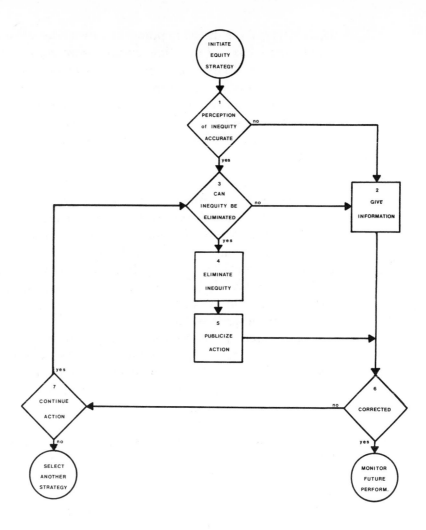

Figure 4-8. Restoring Equity: Strategy Guide

employee. Managers have information about work situations different from the information employees possess. While the employee's
information may be highly specific and detailed about an individual
job or process, the manager's information is more general. The
manager gathers information for the purpose of integrating the output from many jobs. The differing sets of information about a job,

89   *Treating Employees Fairly*

which derive from differing points of view about the work situation, may be the source of the "inaccurate" perceptions of employees.

Managers, like employees, may also lack information about a situation. Not only their perceptions about equity, but their judgments about the accuracy of an employee's perception of inequity may be based on incomplete or faulty information. The gathering of information is critical to this step in the implementation of the equity action.

Step 2 Give Information. The impulse to manage by "knowing more" than the employee leads some managers to fear that if the employees know what the manager knows the manager will "lose control." This misses the point. By the time the manager reaches this step, control has already been lost. Worse yet, control has diminished precisely because employees with inaccurate or insufficient information are operating on the basis of their fantasies and conjecture rather than fact.

A frequent problem when wages and salaries are secret (a common practice) is that employee "A" feels inequitably treated because employee "B" is paid much more for the same work. Employees who feel inequitably compensated tend to greatly overestimate the compensation of others and thus tend to exaggerate the felt inequity. Many organizations (and employees) will not tolerate the publication of each employee's and manager's exact compensation rate. Most organizations, however, can easily publish the ranges of pay for various job classifications (for example, Figure 4-2, this chapter) and thus overcome the gross overestimation in guessing about the relative pay rates within employee groups.

When inaccurate beliefs about a situation are the basis for feelings of inequity, accurate information should be given whenever possible.

Step 3 Can Inequity Be Eliminated? If the employee accurately perceives an existing inequity, the simple solution is to eliminate that inequity. In the example, employee "A" may, in fact, be unfairly compensated. Employee "B" may, in reality, make significantly more than employee "A" and the felt inequity is based on accurate perception. In this situation, employee "A" probably should receive an increase in compensation.

Unhappily, elimination of the inequity felt by an employee is not always a possible option for the manager. This can be true for one or more of the following reasons.

There may be personal, contractual, or organizational reasons for the existence of the inequity. If the manager has personally decided that an employee will not be paid more than the current rate, then the manager must either alter this decision or select some action other than the implementation of an equity action.

Contractual reasons for inequity are the responsibility of the agents who negotiated the contract. Problems can arise from contracts because of some traditions of organized labor. Younger employees, for example, may not accept seniority as a valid basis for different compensation rates. Nevertheless, seniority is a common factor in determining compensation stipulated by many labor unions during negotiation. In this situation as well the manager is unable to eliminate inequity and the best course of action is to inform the employee of the source of the inequity.

Organizational reasons for inequity may take many forms. An outright case of apparent nepotism like the one that began this chapter is only one possible situation. The relatives of owners or of top management may be compensated at an unrealistically high rate. Since the social distance of most employees from this group is relatively great it is rare for the employee to seriously treat this as a case of inequity. If, however, an owner's relative works near to an employee at a similar job, such blatant inequity may be expected to cause some problems.

Organizations may have an overall rate of compensation, fringe benefits, level of working conditions, and so on, well below the average of similar organizations in the surrounding geographic area. This will allow widespread perceptions of inequity on the part of most employees in the organization, although this consequence is far from inevitable. When managed improperly, the situation can result in invasions of labor union organizers and various other forms of conflict. If managed properly, increased employee solidarity, increased job involvement, and employee loyalty to the organization are possible. Obviously, unless the manager is an owner or a top executive of the organization, little or nothing can be done to change many situations of organizational inequity.

The manager may not have the power or authority to change the situation and eliminate the inequity. Two options exist in this case. Either take steps to gain the necessary power and authority or cease attempting to create equity. Admit you are unable to alter the situation and select another action.

To summarize the implementation of this step, the manager should eliminate the inequity if possible or advisable. Otherwise another action should be selected.

Step 4 Eliminate Inequity. For this step the manager should briefly refer back to Figure 4-6 (Four Ways to Regain Equity). Two factors need to be considered in the elimination of inequity. First, as discussed previously, perceived outcomes and inputs may be altered by either giving accurate information or by actually increasing outcomes. Note that the outcomes are primarily under the control of the employer while the inputs are ultimately under the control of the employee. Second, the person with whom the comparison is being made may be changed under certain conditions. The inputs and outcomes of the "comparison other" serve as standards upon which the perception of equity or inequity are based.

One small college known to the authors made the salary schedules of similar small colleges available to its faculty. These salary schedules showed that the compensation rate of the comparison colleges was equal to or lower than that of the home college. Faculty were encouraged to conclude that their rate of compensation was not only fair but above average. This maneuver occurred during an organization effort by a faculty union. The union, of course, reciprocated by supplying additional salary schedules with a much higher rate of compensation than the set supplied by the employer.

In this example, both the union and management were attempting to produce perceptions of equity or inequity by changing the comparison group used by the faculty in making judgments about equitable treatment. The outcome was that management's effort to alter the comparison group used by the faculty was executed with insufficient skill and strengthened the position of the faculty union. It is ironic that without this and other management overreactions to the union's efforts the initially conservative faculty would never have ratified the union on the election date. The transparent manipulation itself was viewed as yet another instance of inequity. If there is any moral to this illustration it may be that there are pragmatic reasons for ethical management behavior.

In summary, equity may be regained by:

1. altering perceived or actual outcomes
2. altering perceived or actual inputs
3. altering the selection of comparison others

Step 5 Publicize Action. In the Stanley Kubrick film "Dr. Strangelove," a "Doomsday Machine" has been activated which will obliterate all life on earth if anybody uses a nuclear bomb. The

Doomsday Machine is thought to be effective in preventing nuclear war because all possible participants know that the detonation of a single nuclear weapon will destroy life on earth. Because the makers of the Doomsday Machine wanted to surprise their head of state on his birthday, announcement was delayed although the machine was activated. More people than the head of state were surprised. Somebody who did not know about the Doomsday Machine dropped an atomic bomb. As the film ends the world is being destroyed.

If the manager takes steps to eliminate inequity and nobody knows about the effort made, the effort will have no effect. Information that the inequity has been eliminated should be provided immediately to relevant others in order to receive the benefits of this action.

Step 6 Corrected?   This step is appropriate after information has been given to correct an inaccurate perception (Step 3) or after an actual inequity has been corrected and publicized (Step 7). The manager should determine at this point whether or not the preceding steps have corrected the original problem. As indicated before, immediate change cannot be expected and the manager must develop the skill of determining how long to wait before expecting the behavioral changes for which this action was initiated.

Step 7 Continue Action?   If the expected change does not occur within a reasonable time the manager must decide if it will be worthwhile to continue the action. Generally, if there has been no effect or an unfavorable effect the action should be terminated. If, however, marked but insufficient change has occurred the manager may decide to either wait somewhat longer for feedback or continue with a revised implementation of the action. If a decision to discontinue the action is made, return to Step Five and select another action.

SUMMARY

In this chapter we have discussed the action of treating people fairly. We have cited examples of how a number of organizations have attempted to implement this action. We discussed how people determine if they are being treated fairly and have outlined the negative consequences which an organization may experience if it is not treating its employees fairly. Finally, we discussed how equity actions may be implemented to resolve present employee performance problems.

As compared to the other strategies, the strategy of treating employees fairly is somewhat unique. Like positive reinforcement and shaping, it can be easily used in conjunction with any other strategy. Indeed, the general notion of equitable treatment is virtually a necessity when using most, if not all, of the other strategies if they are to be optimally successful. For example, if disciplinary actions and procedures are to be fully effective, employees must perceive that they are being disciplined fairly. Thus, this approach has the flexibility to serve as an important adjunct to other strategies. Other approaches may be used independently, but the likelihood of their success increases when employees are treated fairly.

The equity approach is similar to some of the other approaches in that it is frequently, although not always, financially inexpensive to utilize. For example, if an employee feels unfairly treated as a result of a misunderstanding, the manager need only communicate with the employee to remedy the misunderstanding. The only cost involved is the manager's and the employee's time to communicate with each other. Usually, this is a minimal amount. Or, to take a second example, if an employee feels unfairly treated because of something the manager has inadvertently done (such as failing to pay for legitimate overtime) or someone else in the organization has done (for example, another manager improperly asking the employee to perform a task), the required action frequently can be effected with minimal expense. There are situations, however, in which utilizing this strategy will entail considerable costs. If an employee feels unfairly treated because of truly intolerable working conditions, it may cost the organization a considerable amount to make the necessary changes. New buildings, facilities, and/or equipment may be expensive. Fortunately, for most organizations, these latter situations are not too common. Thus, while the strategy of treating employees fairly can be expensive to carry out, it usually is not, which is a definite advantage in its use.

A final attribute of the equity approach which is worthy of note is that managers who use the strategy earn employee respect and are held in relatively high regard by their subordinates. All psychologically healthy employees want their boss to treat them fairly since equitable treatment reflects a respect for employees and a concern for their welfare and feelings. Hence, when managers use this approach, they are viewed more favorably by their subordinates, increasing their real ability to exercise influence. Thus, there is something for the manager to gain personally by using this strategy.

RECOMMENDED READINGS

Adams, J. S. "Toward an Understanding of Inequity." *Journal of Abnormal and Social Psychology* 67, (1963): 422-36.

Adams, J. S. "Wage Inequities, Productivity, and Work Quality." *Industrial Relations* 3, (1963): 9-16.

Adams, J. S. and Jacobsen, P. R. "Effects of Wage Inequities on Work Quality." *Journal of Abnormal and Social Psychology* 69, (1964): 19-25.

Andrews, I. R. "Wage Inequity and Job Performance: An Experimental Study." *Journal of Applied Psychology* 51, (1967): 39-45.

Berscheid, E., Boye, D. and Walster, E. "Retaliation as a Means of Restoring Equity." *Journal of Personality and Social Psychology* 10, (1968): 370-76.

Evan, W. M. and Simmons, R. G. "Organizational Effects of Inequitable Rewards: Two Experiments in Status Inconsistency." *Administrative Science Quarterly* 14, (1969): 224-37.

Evans, M. G. and Molinari, L. "Equity, Piece-rate, Over Payment, and Job Security." *Journal of Applied Psychology* 54, (1970): 105-114.

Goodman, P. S. and Friedman, A. "An Examination of the Effect of Wage Inequity in the Hourly Condition." *Organizational Behavior and Human Performance* 3, (1968): 340-52.

Lawler, E. E. "Manager's perceptions of their Subordinates' Pay and their Supervisors Pay." *Personnel Psychology* 18, (1965): 413-22.

Lawler, E. E. "Equity Theory as a Predictor of Productivity and Work Quality." *Psychological Bulletin* 70, (1968): 596-610.

Leventhal, G. S. and Michaels, J. W. "Extending the Equity Model: Perception of Inputs and Allocation of Reward as a Function of Duration and Quantity of Performance." *Journal of Personality and Social Psychology* 12, (1969): 303-309.

Leventhal, G. S., Weiss, T.; and Long, G. "Equity, Reciprocity, and Reallocating Rewards in the Dyad." *Journal of Personality and Social Psychology* 13, (1969): 300-305.

Prichard, R. D. "EquityTheory: A Review and Critique." *Organizational Behavior and Human Performance* 4, (1969): 176-211.

Weick, K. E. "The Concept of Equity in the Perception of Pay." *Administrative Science Quarterly* 11, (1966): 414-39.

Weick, K. E. and Nesset, B. "Preferences among Forms of Equity." *Organizational Behavior and Human Performance* 3, (1968): 400-416.

5

Satisfying Employee Needs

INTRODUCTION

In the early 1900s a United States company reportedly built a plant in a foreign country. While operating the plant for several years, they noticed that the local employees would work for about one year and then quit, and disappear never to be seen again. The company speculated that the reason the employees were quitting was because the pay was quite low. They, therefore, decided to double the amount of compensation, thinking this would eliminate the turnover problem. To their consternation, they found that the turnover doubled. Instead of working for one year, the average employee worked for six months and then disappeared. Puzzled by what was happening, the company hired an interpreter to interview the workers and find out why the turnover doubled. The company learned that each employee would work ONLY LONG ENOUGH TO SAVE UP A GIVEN AMOUNT OF MONEY. When the required amount was reached, they would quit. Thus, when the company doubled the amount of pay, it took the workers only six months to save the desired amount rather than one year.

ACTION

The preceding example demonstrates the motivation strategy which is of concern to us in this chapter, that is, determining and satisfying employee needs. Obviously, the company management did not know what the workers wanted from a job, and its action only aggravated the turnover problem.

It is important at the onset to observe that the strategy discussed in this chapter entails two separate actions. First, a manager needs to determine what it is that an employee needs. More specifically, a manager wants to determine which needs employees want an organization to satisfy or help satisfy. Do they want money? Security? Interesting work? Prestige or status? Recognition or what? Secondly, a manager must attempt to satisfy those needs.

Needs Versus Wishes

This second action deserves some elaboration. Managers, of course, are not typically in a position of being able to provide employees with virtually everything they want. Even if they were, it probably would not be a wise strategy to do so. For example, if a carpenter wants a $50,000 annual raise, what manager would or could grant it? Obviously, a manager can realistically only satisfy employee needs within the constraints provided by the organization. Managers can, of course, attempt to change these constraints, but there are limitations to this.

It is important for a manager to distinguish between what an employee wishes and what an employee actually needs. You may wish you had three cars, but do you really need that many? A wish relates to something a person would like or desire. It is not a physical or mental necessity. A person can live a full life even if a wish is not granted. Managers should attempt to satisfy employee needs. On the other hand, satisfying employee wishes should be considered as icing on the cake. A manager should attempt to do so only if it achieves organizational purposes, and even then, mistaking a wish for a need can open "Pandora's Box."

Knowing What Employees Need

What, then, do employees need? Later in this chapter we will discuss this issue at length. It will suffice to say at this point that people have both physical and psychological needs. One's physical needs relate to all of those things which are required for an individual to survive biologically. They are all of those things which a person needs to physically maintain himself. Included in this category are such items as food, water, clothing, shelter, exercise, and rest.

While physical needs are relatively easy to conceptualize, psychological needs are much more difficult to assess and categorize. Psychological needs include such things as a need for self-esteem, need for achievement, praise and recognition, need for friendship, and a need to develop one's potential. While physical needs relate to one's biological survival, psychological needs relate to one's mental survival or well-being. People share physiological needs but not necessarily psychological needs. It is important to observe that while almost all people have similar psychological needs, they differ considerably in the strength of those needs. One person may have a strong need for companionship, whereas another may aspire to the life of a hermit. Or, one person may have a strong desire for security, whereas another may enjoy engaging in highly risky ventures throughout his life.

Employee Needs Are Satisfied Off the Job, Too

Must a manager attempt to satisfy all of an employee's needs, both physical and psychological? The answer to this question is clearly no. Most employees satisfy many of their needs off the job. Remember that the average employee works only about 250 days a year and then only eight hours out of a 24 hour day. Thus, employees potentially have many off-duty hours to satisfy many of their needs. Employees frequently satisfy their needs for affiliation off the job by joining various social organizations or clubs. These same organizations also help to satisfy other employee needs for recognition, status, and prestige. Perhaps the major point to be made is that employees differ in terms of the extent to which they satisfy their needs off the job. Some employees satisfy a large number of their needs away from work, whereas others want and expect a job to provide them with considerable need satisfaction. Thus, while employees have similar needs, they differ in terms of need strength and in terms of the extent to which they expect a job or the organization to provide them with need satisfaction. The logical consequence of this conclusion is that if a manager intends to motivate a given employee, he or she must determine which needs the employee expects to satisfy by working, and how strong each of these needs is. Ideally, this would be done for each employee.

Earlier in this chapter we stated that the need satisfaction strategy entails two actions: determining employee needs, and satisfying those needs. Now the reader can see why the first action is so essential. What remains is to explain what a manager has to gain by doing the second.

Why Satisfy Employee Needs?

Some people argue that managers should attempt to satisfy the needs of their employees for humanitarian reasons. They add that organizations have a moral obligation to help employees by creating an environment which optimizes each employee's welfare. While this argument may have some merit, most managers in profit-making organizations do not feel this is the only reason for satisfying employee needs. They believe that it also must be in an organization's own best interests to do so. Most believe that the organization must also benefit from taking this action.

Over the years, numerous studies have been conducted which have investigated the relationship between job satisfaction and various organizational consequences. These studies are relevant here because job satisfaction is closely related to an employee's need satisfaction. The results of these studies show that employee job satisfaction is correlated with absenteeism and tardiness. More specifically, they show that the higher the employee's job satisfaction, the less likely the employee is to be absent or tardy. In addition, these studies show a similar finding with reference to employee turnover. The more dissatisfied employees are with their jobs, the more likely they are to quit, arrive late, or just disappear for a day or so. In addition to its effects on absenteeism, tardiness, and turnover, employee job satisfaction appears to be related to other forms of dysfunctional employee behavior. Dissatisfied employees are more apt to break company rules and become discipline problems than are satisfied subordinates. They are also more apt to sabotage the company plant and equipment, to file grievances, and to go on strike. One of the most surprising findings with regard to employee job satisfaction is that it does not appear to be highly correlated with job productivity as such. In other words, high job satisfaction does not always result in high productivity, nor does low job satisfaction always result in low job productivity. Obviously, variables other than job satisfaction or dissatisfaction can and do affect an employee's job productivity. As an example, consider an employee who hates his job but works hard at it because he is afraid of being fired. He knows that it is very difficult to get a better or equal job elsewhere.

To summarize, while a highly satisfied worker may not always be more productive than a dissatisfied one, he is less likely to be absent and tardy, quit the job, and to engage in other forms of behavior which are dysfunctional to the organization. All of these are very practical non-altruistic reasons why a manager may want to try to satisfy an employee's needs.

How Does This Strategy Differ From Others?

At this point the reader may be asking: Are not all strategies for increasing employee productivity based on the notion of satisfying employee needs? If so, how does this strategy differ from the others?

While it may not be clear at this point in the book, all motivational strategies do have their roots embedded in employee needs. Administering penalties, for one, attempts to motivate people not by satisfying needs but by threatening the satisfaction of one or more needs. The goal-setting strategy, too, attempts to increase employee productivity through the setting of clear, somewhat difficult, objectives rather than easy, poorly defined ones. While this strategy ultimately may serve to satisfy the needs of an employee, that is not its explicit intent.

In general, it could be said that while all motivational strategies involve employee needs in some way, the strategy presented in this chapter is the only one which focuses solely on employee needs. It is the only one which argues that a manager should specifically attempt to identify the wide range of job-related needs employees possess and satisfy those needs. All of this will become even more clear when the entire book has been read. Now it is time to look at specific examples which show how organizations can identify an employee's job related needs and how organizations can attempt to satisfy the needs which are identified.

EXAMPLES

As we suggested earlier, many actions taken by a manager have the effect of satisfying the needs of one or more employees even though that may not have been the manager's intent. For example, if a manager simply says "Hi!" to a subordinate who is working late, it may help satisfy the employee's need for recognition even though the manager was only trying to be polite. The examples cited in the following pages will be limited to overt attempts made by organizations to identify and satisfy the needs of one or more employees. Since the need-satisfying strategy consists of two parts, we will focus on each separately, beginning with organizational attempts to determine employee needs.

Determining Employee Needs

Attitude Questionnaires.   Many organizations and managers who attempt to determine the needs of their employees do so by either interviewing one or more of them or by asking them to complete an attitude questionnaire such as a job satisfaction survey. A host of questionnaires have been developed for this purpose, and a manager has the choice of either using one of these or of developing a new one using his own set of questions. A description of a number of attitude questionnaires which can be purchased is given in the Buros' *Mental Measurement Yearbook* available in many libraries. The Psychological Corporation and Science Research Associates are two large organizations which sell questionnaires. One of the benefits of using a ready-made instrument is that norm tables are frequently available which can aid considerably in interpreting the results obtained. It is not uncommon for an organization to administer an attitude questionnaire to all employees and then follow it up with interviews covering a random sample of employees.

Now let us look at two specific examples of the use of questionnaires.

Minneapolis Gas Company.   The Minneapolis Gas Company conducted one of the most elaborate studies ever done which relates to what potential employees desire from a job. The study, which spanned a twenty-year period from 1945 to 1965, asked people applying for a job with the company to rate each of ten specific items in terms of the item's desirability to them. The results of the study were quite revealing. The company reportedly (Jurgensen, 1967) found that security, type of work, advancement, and "working for a company one could be proud of," were rated highly by both men and women. On the other hand, benefits, working conditions, and work hours were rated relatively low by both sexes. The actual ratings were (highest rated items first):

FOR MEN	FOR WOMEN
Security	Security
Advancement	Type of work
Type of work	Company
Company (Proud to work for)	Advancement
Pay	Coworkers
Coworkers (pleasant, agreeable)	Supervisor
Supervisor (considerate and fair)	Pay
Benefits	Working conditions
Hours	Hours
Working conditions	Benefits

There are several aspects of this study which warrant our attention. First, the study involved an extraordinarily large number of participants—30,746 men and 12,783 women—which adds credence to the results. Keep in mind that most studies involve less than 300 participants. Secondly, whereas most studies focus strictly on an organization's present employees, this study is quite unique in that it surveyed job applicants. The company's approach provides it with information regarding what all potential employees desire, not just those who are ultimately hired. The benefit of having this type of information is that the company can use it to develop jobs and careers which will not only satisfy the needs of its work force but will attract new employees as well. Third, it is clear from these data that men and women (at least in the twenty years from 1945 to 1965) differed somewhat in what they wanted from a job. Despite apparent differences there was approximately a 75 percent overlap in the rankings of employee needs between sexes.

Since the Minneapolis Gas Company study is based on such a large sample size and involves job applicants, the reader will undoubtedly be tempted to generalize these findings to his or her own organization and its employees, that is, to assume that the employees in one's own organization would rate the ten items in the same way that the Minneapolis Gas Company applicants did. As tempting as this is, it would be unwise to do so, for other studies indicate that specific groups of employees often rate these ten items in a substantially different way. Accountants, engineers, computer programmers, secretaries, plumbers, and so on, often differ significantly in what they want from a job. Practically speaking, there is no easy substitute for surveying one's own subordinates or job applicants to determine their job related needs.

Labor Relations Institute Study. In 1946, the Labor Relations Institute of New York reportedly (Kovach, 1980) conducted a study to determine what employees want from a job and what supervisors think their employees want from a job. In conducting the study, the Institute first asked a group of employees to rank ten items in order of importance to them. They then asked the first line supervisors of these employees to rank the same items as they thought their employees would. The results of this study are presented in Figure 5-1 and show a wide variance between what employees actually want from a job and what supervisors think their subordinates want.

In 1980, Kovach presented the results of a follow-up study administered to a group of over 200 employees and their immediate supervisors. While the study necessarily involved a different set of subjects than did the one conducted by the Institute, the question asked in each study was the same, as were the results (Figure 5-2). Interestingly, the gap between supervisors and subordinates had changed little over the years. While some greater correspondence is apparent, most of it can be attributed to only one factor: "sympathetic help with personal problems."

The major conclusion one can draw from these two studies is that supervisors typically are not adept at estimating the needs and desires of their subordinates. They do not really know what motivates their subordinates. On the other hand, this finding is quite surprising, for one might expect that since supervisors typically come into contact with their subordinates quite frequently, they would know what motivates them. However, it is important to remember that managers are not often trained to be psychologists. In addition, managers do not usually talk with their subordinates about the latter's needs. Furthermore, while employee behavior always stems from one or more needs, it may be difficult for a manager to determine all of the interrelationships which exist be tween employee needs and behaviors. Inspection of the rankings in 1980 as compared with 1946 also indicates that what employees want from their work has changed somewhat in the last thirty-four years. The moral of this story appears to be quite clear: the only way to determine an employee's needs is to ask him and to pay close attention to casual comments made by employees regarding their needs. If you want to know, *ASK!*

Satisfying Employee Needs

Now let us look at some examples of overt actions some organizations are taking to satisfy their employees' needs and, simultane-

Employee Ranking	Supervisor Ranking
1 Full appreciation of work done.	8
2 Feeling of being in on things.	9
3 Sympathetic help with personal problems.	10
4 Job security.	2
5 Good wages.	1
6 Interesting work.	5
7 Promotion and growth in the organization.	3
8 Personal loyalty to employees.	6
9 Good working conditions.	4
10 Tactful discipline.	7

Figure 5-1. What People Want From Their Work (1946)

Employee Ranking	Supervisor Ranking
1 Interesting work.	5
2 Full appreciation of work done.	8
3 Feeling of being in on things.	10
4 Job security.	2
5 Good wages.	1
6 Promotion and growth in the organization.	3
7 Good working conditions.	4
8 Personal loyalty to employees.	7
9 Sympathetic help with personal problems.	9
10 Tactful discipline.	6

Figure 5-2. What People Want From Their Work (1980)

ously, to improve organizational effectiveness. We will begin by looking at "Flexitime" and "Compressed Work Schedules" followed by a discussion of "Job Sharing" and "Phased Retirement." We will then look at "Leaves of Absence and Vacations," "Cafeteria Style Incentive Systems" and, finally, "Music."

Flexitime. Flexitime, which refers to flexible working hours, is a system under which each employee decides, on a daily or weekly basis, when he or she will arrive at work and when he or she will depart. Employees typically do not have an unlimited choice in this regard. Instead, an organization creates a core set of hours during which they want all employees to be present (for example, 10:00 a.m. to 2:00 p.m.). Two or three hour bands of time are then created both before and after the core time, and employees can then decide which eight hours during the day they want to work. To illustrate, some employees may choose to work from 6:00 a.m. until 3:00 p.m. (one hour for lunch), whereas others may work from 10:00 a.m. to 7:00 p.m. Some organizations allow employees to work less than eight hours one day if they work more than eight hours on another day. Others prescribe few, if any, core hours and even allow workers to select the length of their breaks and meal times.

Flexitime has been used by many companies, both large and small, in various industries and in various countries. Glueck (1979) reported that in 1979 about 1,000 United States enterprises used flexitime covering about 500,000 employees. Among the major organizations which have used it are Prudential Life Insurance, First National Bank of Boston, Canada Trust, Hewlett-Packard, Control Data Systems, Lufthansa, General Motors, and several Blue Cross/Blue Shield plans.

How effective has flexitime been? It is quite difficult to determine the answer to this question because most organizations which have used it did not keep comprehensive records or report their results. The literature does suggest, however, that flexitime is viewed quite favorably by subordinates. They seem to prefer it to standard work schedules. In addition, reductions in absenteeism, tardiness, and turnover are frequently reported by the companies using flexitime. Interestingly, productivity does not appear to change significantly under a flexitime system. Studies show that most organizations report no increase or only slight increases in employee productivity. Keep in mind, however, that the literature relating to this question is sparse, so the "jury" is still out.

It is important to note that flexitime does have some potential disadvantages. Among the most severe are tabulating each employee's work hours, insuring supervisory coverage during the entire work day, scheduling meetings with employees, coordinating projects, and insuring that necessary but unpredicted work can be done when required.

Compressed Work Schedules. The typical organization requires its employees to work five days a week, eight hours a day. A large number of organizations, however, have experimented with compressed work weeks such as four ten-hour days or three twelve-hour days. Some other organizations have utilized compressed work months. Some riverboat pilots work thirty days and are off thirty days. Reportedly (Glueck, 1979) about one million Americans representing over ten thousand organizations work a compressed work schedule.

In 1979 Glueck analyzed all the studies which had been reported to date on compressed work weeks. He found that companies differ considerably in terms of their experience with it. Some companies reported favorable results, while others were not pleased. Glueck concluded that middle-aged employees whose jobs do not require heavy physical or taxing mental work can be expected to have favorable attitudes toward compressed work weeks. In addition, companies whose business does not require that employees be present every weekday, who do not have capital intensive technology, and whose sales are fairly constant are most likely to have a favorable experience with compressed work weeks.

Phased Retirement. Phased retirement is a relatively new approach that focuses on the needs of older workers who are approaching retirement age.

As the phrase "phased retirement" implies, those organizations using this approach attempt to develop flexible work options for older employees which ease their transition to retirement.

Two organizations which have reportedly (McCarthy, 1979) developed phased retirement programs are Teledyne Continental Motors of Milwaukee, Wisconsin, and Varian Associates, Palo Alto, California.

Teledyne offers a "Golden Bridge" program to workers who are fifty-eight years old and have at least thirty years employment. Under the program, qualified employees between the ages of fifty-eight and sixty-one reportedly receive 160 extra hours of paid vacation, while those between sixty-two and sixty-eight receive 200 hours extra vacation. Payment for the vacation can be taken at the end of the year, or it can be deferred until after retirement.

Varian Associates reportedly has established a "Retirement Transition Program" for employees who are sixty years old and have five years of service. Under the program, employees can reduce their work schedule during the two-year period prior to their planned retirement. For example, if a worker, aged sixty, decided to retire at age sixty-five, he could reduce the number of days worked per week when reaching the age of sixty-three. The program requires that each employee work a minimum of twenty hours per week. Employees can reduce their work schedules to four days the first year and three days the second year. Interestingly, full medical and dental benefits are provided and those which are salary-related are prorated.

Since so few companies have experimented with phased retirement, little evidence exists as to its effectiveness either from the employee's or the organization's point of view. One could surmise, however, that organizations could potentially benefit from this approach in numerous ways. The employee's productivity per working hour may increase as the result of working fewer total hours. In addition, the promotion route could be expected to open up, and unauthorized absenteeism among older workers could decrease because of their reduced work schedules. Retirement fund costs may also be reduced. From the employees' standpoint, phased retirement may make it easier for them to adjust to and prepare for retirement. It gives them a taste of what retirement will be like. In addition, it provides them with additional free time to develop and pursue outside interests.

Job Sharing and Job Pairing. *Job sharing* refers to a situation in which two equally qualified part-time employees divide the hours, responsibilities, and benefits of a full-time job by performing complementary tasks. Closely related to the notion of job sharing is *job pairing* which is identical to the former except that each employee is accountable for everything that is done on the job, not just what he does. Job sharing and job pairing is a form of part-time employment. However, unlike most part-time positions, people engaged in these two approaches actually split a full-time job. In addition, unlike many part-time workers, the skills and education of job sharers and pairers are equal to those of full-time workers.

At the present time, job sharing or pairing reportedly (Frease and Zawacki, 1979) is used in a number of different organizations including banks, libraries, museums, legal firms, and governmental organizations. Over 100 college professors share jobs. Many of these are husband-wife teams who share one salary and one teaching load.

There are numerous potential advantages from the use of job sharing and job pairing. Productivity may be higher because job sharers/pairers have found a job that conforms to their special needs and because two people working four hours per day could be expected to suffer from less fatigue and boredom than one person working eight hours per day. Absenteeism and turnover could be lower for the same reasons. Allowing workers to share a job may increase the number of highly qualified job applicants who apply for a job. At the present time, many well-qualified individuals often do not apply for a job because it requires their full-time effort. Offering these individuals a part-time job may encourage them to enter the work force and net the company an excellent employee. A further advantage of job sharing and pairing is that it helps to reduce problems caused by employees taking vacations, going on lunch breaks, and being absent. When full-time employees are absent from work, organizations frequently must find temporary replacements for them. With job sharing this problem may be reduced considerably since one job sharer/pairer may be able to cover for the other.

While the potential advantages of job sharing/pairing are many, there are also some potential problems associated with its use. Coordination between those sharing a job can create problems unless both parties make a conscientious effort to communicate effectively with each other. The same is true regarding coordination between the supervisors and the job sharers/pairers.

Accountability can represent a problem with job sharing. When two people share a job, it is obviously more difficult to affix responsibility than when only one person is involved. Interestingly, with job pairing both employees are held responsible for the entire job which helps to reduce this problem.

Yet another potential disadvantage of both job pairing and job sharing is increased costs of fringe benefits. While salaries and many fringe benefits like life insurance and retirement benefits can be prorated if management desires, statutory benefits such as FICA and unemployment insurance may be higher, depending on the amount of earnings involved.

How successful has job sharing and job pairing been overall? One study at a mass-assembly department in a northeastern firm reported that job sharing resulted in a seven percent higher output and a twelve percent lower scrap rate. A second study of fifty Massachusetts welfare caseworkers showed that each job sharer handled eighty percent of a full-time caseload. Reportedly, when people work only two or three days a week or only four hours a day, they come to work with great enthusiasm and find it hard to leave their job behind.

While the results of these two studies are favorable, it is still far too early to reach a verdict regarding the efficacy of job sharing and job pairing. Certainly organizations that are thinking of using this approach should tread slowly. The old adage "Look before you leap" is certainly applicable here.

Leaves of Absence and Vacations. Two of the most common ways organizations attempt to satisfy employee needs are by granting vacations and by granting leaves of absence. Because most readers are undoubtedly quite familiar with vacation policies of various organizations, we will not elaborate on them. Instead, we will focus solely on leaves of absence.

One of the most common leaves is for medical reasons. One type of medical leave of absence is typically made available to employees who have short-term illnesses. A second type is for those who have extended mental or physical illnesses or who are pregnant. Both forms of medical leaves allow employees to miss work for the length of their illness or pregnancy and yet not lose their jobs. While an employee is out of work, he or she continues to receive some form of compensation. If the illness is of short duration the employee continues to draw his or her usual salary. If it is a long-term leave, compensation is usually in the form of a long-term disability insurance benefit.

Besides medical leaves of absence, some organizations grant personal leaves of absence to employees. One large auto manufacturing company, for example, grants each employee three days personal leave per year with pay. The employee can use it at any time and for any reason. Under the plan supervisors are not permitted to ask employees what they plan to do during these "personal business days." One mental health organization grants its own employees three paid "mental health days" per year for use when the employees simply do not feel like coming in to work. In addition to short-term personal leaves, some organizations grant employees extended personal leaves of absence as well. For example, one large hospital grants its employees, on a case by case basis, up to thirty days unpaid leave of absence for good cause. The leave can be extended up to a period of eighteen months if the employee establishes a satisfactory reason for the request. Hospital administrators, of course, determine what constitutes a "satisfactory reason" and a "good cause."

Funeral leaves of absence are common in many organizations. Frequently, employees are granted up to three paid days leave to attend a funeral of a close relative. A "close relative" is usually defined as a wife, husband, son, daughter, father, mother, brother, sister, or parent of spouse.

One large retail organization offers its employees a marriage leave of absence. Under the plan employees receive a paid absence day for the day of their wedding. If the wedding falls on a Saturday or

Sunday, employees are paid and allowed to take off work the preceding Friday.

Companies grant military leaves of absence for employees who serve in the armed forces. One organization's policy, which is typical of many others, states:

> If Uncle Sam wants you, you'll be released from the company for regular, full-time military duty. If you come back to work within 90 days of your military separation, you'll be reinstated and given your most recent service date, your former salary plus any automatic increases employees received while you were away. The company allows military leaves up to 10 working days a year for reservists and national guardsmen required to participate in active duty training. You'll receive your full salary, minus your military pay.

Some organizations, usually larger ones, allow their employees a leave of absence to engage in civic, educational, professional, or governmental activities, including politics. One large computer manufacturer allows its employees with one year employment an opportunity to take an educational leave of absence. Approval of the leave is based on the relevancy of the employee's study program to company interests, the employee's academic and work record, and the appropriateness of the school to the employee's educational objectives. A large oil company grants qualifying employees leaves up to ninety days to run for political office.

All of the leaves of absence policies described above, as well as vacation policies, are designed to satisfy the needs of employees. However, they typically have positive consequences for the organization as well. They help organizations to attract new employees and to keep older ones. In addition, both potentially have a positive effect on company productivity in the long run. This is most obviously true for sick leaves because the productivity of sick employees is usually low, and they may spread their illness to other employees, thereby reducing productivity further.

Cafeterial Style Incentive Systems. A rather new and innovative approach to satisfying people's needs is the cafeteria style incentive system which is being used by several major and undoubtedly many small organizations at the present time. The basic notion behind this approach is that each employee should be given a choice regarding the compensation and benefits package he or she receives rather than having management make the choice for them.

American Can Company is one of the best known innovators in allowing employees to design a benefit package to meet their own needs and preferences. In 1979 they reportedly (Tavernier, 1980) instituted a plan covering nine thousand salaried employees which provides them with a core of nonoptional benefits and then allows them to select additional benefits from a group of options on the basis of credits which are granted to each employee. Employees are also permitted to purchase additional benefits through payroll deduction.

Under the plan employees reportedly have a choice of options regarding medical coverage, life insurance, disability income, vacation, and retirement and capital accounts.

In terms of medical options, employees have a choice in terms of the percentage paid by the plan and the amount deductible. Employees can also choose coverage for vision, hearing, and health examinations, or a dental plan.

Additional life insurance for up to four times an employee's annual salary can be chosen. This is in addition to the core coverage which provides coverage equal to one's annual salary. Furthermore, an employee can select survivor income benefits equal to either twenty percent or forty percent of his base salary. There are options covering accidental death or dismemberment and life insurance for spouses and dependent children.

The vacation option permits employees to use their credits to purchase up to five additional vacation days in any year. The cost of the option depends on the employee's pay level.

Employees can choose an option to extend their disability insurance coverage beyond the core amount with the cost depending on the employee's age and salary.

The retirement and capital accumulation options permit additional retirement income beyond that provided in the company's regular pension plan. Employees can allocate money to American Can Company stock, a diversified investment fund, or to a guaranteed interest fund.

Employees are permitted to change their benefit options once a year. Each September, American Can sends employees a form showing their existing program and the number of credits to which they are entitled. The employees can then choose to keep the same program or select new options. Changes go into effect January 1. New employees are given sixty days to select their benefits.

American Can Company management is reportedly quite pleased with this plan. Employees appreciate receiving a choice in their benefits, and the company has found that the new plan helps to attract and retain good employees. The cost of administering the program, while significant, was less than expected. A total of fifteen people, mostly design personnel and computer programmers, worked full-time for eight months to develop the plan. The plan is reportedly being administered by five employees, although additional clerical help is needed at the end of the year when selection forms are submitted for processing.

The notion of allowing employees to choose the rewards they desire is an intriguing one. One could easily envision extending the approach being used by American Can to include other options such as office size and furnishings, length of lunch breaks, clothing allowances, automobiles, membership in various organizations, and the amount of clerical help and other support provided.

Music.   The use of music to increase employee satisfaction and productivity has been studied in a number of organizations. Generally speaking, the results of these studies are quite favorable (Fox, 1971). Studies have generally shown that music increases productivity on monotonous tasks; it decreases errors, tardiness, turnover, accidents, and increases work quality in some settings. To what extent music can improve productivity on complex mental tasks is unclear. Some studies show that the introduction of music in settings which require demanding mental attention results in positive organizational consequences, whereas other studies show the opposite.

It is important to remember that not all forms of music have equal effects on employee performance. For example, the constant playing of loud bagpipe music or acid rock would likely be quite disruptive. While studies are not clear as to which type of music is optimal in given situations, Grandjean (1969) has concluded, based on a number of studies, that continuous loud music should not be played during the day. A short rousing selection of music is recommended to start the day, and a more festive selection is suggested at day's end.

How long music should be played during the day is subject to debate. Fox (1971) argues that music should definitely not be played continuously, or it will lose its stimulating value. He recommends that music be timed to counteract the peaks of fatigue during the day. One study recommends that music will be optimally effective if it is played thirty-three percent of the day, while another recommends that it be played twenty-five percent of the work day.

It is also possible that the effect of music differs from individual to individual. Perhaps the simplest solution to differing preferences for loudness and presence or absence of music would be to have a volume control in each office area.

REASONS

Up to this point we have examined the action of satisfying employee needs itself and described numerous examples of organizations using it. Now it is time to present the logic or rationale behind the action.

Maslow's Hierarchy of Needs

Perhaps the most well known of all motivation theories is that of Abraham H. Maslow who, in 1943, wrote an influential article entitled "A Dynamic Theory of Human Motivation." In this article he outlined his now famous hierarchy of needs approach to motivation. Maslow's theory can be summarized and understood effectively in terms of four major propositions.

People Are Motivated by Needs.   Maslow contends, as do many other theorists, that people have needs and are motivated to satisfy them. In this context a need is generally conceived of as an internal stimulus which causes a person to act and has a physiological or psychological basis. Needs, of course, must first be translated into goals before any action can occur.

At this point it is helpful to remember that people differ in terms of the strength of their needs and perhaps in terms of the needs themselves. In addition, the needs of a person frequently change over time. When one is a small child, the offer of a lollipop or ice cream cone may be sufficient to motivate one to do a household chore. However, when that same child reaches the age of seventy, a lollipop or ice cream cone will undoubtedly no longer serve to induce the same behavior.

It is also important to observe that any given behavior can be determined by more than one need. For example, a person's desire to collect antiques can be caused by a combination of several, even many, different needs such as the need to furnish one's house and the need for investment. Conversely, engaging in a single activity can satisfy more than one need. It should also be observed that people may engage in the same activities for different reasons. To illustrate, you may collect antiques because of your need for furnishings, whereas your brother collects them to satisfy his need for a good investment.

Satisfied Needs Are Not Motivators.   One of Maslow's most important propositions is that satisfied needs do not motiviate employees, only unsatisfied needs do. While this proposition may appear to the reader to be obvious, it is remarkable how many supervisors take actions which are contrary to it. Many persist in giving or offering employees more of the types of rewards they no longer desire. They fail to recognize that employees are not motivated to work for "rewards" they do not want. Employees can only be motivated to obtain something they do want.

Perhaps an illustration is in order. Offering a dental plan to a worker whose teeth need cleaning and gold caps may serve as an incentive to that worker. Offering the same plan to an employee whose spouse is a dentist will probably not be effective in improving performance.

Managers must be aware, then, of what employees do in fact want and appeal to those needs. Clearly, there is little to be gained from offering employees "rewards" which they do not consider as rewards. Previously we described the cafeteria style incentive system used by American Can Company. Now the reader can clearly see that this system is one of the practical applications of the proposition that only unsatisfied needs motivate people's behavior.

Unsatisfied Needs Can Result in Dysfunctional Behavior.   What happens to employees whose dominant needs go unsatisfied over a prolonged period of time? In many organizations employees are unable to satisfy their most important needs regardless of how long they wait or how hard they try. This may be the result of many factors, such as repressive company policies, incompetent managerial personnel, or a poorly designed job. Given this situation, employees have little choice other than to quit the job or engage in some form of coping behavior. Unfortunately, this coping behavior may have many negative side effects. Some employees may vent their frustration directly at the company or supervisor by engaging in some form of sabotage such as destroying company property or being insubordinate. Others may simply complain and bicker incessantly, and in doing so have an adverse impact on coworkers. Still others may develop severe mental problems or physical ailments such as headaches and ulcers. The major point that the "need theorists" make is that if an employee's needs are not eventually satisfied, dysfunctional consequences for the organization are likely to occur. Remember, unsatisfied needs motivate employees, for better or worse.

People's Needs Form a Hierarchy.   Perhaps the most profound and widely known aspect of Maslow's approach is his proposition that people's needs are arranged in a hierarchy of importance (Figure 5-3). Not all needs are equally important; some are more potent than others.

One of the easiest ways to understand and remember Maslow's need hierarchy is to picture yourself on a island located somewhere in the Pacific. You have just survived an airplane crash. Which of your needs would be most important to you at that time? For most people, it would be physical survival or taking care of one's bodily needs, such as obtaining water and food. Maslow calls these "physiological needs," and they are ultimately the most important of all of our needs.

After your bodily needs are satisfied on the island, what needs would then become important to you?

The answer is probably a concern with safety and security. People need to find shelter to protect themselves from the elements. They want to provide themselves with shoes, hats, and other clothes. Maslow labels these desires as "safety or security needs," and they are rated second in importance on the need hierarchy.

Both physiological and safety needs can be thought of as needs related to the preservation of the human body. But, for most people, mere preservation or survival is not the only concern which is important to them. They want to enhance themselves as well. One of the major desires people have beyond satisfying their survival needs, and the one rated third in importance by Maslow, is the need for affiliation and companionship. This includes the desire to be accepted by others, to be loved, and to be understood. Maslow refers to this group of wants as "social needs." One can easily

Figure 5-3. Maslow's Hierarchy of Needs

Emerge LAST –	*Self-actualization Needs*
	Esteem Needs
	Belonging Needs
	Safety Needs
Emerge FIRST –	*Physiological Needs*

---

envision that a person on an island would want to find others to converse with after his physiological and safety needs were fairly well-satisfied.

Enhancing oneself goes far beyond the enjoyment companionship brings, however. People typically also have a need for recognition and admiration, even prestige. They want to feel that they make a difference, that their presence is important to the company, the supervisor, and to others. They want to know that what they do counts and is appreciated. In addition to these needs which relate to one's reputation, people also have needs which relate to their self-esteem. These include self-confidence, self-respect, and feelings of competence. The need for recognition or status combined with the need for self-esteem are referred to as "esteem needs." Maslow contends that these needs rank as the fourth most important needs for most people, including the person on the remote island.

The fifth and last set of needs in the Maslow hierarchy is called "self-actualization needs." This is perhaps the hardest of the five needs to grasp. It refers to the notion that people want to become all they are capable of becoming. They want to realize their potential. It encompasses one's desire to feel a sense of accomplishment, of growth, and of fulfillment. It includes the desire people have to feel they are competent to deal with reality, to experience a sense of mental efficacy and mastery.

There are several aspects of Maslow's need hierarchy which deserve further consideration. Maslow argues that a person is motivated by the needs that are dominant at a particular point in time. One's physiological needs are the most dominant initially. However, as these become satisfied, safety or security needs then become the dominant ones and, hence, are the motivators of behavior. After one's physiological and safety needs are both relatively satisfied, a desire to fulfill one's social needs then start to dominate an individual's behavior. Subsequently, in a step by step fashion, as the first three needs are relatively satisfied, esteem needs start to dominate one's behavior. Ultimately one's behavior is concentrated around a desire to satisfy one's need for self-actualization. As the reader can see, as the need in one category becomes satisfied, it causes the strength of the need in the next higher category to increase.

What happens when all five of an employee's needs are fully satisfied? How does a supervisor motivate his employees under this condition? Maslow and other need theorists argue that this hypothetical situation cannot possibly occur because people cannot ever satisfy all of their self-actualization needs! One can always develop his potential more fully. One can always achieve greater competency and mastery in what is done. In addition, Maslow contends, with reference to self-actualization needs, that their increased satisfaction leads to increased need strength rather than decreased need strength. The more one attempts to gratify one's need for self-actualization, the stronger and more dominant this need becomes. To illustrate, when a basketball player gains competency in shooting jump shots, it increases the desire to obtain competency in shooting free throws, hook shots, and so on.

Another question which is frequently asked with reference to the need hierarchy is whether it is the same for everybody. In other words, are everyone's needs arranged in the same order of importance, that is, physiological needs, safety needs, social needs, esteem needs, and self-actualization needs? Need theorists typically state that people do, in fact, differ in terms of the importance they place on various needs. A hermit, for example, who lives miles from anyone else, may indeed place little emphasis on social needs. A stunt pilot or oil well fire fighter may have weak safety and security needs. Perhaps the major point is that Maslow's hierarchy of needs may not accurately describe everyone's need structure, but it probably does portray it accurately for a large number of people. In any event, it is a good conceptual framework from which to start analyzing employee motivation.

Maslow's Theory—A Capsule Summary.   Since Maslow's theory is a bit complex, perhaps a capsule summary of it is in order. This summary can serve as a double check on the reader's understanding of this conceptual framework.

Maslow contends that people are motivated to satisfy their unfulfilled needs. Most people's needs are arranged in a hierarchy of importance: physiological needs, safety needs, social needs, esteem needs, and self-actualization needs. The more basic needs are inherently more important than are the higher level ones. However, once a lower level need has been satisfied, its strength and importance decreases, and the next higher level of need becomes the strongest motivator of behavior. This process repeats itself in a step-by-step fashion until the highest level in the hierarchy (self-actualization needs) is reached. No one can ever satisfy all of his self-actualization needs, since the more it is gratified, the stronger it becomes.

As a final analogy consider the following. You are a manager with five items on your agenda. The first item must be completed before the second can be begun. This might be due to information required to perform item two which is generated by item one. Item two must be completed before item three is begun, for similar reasons. Similarly, item three must precede four, and four must precede five. In this situation there is no question about where any competent manager would begin. Now consider the five items to be the five needs which Maslow speaks of, item one being physiological needs, and so on. All Maslow intended with the hierarchy notion was that some needs must be satisfied before others will receive attention.

IMPLEMENTATION

The steps a manager can potentially follow when implementing the need-satisfying strategy will now be described (Figure 5-4). Keep in mind that there is nothing absolute about the steps themselves. They are general guidelines which the reader may want to modify to his

Figure 5-4. Satisfying Employee Needs: Strategy Guide

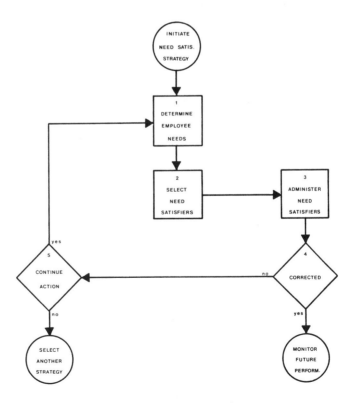

own particular situation. Remember that all of the action strategy guidelines presented in this book are designed to encourage a logical step-by-step approach to increasing employee productivity. They are not designed to encourage robot-like managerial behavior.

Step 1 Determine Employee Needs.   At the start of this chapter, we stated that the need-satisfying strategy consisted of two separate actions: determining employee needs and satisfying them. Of course, one must determine employee needs first and, hence, the strategy guide begins with that step.

In the previous section we described several different methods organizations use to determine employee needs. We stated that some organizations administer attitudinal questionnaires or job satisfaction questionnaires to their employees, while others conduct interviews with workers.

Managers, of course, can utilize these approaches with their own employees. One may want to use an attitudinal questionnaire when many employees need to be surveyed and it is desirable to make comparisons across various departments. On the other hand, if a manager has only a few employees or is concerned with just a single employee, it will probably be advantageous to use an interview. The word *interview* often connotes a formal meeting between a boss and an employee. During an interview the manager asks the employee a series of questions. While some managers may want to follow this approach, a short informal meeting between a manager and an employee can often prove quite useful in determing employee needs. If they are alert, supervisors can often uncover quite helpful information about an employee's unsatisfied needs when talking about ordinary job-related problems with the employee. It is not uncommon for employees, during job-related discussions, to make statements such as, "I'd really like to learn more about..." or, "I don't like to... ." While these statements may seem rather innocuous, they frequently can tell a supervisor quite a bit about an employee's needs. Surely they should not be overlooked.

On occasion, a manager may want to ask an employee directly about what he wants from a job or feels about his present job. To ask an employee questions like, "What are your dominant needs?" or, "Which of your needs are presently unsatisfied?" or, "How satisfied are your physiological needs compared with your self-actualization needs?" is simply not effective because most employees will not know what you are talking about. Instead, a manager may want to experiment with questions like, "What could I or the organization do to make your job more enjoyable?" or, "What changes would you like to see made in your work situation?" Even questions like, "How could I or the company help you to improve your job performance?" or, "What job would you like to be doing two years from now?" might prove fruitful under some conditions. Ultimately, each manager will want to word the questions he uses in a way that best matches his own personality and the situation.

Be careful of asking negatively-oriented questions like, "What don't you like about working for this organization?" Such questions are technically called *reactive* because they may produce an attitude change just by being asked. Sometimes formerly satisfied employees respond to this question by thinking of things they do not like that were never on their minds before.

We mentioned that employees are often unable or unwilling to report their needs to a manager in a valid way. For example, some may report that they want more pay when, in fact, they might really want greater recognition or responsibilities. A manager needs to remember that what employees say they want is often affected more by the need satisfiers they believe they can get than by those they want.

To illustrate, assume an employee believes that a manager can only provide him with need satisfiers W, X, and Y. When a manager asks the employee about his needs, it should come as no surprise when the employee responds that he wants more of W, X, or Y. Why ask for Z when one knows it cannot or will not be provided by the company or supervisor? There is no use asking for apple pie at a restaurant which serves only cherry pie.

There is one particularly important situation that occurs in many organizations and deserves further discussion. Many organizations provide workers with an opportunity to satisfy their physiological, safety, and social needs but not their esteem and self-actualization needs. When asked about their unsatisfied needs, workers in these organizations typically respond that they want more job security or pay. The rationale behind their answer is quite simple. They have learned over the years that the organization will not or cannot provide them with opportunities to satisfy their esteem and self-actualization needs. They feel they have no alternative but to try to get more of the rewards which the organization has provided in the past. The important point is that money and other relatively lower level need satisfiers often serve as substitute requests for higher level need satisfiers. Hence, when managers hear their employees asking for lower level need satisfiers, they should attempt to determine whether this is really what the employee needs or whether this demand represents a masked desire for higher level need satisfiers. It is wise to remember in this context that many people whose jobs pay minimal wages and provide poor working conditions often are more highly satisfied with their jobs. Peace Corps and VISTA members, as well as members of hundreds of volunteer organizations, are prime examples of this.

In summary, a manager can determine employee needs by using job satisfaction questionnaires, conducting a formal or informal interview regarding the employee's needs, or by being attentive to casual employee comments regarding their likes and dislikes. It is important, however, for a manager to exercise caution when interpreting what an employee says regarding his needs. Ideally, a manager would have-- as a result of using one or more of these approaches-- a general understanding of:

1. which needs of the employee are presently satisfied
2. which needs of the employee are presently unsatisfied
3. which of the unsatisfied needs is most important to the employee.

Step 2 Satisfying Employee Needs.   In the example section of this chapter we described seven different actions that organizations take to satisfy the needs of their employees. We stated that these actions are not only designed specifically to satisfy the employee's needs, but also serve worthwhile organizational purposes as well.

At this point it is important to observe that these seven actions are designed primarily to satisfy an employee's physiological, safety, and social needs. What about an employee's esteem and self-actualization needs? How can they be satisfied?

Perhaps the reader has already come to the realization that job redesign (Chapter Seven) provides one avenue of action. Keep in mind that increasing an employee's responsibility, job meaningfulness, and knowledge of results are all designed to appeal to an employee's esteem and self-actualization needs.

Most of what was said about Maslow's hierarchy of needs approach is relevant to selecting need satisfiers. Of particular importance is Maslow's proposition that people's needs are arranged in a hierarchy of importance and that only unsatisfied needs are motivators. A manager should attempt to select those need satisfiers which are relevant to an employee's dominant unsatisfied needs.

In many organizations employees face what are described as job irritants, that is, minor inconveniences or problems which occur periodically on an employee's job. For example, a teacher might find that there is no chalk in a classroom, or a secretary might be asked to retype a twelve-page report because someone spilled coffee on the original. While most of us can tolerate a few of these nuisances from time to time, a steady diet of them can become intolerable and can lead to considerable need dissatisfaction. These problems surface in many ways and usually differ from organization to organization. They can relate to or tie into any of the five need categories suggested by Maslow. In selecting need satisfiers a manager may be wise to begin by focusing his attention on reducing or eliminating these irritants. Fortunately, employees can usually identify nuisances quite accurately and quickly, and the action required by the manager is typically apparent.

Step 3 Administer Need Satisfiers. After the manager has determined which satisfiers are likely to motivate his employees, the next step is to make the satisfiers available to the workers. There are several considerations which are noteworthy in this regard. First, a manager should give some consideration as to when the need satisfiers are given. No specific rules can be offered in this regard. A manager must simply rely on his own best judgment.

A consideration more important than timing relates to which employees are to receive the need satisfiers. Normally, those given the need satisfiers are the ones whose job performance the manager is trying to improve. In some cases this may be just a single worker. The important point is that managers should attempt to administer need satisfiers in a way that is fair. In Chapter Four we discussed "treating people fairly" as a motivation strategy. Certainly many of the principles and considerations suggested there are relevant here. A manager should not forget that what he does for one employee he may need to do for another.

One final consideration that is important in administering need satisfiers is this: Managers should observe that they cannot, in fact, directly satisfy employee needs, particularly esteem and self-actualization needs. All a manager can do is provide employees with an environment which gives them an opportunity to satisfy their needs. A manager can provide the employee with an opportunity to achieve his potential, for example, but the employee always has the option of not taking advantage of this opportunity. Obviously, the phase "administer need satisfiers" should be construed in the broad sense and not literally. A manager cannot inject an employee with "need satisfiers" which instantly satisfy the employee's needs in the same way a dentist can give a patient an anesthetic to eliminate pain.

Step 4 Checking For Correction. As with all of the other strategies, a manager may find after attempting the need satisfying strategy that it was not successful, that is, the employee's job behavior has not improved. Typically this occurs because what the manager thought would satisfy an employee's dominant unsatisfied needs did not. Keep in mind that managers cannot expect all of their actions to be successful. Given that the manager's actions were unsuccessful, what course should be followed? One possibility is to try the need satisfying strategy again, using a different need satisfier.

Step 5 Continue Action? Alternately, a manager may simply want to utilize a different motivation strategy altogether or use an outplacement approach. It is important to remember in this regard that it is very hard to satisfy the needs of some, albeit few, employees because of early "need-starvation" as a child. These employees, whose parents repeatedly ignored one or more of their early childhood needs, may have an insatiable desire for satisfaction of these needs. Regardless, then, of what the manager does, the employee will continue to feel deprived. To repeatedly try to satisfy the needs of these employees would be futile. Instead, a counseling referral is appropriate.

SUMMARY

In this chapter we have described the motivational strategy of satisfying employee needs. We have observed that this action consists of two separate parts: determining employee needs and satisfying them. We have cited numerous examples of organizations which have used this approach and how they have done it. The reasoning or rationale behind the action was discussed in terms of Abraham H. Maslow's need hierarchy theory. This theory suggests that people's needs are arranged in a hierarchy of importance. The hierarchy, in order, is as follows: physiological needs, safety needs, social needs, esteem needs, and self-actualization needs.

The theory also argues that satisfied needs are not motivators, only unsatisfied needs are. Finally we have presented an action guide for use in implementing the satisfying need approach. Potential pitfalls to avoid and decisions that must be made when using this approach were discussed.

The use of the need satisfaction strategy has several important advantages for a manager. First, to the extent that a supervisor can, in fact, satisfy employee needs, workers will be relatively happy. It is easier and far more enjoyable to supervise satisfied employees than ones who are dissatisfied with their work situation. Unsatisfied workers are often less cooperative and less friendly, and are more likely to be tardy or absent, to break company rules, and to quit.

Secondly, managers who use this strategy are generally viewed more favorably by employees than are those who do not. They are thought to be more considerate, supportive, and interested in their employees' welfare. This is true even if they are not always successful in obtaining what is wanted for the employees. Almost all managers find it more personally rewarding to be liked than to be disliked.

Finally, to the extent that managers can satisfy employee needs, the employee will see the organization as a central part of his life. Employee commitment to organizational goals, and, indeed, to the manager's own goals is directly related to the centrality of their work to their lives. Thus, when need satisfaction is high, commitment is usually high. Both the organization and the manager gain when this occurs.

RECOMMENDED READINGS

Atwood, Caleb S. "A Work Schedule to Increase Productivity." *The Personnel Administrator* 24, (1979): 29-34.

Cohen, A. R. and Gadon, H. *Alternative Work Schedules: Integrating Individual and Organizational Needs*. Reading, Mass.: Addison-Wesley Publishing Co., 1978.

Fox, J. G. "Background Music and Industrial Efficiency— A Review." *Applied Ergonomics* 2.2 (1971): 70-73.

Frease, M. and Zawachi, R. A. "Job Sharing: An Answer to Productivity Problems." *The Personnel Administrator* 24(10) (1979): 35-39.

Glueck, W. F. "Changing Hours of Work: A Review and Analysis of the Research." *The Personnel Administrator* 24 (1979): 44-67.

Golembiewski, R. J. and Proell, Jr., C. W. " A Survey of the Empirical Literature on Flexible Workhours: Character and Consequences of a Major Innovation." *Academy of Management Review* 10 (1978): 837-53.

Hodge, B. J. and Tellier, R. D. "Employees' Reaction to the Four Day Week." *California Management Review* 8(1) (1975): 31-35.

Hutton, T. A. "Involvement Through Music." *The Personnel Administrator* 25 (1980): 61-62.

Jurgensen, C. E. "What Job Applicants Say They Want." From *Studies in Personnel and Industrial Psychology,* edited by E. A. Fleischman. Homewood, Ill.: The Dorsey Press, 1967.

Kovach, K. A. "Why Motivational Theories Don't Work." *Advance Management Journal* Spring 1980, pp. 54-59.

Krakauer, D. "Now We Know What Our People Want." *Personnel Journal* 32(7) (1953): 246-52.

Maslow, A. H. "A Dynamic Theory of Human Motivation." *Psychological Review* (1943): 50.

McCarthy, M. "Trends in the Development of Alternative Work Patterns." *The Personnel Administrator* 24(10) (1979): 25-28.

Newstrom, J. W. and Pierce, J. L. "Alternative Work Schedules: The State of the Art." *The Personnel Administrator* 24(10) (1979): 19-24.

Poor, R. *4 DAYS/40 HOURS*. New York, N. Y.: NAL, 1973.

Swart, G. W. and Guthrie, A. "Alternative Work Schedules: Which One Fits Your Operation?" *Supervisory Management* 6 (1976): 2-19.

Tavernier, G. "How American Can Manages Its Flexible Benefits Program." *Management Review* 69(8) (1980): 8-13.

6

Setting Employee Goals

INTRODUCTION

Most managers are already familiar with goal setting, although it may not be apparent at first. To open this chapter we present two common examples of goal setting.

Military Field Manual Example

a. Give clear, concise orders. Be sure they are understood. Then supervise to make sure the order is promptly executed. The able leader makes wise use of his subordinates to carry out his orders effectively. Any commander who fails to make proper use of his staff and subordinates in accordance with their capabilities demonstrates a fundamental weakness in leadership ability.

b. Men will respond more quickly to orders which are clear, concise, and easily understood. On the other hand, they may become confused if you overstate the order or instruction by giving too many details. Your subordinates like to know that you are available for advice and counsel if and when needed. However, they will resent oversupervision and harassment. Individual initiative is developed within subordinates when they can use their imagination in developing their own techniques in accomplishment of tasks or missions. (Principle VI: Military Leadership (FM 22-100; Nov. 1965)

Job Description Example

Credit Analyst:

1. Analyzes credit data to estimate degree of risk involved in extending credit to present customers and prospects.

2. Prepares reports of findings including suggested credit limit.

3. Contacts banks, trade and credit associations, salespeople, and others to obtain credit information.

4. Analyzes paying habits of customers who are delinquent in payment of bills and recommends action.

5. Reviews files to select poor-pay accounts for collection; recommends collection techniques to be used.

6. Interviews customers in person or by telephone to investigate complaints, verify accuracy of charges, or to correct errors in accounts.

7. Verifies credit standing of customer from information in files and approves or disapproves credit.

Both employee manuals and job descriptions contain statements of job duties and goals to be reached. Let us look more deeply, now, into the nature of goals and their significance for both employees and the organization.

Goals and Intentions

The conscious, rational activities of people are the subject of this chapter. Some of the other six approaches which we present rely on the less than fully-conscious activities such as response to rewards or punishment, the feelings people have about equity or inequity, the worth of jobs, the fulfillment of needs, and so on.

Here, however, we deal with people's conscious intent, their goals, their plans. The management of such intentional activities of employees is very much a part of a manager's role.

In this chapter we emphasize first the setting of individual goals, then the integration of these goals into sets of individual goals.

These sets of goals, each normally the goal of an individual, are the common goals of people in positions which have related or interdependent functions. These sets of goals become the group goals.

Is Goal Setting New?   It is truly remarkable that the idea of setting goals for oneself or for one's employees is regarded as new. All of us, from time to time, decide that there is something we want. Most of us follow this decision with some sort of plan for getting what we want. It is all very simple—so simple there is really nothing to argue about—we just do it.

The idea that a person can work toward a goal without knowing what the goal is seems absurd. Without some kind of definition of where it is we want to arrive we cannot tell if we are progressing nor can we tell if we have arrived.

If this is so obvious for any individual, it must be even more so for when directing those we hire or manage toward a goal we desire. After all, unless our employees develop the ability to read our minds we cannot reasonably expect them to know what we want unless we tell them.

There is another side to this as well. Most employees are actually interested in doing a good job. They want to know what is expected of them so that they, too, can tell if they are doing the right things in their work. The same rules apply to employees as well as to managers. We need to define our goals and objectives before we can say we have attained them.

Just like managers, employees also need a definition of goals, and for the same reasons: so they can tell if the goals have been reached.

ACTION

The action of setting employee goals is one in which the manager directs and gives information while the employee does the actual goal setting.

Instructions to the employee and the training of the employee in setting appropriate goals is the substance of the manager's activity in this strategy.

What is an "appropriate goal" and how does the employee set such a goal? First, the goal must have some level of difficulty or challenge. It must be neither extremely easy to achieve nor impossible to achieve.

Second, the goal must be specific enough so that both the employee and the manager will know quite clearly whether or not the goal has been achieved.

There are additional and, in fact, optional attributes which the goal may have. Research indicates that these additional attributes may make the goal-setting effort more productive in certain situations. Just which situations is not clear at present and so for the practicing manager it may be advisable to include these optional attributes when feasible, just in case they are needed.

Feedback

Most of the work on feedback is found under the term *knowledge of score* which was used by Locke and Bryan in a 1967 series of studies. An addition task was used. Subjects were split into two groups, distinguished only by one of the groups receiving feedback frequently about their score on the progress of their task. Those subjects with hard goals who were given frequent feedback on progress toward the goal did best. The authors interpreted these data as indicating that the goal mediates the effect of feedback. We cannot say how far one might generalize these findings to tasks more real than an addition task. However, it makes sense that workers attempting to reach a goal will be more likely to do so if they are informed of their progress.

Other Incentives

Money, time limits, competition, and even praise or reproof are reported to also show effects which are mediated by goals. Why should this be so? Each of these commonly used incentives is normally linked to the attainment of some goal in actual practice.

We would argue that Locke's contribution may be that a specific and somewhat difficult goal provides two important cues about whether or not the performance is sufficient to achieve the incentive. First, whether one is close to a specific goal is logically easier to determine than for a nonspecific goal. Second, a difficult goal may augment the effect of the incentive by adding to it the intrinsic reward of reaching a difficult goal.

When Goals Are Set

Setting work-related goals with your employees is not simply a matter of implementing yet another fashionable management technique (usually the high-glamor Management By Objectives). Rather, it is a method of harnessing the intangibles of human experience and motivation. It is all too easy to believe that MBO or its cousins work because of hard-nosed principles and football game-like goal pursuit of the need to achieve.

What you will actually be doing in goal-setting is far more subtle. You will be manipulating the conscious goals and intentions of employees, using their own self-concept and the fact of public (in front of their peers) commitment to goals as a motivating force in their work behavior.

In Chapter Seven you will find that a major means of increasing the meaningfulness of a job is to increase two dimensions: Task Identity and Task Significance. These two dimensions together with increased worker skill variety largely determine the meaningfulness of the job in the worker's experience.

In a sense, goal setting works on the same dimensions. This chapter differs from the next in that its focus is not on the structure of the job itself but on the cognitive environment in which the job is done. Workers can become involved in their jobs in several ways. Among the most useful to the manager are the redesign of the job in order to allow more meaning to attach itself to the work done and the redesign of the cognitive environment of the job in order to produce the same effect.

The Cognitive Environment

Just how do we define the "cognitive environment of the job" and what can we do to change it?

Of course it is evident that much learning of how the goals are to be set realistically is of greatest importance since it takes considerable experience (more than most employees have) before truly realistic goals can be set with regularity.

The previous point makes it clear that the manager who wishes to make use of goal-setting as an employee productivity improvement device must also be a trainer of employees in the goal-setting process.

It is apparent that if a person wants to or intends to do something that she is actually likely to do that thing. If a person desires to make a certain thing (like a piece of work) and, in addition, we find upon asking her that she intends to produce the piece of work, then it is never surprising (except to the most ardent ivory tower Platonists and Pythagoreans) when the piece of work is actually produced.

In modern industrial enterprises it is rarely so simple as having a single person produce a piece of work since most work of any consequence and frequency is the joint product of the highly interdependent work efforts of many people (an automobile, for example) and thus there must be some sort of integration of the work of several people if we are ever to get a finished product.

Here is where goal-setting can be of enormous help in simplifying—after a somewhat long lag period—the work of the manager. When workers with interdependent tasks are setting their goals it is always necessary that they communicate with their fellow workers to find out how the parts fit together to make a whole. Now, normally this is the job of the manager, but under the goal-setting method it becomes necessary for each person to know what every other person is doing and why. It is neccessary for a person who uses the product of worker X to know what X is doing when the work is done. It is also extremely important that X know what the work produced is to be used for so that X will know what is important about the work, just which mistakes are serious and which are trivial.

Thus, it is apparent that the setting of goals is never a solitary activity. Rather, the setting of my goals is partially determined by what I get from others and partially determined by what others get from me. After, and only after, these things are known is it possible for me to make a suitable and practical statement of my goals.

The cognitive environment of the job, then, is the expectation that employees will communicate with each other and with the manager about their jobs. Based on the exchange of information and the stated intentions to do certain things the employees also set challenging goals which they intend to reach in their work.

EXAMPLES

The reader will have noted that the authors exhibit some skepticism about how well one can generalize from Locke's addition task to real work behavior. This skeptical posture is due more to the marginally relevant content of the academic studies conducted by Locke and others than to the usefulness of goal setting as a strategy. In this section we present two studies using real workers in real environments: loggers working on the West Coast of the United States and sewing machine operators working in the garment industry.

The Logging Study

The making or saving of money is considered by many to be the only true test of a theory's practical value. While we cannot agree with this extreme view, an experiment by Latham and Baldes, reported in 1975, provides one compelling example. The report was entitled "The 'Practical Significance' of Locke's Theory of Goal Setting" and it appeared in the *Journal of Applied Psychology*.

In the Latham and Baldes experiment, using logging truck drivers who were paid on an hourly basis and were union members, goals were assigned for loading trucks with logs. Before the goals were assigned the workers had been urged to "do their best" and the resultant loads appeared to be about sixty percent of the legal truck net weight. Following three months of the "do-best" condition a specific goal of ninety-four percent of the legal truck net weight was assigned.

> At the onset of the goal setting, the drivers were told that this was an experimental program, that they would not be required to make more truck runs, and that there would be no retaliation if performance suddenly increased and then decreased. No monetary rewards or fringe benefits other than verbal praise were given for improving performance. No special training of any kind was given to the supervisors or the drivers.

The test was run for a nine-month period (October to June) and for the final six months of this period the loads were near the set goal of ninety-four percent, consistently at the ninety percent level or above.

Now to practical significance. The increased efficiency due to this goal setting experiment could have been achieved (the authors report) by purchasing additional logging trucks. The cost of the additional trucks necessary to produce an increase in productivity comparable to what the experiment obtained by goal setting was estimated to be $250,000. This figure does not, however, include the additional costs of diesel fuel to run the additional trucks or the recruiting and hiring costs for additional truck drivers.

*Goals and Feedback
on Sewing Machines*

In 1979 James Koch reported an investigation into the joint effects of goal setting and feedback on sewing machine operators.

The research used 150 sewing machine operators in a south-western garment factory. These workers assembled pairs of pants using an "assembly line" on which thirty-four separate operations were performed. Each operation took an average time of eighteen seconds.

Quality of the work done was inspected at the end of the line by full-time inspectors. Each garment was inspected. Sewing errors were called to the attention of operators only if the number of errors for a particular operator's segment of the total task was excessive in a sixty-unit bundle of pants. Mending of errors was done by menders, not operators.

The plant where the study was conducted was experiencing more than twice the turnover normal for the garment industry at the time. Annual turnover, when the study began, was 216 percent and absenteeism was 9.4 percent per day.

One purpose of the study was to determine the effects of goal setting and feedback on the work. Challenging goals were set. The goal was to reach the quality level of the best plants owned by the manufacturer. Feedback was accomplished by erecting large plexiglas display boards on which the daily results were posted for the workers by management.

The sewing errors detected dropped from 3.6 percent to 1.2 percent and the improvement in quality is reported to have begun at the same time as the goal setting and feedback interventions. Koch also reported that a decrease in turnover was observed.

REASONS

Locke's Goal Setting Hypothesis

In 1968, Edward Locke advanced his goal setting hypothesis which was a motivational theory about why the setting of goals with employees should result in various positive effects.

Locke began with the stated intent of studying the role of conscious factors in task performance. He built on the prior work of Ryan (1958), Mace (1935), and others. The problem he addressed is this:

1. How do the conscious goals and intentions of the people who perform a task affect that task performance?
2. Are difficult goals better or worse than easy goals in obtaining the maximum performance level?
3. Is it better to use general goals or specific goals in terms of performance obtained?

After an initial series of research studies Locke felt able to state: "The results are unequivocal: the harder the goal the higher the level of performance." (Locke, 1968).

The notion that specific goals produce better performance than general goals seems, at first, to be only common sense. However, two notes need to be made regarding this part of the hypothesis. First, the goals which Locke explored in the research cited are not what one might think of given the terms "specific" and "general" as we have used them. What Locke actually did was to use "...specific quantitative hard goals..." as the specific goals and an assigned goal of "do your best" as the general goal. Commenting on the "do your best" goal Locke says that it "...was chosen for research by the present writer because it is used, explicitly or implicitly, in virtually all psychological experiments. Yet, just what it means is not exactly clear."

The more serious problem posed by the definitions used in the studies is the definition of the specific goal as one which is quantitative. This definition severely restricts the research to goals with measurable aspects. As we shall show later, Bavelas (1978) has shown in a number of studies that when a "hard" quantitative goal is specified the quality of performances decreases with goal difficulty while (as Locke predicts) the quantity increases with goal difficulty. In those situations where quantity is important and where quality is not important these findings should pose no practical problem. Unhappily, we are at a loss to think of any significant sort of work where quantity is important and quality is not (except certain fly-by-night operations).

Attention must also be given to the definition of the term "difficult" in describing a goal. Just how difficult is difficult? Some authors have defined difficulty in terms of the probability of success attached to an effort. This, in turn, raises another question. Is the probability of success objective or subjective?

The game of poker is a good example of the distinction between an objective and subjective probability of success. Suppose two people are holding poker hands and each has four-of-a-kind; one has four kings and the other has four tens. Now, objectively, both hands are about equally unlikely, and the game of poker is such that the person with the most unlikely hand wins. This is why three-of-a-kind beats a pair. The probability of four-of-a-kind (dealt in sequence from the top of the deck) would be 4/52 times 3/51 times 2/50 times 1/49. This computed probability is an objective probability. Given the way hands are dealt (in alternation) in a two-player game with only four cards dealt apiece, the person receiving cards second has a slightly higher objective probability of getting four-of-a-kind:

First Player (Kings)	Second Player (Tens)
4/52	4/51
3/50	3/49
2/48	2/47
1/46	1/45
24/5740800	24/5285385
(.0000041806)	(.0000045408)

The point of all this is not to prove that your authors are able to compute joint probabilities, but that objective probabilities are simply outside the normal thinking of most people. (Readers who experience the above as simple and obvious are cautioned not to expect their employees to react in a similar manner.) What, then, is the usual way in which a person experiences probabilities? Most will simply say that four aces in a poker hand is both very good and very unusual. It is so unusual, in fact, that most players with a mere three-of-a-kind will bet heavily that their opponent does not hold a better hand (that is, less probable). The crude estimate of likelihood is a subjective probability.

There is another way to look at subjective probability in the game of poker. This is the "gambler's fallacy," the idea that since no recent hands have been good it is time for a winning hand to appear.

Finally, apart from the arena of poker, there is the subjective probability of a person estimating how well he will do in attempting a given task. A salesperson who has just left a pep-meeting of the vacuum cleaner sales force is more likely to believe she can sell to the most resistant prospect than is the same salesperson who has just been turned down by seventeen prospects in a row. The subjective probability of an accomplished craftsman for the successful completion of an intricate piece of work is much higher than the subjective probability of the apprentice for the same piece of work. The subjective probability is, in essence, the personal belief that success will follow effort. This personal belief is a function of many factors, the least of which is the actual objective probability, particularly as seen by some outside observer.

What is the point of all this? Simply that people operate on the basis of their own perceptions, not the perceptions of others. What is hard to one person (perhaps an experimenter) may or may not be hard to another (perhaps the subject in the experiment). Here lies the most critical fallacy in Locke's hypothesis and the most critical practical difficulty in the experiments which have been done to examine the hypothesis.

Despite the logical and operational problems which lie in the ways in which Locke's theory is presented, the theory has considerable practical significance. Workers with specific goals do, indeed, tend to reach those goals. Specificity seems to reduce worker confusion and discomfort frequently found when what is required is not made clear. Difficult goals also seem to be followed by higher performance. We are not certain about how this comes to pass, but it does. Does an employee work harder because more is expected? Does the hard goal redefine the task as a challenge and thus increase the intrinsic reinforcement which the worker gets from the task? While these are important questions, insufficient information is currently available to answer them. The simple fact that goal setting using Locke's prescription of "specific" and "difficult" usually works qualifies the approach for both applied use and further exploration.

Latham and the Loggers

Gary Latham has published prodigiously in the area of goal setting. The recommended readings at the end of this chapter lists him in conjunction with nine of the forty-eight articles listed. He has done most of this work with the Weyerhaeuser Company, one of the world's largest producers of wood products and most of the research has concerned logging operations. He has repeatedly shown confirmatory evidence for Locke's hypothesis, and we think this is for two basic reasons. First, Locke's hypothesis is basically correct. Second, logging is one set of tasks where "trying hard" in fact does increase productivity. We shall shortly cite areas where this is not true and where, we maintain, Locke's hypothesis does not hold.

Management By Objectives

In addition to Locke's goal setting hypothesis, the system known as Management By Objectives (MBO) underlies the strategy of setting employee goals. Just what is MBO?

MBO is a Philosophy of Management. When using management by objectives a manager places emphasis on employees' accomplishments and results. Accomplishment is defined in terms of the meeting of objectives which are measurable, not just the opinion of some person who evaluates once a year because of company policy.

MBO is a Process Consisting of a Number of Steps. The process followed in MBO consists of four basic steps:
1. Goal setting
2. Planning actions
3. Control
4. Periodic Review

First, the long-range goals of the organization are formulated and specific overall objectives of the organization are stated. Given these, specific objectives for sub-areas and individuals are established. Next, plans of action which should result in reaching the objectives of each level in the organization are laid. As a logical consequence of these plans an ongoing control over the planned actions is exercised by both the employees and management. Finally, both progress toward the objectives and final results are reviewed at appropriate times.

MBO is a System of Management. The MBO process contains within it all of the standard management functions: planning, directing, organizing, and controlling. It also serves as a problem solving, decision-making, and motivational tool. What is different about MBO is that many of these functions are delegated or shared. Control of employee actions becomes self-control.

Locke and MBO. How does MBO differ from the approach Locke has advocated? MBO is a larger, more comprehensive system which manages the entire process of goal setting while Locke's hypothesis addresses the nature of the goals to be set. The two approaches are not competing views of goal setting but rather complimentary views which both underlie the goal setting process.

WHERE TO BEGIN WHEN SETTING EMPLOYEE GOALS

Employees react best to goal setting efforts when they are personally involved. Should the manager assign goals to employees or allow the employees to set their own goals? Lack of involvement in setting goals has been held by some to be no problem. However, fully one-third of the material we have reviewed indicates that there is a problem when goals are simply assigned. For example, in the sewing machine operator study given previously as an example, Koch (1979) noted that while work quality increased and turnover decreased, overall satisfaction and intrinsic job satisfaction decreased. In fact, decreases in intrinsic job satisfaction are reported with some frequency in other studies as well. We find this pattern both significant and troubling in the light of long term consequences for the manager. In the following section, we present our resolution to the dilemma about where to begin.

Top-Down Versus Bottom-Up Goal Setting

With regard to the mechanics of setting objectives for the organization, the area, and the individual, the question is asked whether we begin at the bottom or the top in the process. That is, does top management pass down the objectives to be met by their subordinates to the area and then to the individual, or, do the individuals at the bottom of the organizational heirarchy pass their objectives up to top management with each successively higher level in the organization collating together the objectives of the subordinates into area and finally organizational goals? (Note: Our usage of "organization," "area," and "individual" is further covered on pages 139-142.)

There are severe problems with either approach. However it would seem, at first, that these are the only two approaches which are available to us.

We shall characterize the objectives which have their origin with top management as the "top-down" approach and the objectives which have their origins with the individuals at the bottom of the organizational heirarchy as the "bottom-up" approach.

Top-Down Approach.   In this approach to the setting of objectives, the top management of the organization derives objectives for its direct subordinates from the goals of the organization. These are formulated either by the top management itself or they come from some governing board of directors or trustees. In turn, each level of management in the organization passes the objectives so derived down to their direct subordinates until the lowest level of the organization is reached.

Clearly, the objectives of any given person in the organization (with the possible exception of the chief executive officer) are objectives not derived from the individual's knowledge of the job and its actual requirements, but rather, from the point of view of the immediate superior. This is in accordance with the most traditional practices of bureaucracy as defined by Weber in describing the German civil service.

With each person or position under the direct control of the immediate superior how can there be a problem with this approach?

The traditional answer, of course, is that nothing is wrong. However, what would distinguish this approach to organizational goal setting from the normal operations of a well-run organization? The only major difference we see is that the objectives overtly stated are somewhat more salient than those in the well-run organization. People will pay more heed to them. But is this difference sufficient to justify the amount of time devoted to the implementation of so pervasive a system as a goal setting strategy like MBO?

Probably not.

What is missing in this approach and what accounts for the successes of MBO (when successful) is the personal involvement of the individuals in the organization, their commitment to the achievement of goals and objectives, and the harnessing of the personal and conscious intention of the people who do the work on which the organization depends for its survival.

So, we have the circumstance that the handing down of goals and objectives (are these different from work assignments?) by top management serves to produce sets of objectives which are most likely well-related to the overall operation of the organization but which lack the powerful motivational participatory input of the employees. It also may lack the intimate job knowledge possessed by the employees who actually perform the planned work.

Clearly, then, we ought to use the "bottom-up" approach which has its problems too, as we shall see.

Bottom-Up Approach. It is possible to maximize the personal involvement of employees in the pursuit of work-related goals if the employees themselves generate the sets of objectives toward which they will be working. In this approach to goal setting each employee in a given work group gives the direct supervisor a set of objectives which the employee will seek to accomplish during the ensuing year (or quarter, or other suitable period of time). The supervisor then takes the objectives of all of the employees in the work group, collates them together, and produces the amalgamated objectives for the work group. All of the work groups at the same level go through the same process and their supervisors (who may be considered a group at the next higher level of the organization) pass on their group objectives to the next higher level of supervision or management. This process continues until the areas just below the apex of the organizational pyramid pass their objectives up to the chief operational officer and these objectives become the objectives of the organization.

This process would work perfectly if the following conditions were met:

1. At each level employees know how their work interfaces with that of other groups.
2. Either nothing new is planned in the organization by its top management, or--
3. All employees at all levels know of all of the plans for new action and the implications of these plans.

In reality, however, what employees lack in the bottom-up approach is the information required under each of the three conditions just listed.

This approach has the advantage that high levels of personal involvement in the objects may be present, that there has probably been a public commitment to the attainment of the objectives made in front of the peer group, and the conscious intention of the employee is closely linked to the objectives as stated and therefore to the plans necessary to attain those objectives.

The disadvantage is that the people who make the plans and establish the objectives do so with even less information that an uninformed middle manager might have. This lack of information is so severe that it alone disqualifies the bottom-up approach as a viable solution.

What do we do now? One solution has been to fall back on the top-down strategy, with all of its faults, partially because it leaves management in control (and management makes this decision) and partially out of tradition (''Managers have always made these decisions and should continue to do so.'')

There is, happily, a way around the disadvantages of both approaches which also retains the advantages of both.

How to Use Both Approaches. The key to using the best aspects of both approaches requires that the reader understand the concept of iteration. For those who are familiar with the concept because of their knowledge of systems planning or computer operations this will be a review.

Iteration simply means doing something over and over again, each time with increased precision. In the context of an MBO effort this means that initial plans are made, critiqued by those involved, and then the plans are re-made, or altered according to the feedback from the initial critique. The reformulated plans are then critiqued, and the circular process continues until the plans are acceptable to all concerned. This circular process of plan-to-critique and critique-to-plan yields greater precision and uses more and more relevant information with each iterative cycle.

The Latin verb *iterare*: meaning to say again or repeat, is the origin of the term and portrays quite well what we are recommending here. Under the top-down approach, management passes down instructions, objectives, and assignments. While this procedure can effectively remove personal initiative and involvement from the system, if management were to pass down information instead, these ingredients would be at least potentially present. If employees are given appropriate information using a variant of the top-down approach, then the bottom-up approach should be effective.

What we are proposing is that instead of management saying "Do this and this," the message could just as well be "We want to achieve this and this." In effect, management retains control and organization and direction while it delegates planning to those who will use the plans. Planning of the superordinate goals is also retained. We operate under the assumption that both subordinate goals and objectives which service those goals are best left to the operational levels where implementation takes place.

Of course, the process as we describe it simply will not work if iteration is not included. Even with the best of information in the first cycle (information down, plans up) management at all levels will discover that only seventy percent to ninety percent of the superordinate goals would be achieved given the initial plans. Iteration, performing the cycle of events again, makes it possible for the second and subsequent sets of information to include corrective information. Generally, two types of shortcomings in initial planning will be found:

1. Duplicate efforts by areas or individuals will occur because of a lack of integrative information.
2. Some superordinate goals will not be addressed or will be only partially addressed for the same reasons.

Each time an iteration takes place other than in the very first cycle, management must include information about these two deficiencies. Along with the information, explicit permission must be given for horizontal communication and joint planning to occur before the revised plans are communicated upward.

IMPLEMENTATION

The strategy guide for setting goals (Figure 6-1) has two small differences from the previous ones. The individual steps of the guide are sequentially numbered as usual; however, two additional steps, "A" and "B," feed into Step One. The user should note this departure from the usual format.

Setting work-related goals with employees requires that both the manager and the employee carefully consider what is to be done and then communicate conclusions to each other. The process, however, cannot work effectively in a vacuum.

Step A Organizational Goals. All organizations have goals they must achieve in order to survive; there are additional goals necessary if the organization is to prosper. While many organizations have overtly stated these goals, many have not. If your organization has put a set of goals into writing, frequently in a long-range planning document, then the task is relatively easy. If the organizational goals are not stated, however, some creative "digging" will be necessary.

Step B Area Goals. By *area goals* we refer to the goals of your own area within the organization. The reader should already be familiar with these goals, but we know from experience that this is not always the case. Managers will probably have put a set of goals into writing if the entire organization has done so. As we indicated above, however, many organizations have not done so and, in such organizations, the incentive for the manager to explicitly state area goals is not so strong.

Before continuing with the discussion of goals and goal setting, now is a good time to outline the process which will be followed and to show how the parts go together.

Organizations have sub-units, the number of which depends on the size and structure of the organization. Let us look at a simplified organizational chart (Figure 6-2).

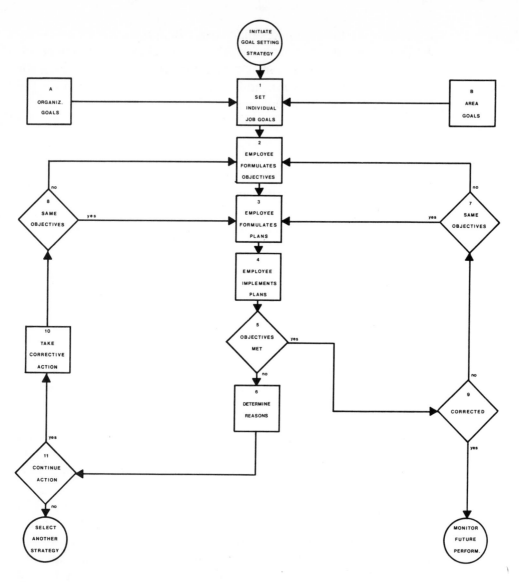

Figure 6-1. Setting Goals: Strategy Guide

When we speak of the organization we refer to the entire chart shown above. The term area is more complex since, in our usage, it could be the entire production sector of the company, or it could be assembly or inspection (both sub-areas of production) or the local or national sub-areas of marketing. Therefore, we have three levels of analysis for goals:

1. The entire organization

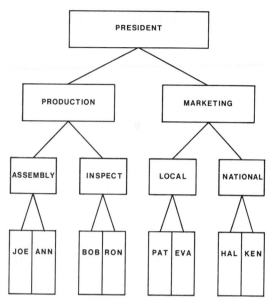

Figure 6-2. Organizational Chart

    2. An area, which is any unit less than the total organization but having more than one individual

    3. Individual employees (for example, Joe, Ann, Bob, and so on.)

Why are we giving so much attention to the nomenclature for parts of the organization? Individual goal setting is the main subject of this chapter. However, individual goals which take no account of either organizational goals (see ''A'') or of area goals (see ''B'') are of little practical value to either the individual or the organization. From the point of view of the individual, the act of setting goals in cooperation with the direct supervisor clarifies what is to be done and what is wanted. In otherwise highly functional work settings there is often a surprising amount of uncertainty about what is expected, what is to be done, what is appropriate.

    Goal setting for the individual employee provides certainty of expectations as well as an objective focus for job-related efforts. In short, employees with clear goals are able to do a good job if they want to, while employees with unclear goals are usually not able to do a good job even if they fervently desire to do so.

    So much for the employee. What does the manager gain from this process? Since the process itself entails a considerable time commitment to initiate, it must have definite benefits in order to justify this time investment.

The manager, by definition, operates either the entire organization or one of its areas, using the nomenclature we have introduced above. The whole point of Management By Objectives or any of the other goal setting schemes now in use is to generate a set of employee goals such that if all employee goals within an area are attained, the goals of the area are automatically attained. Similarly, when all of the area goals within an organization are attained, the goals of the organization are automatically attained.

Stated in this way, the aims of goal setting are powerful, pervasive, and just a bit grandiose. Clearly such a complex effort cannot be expected to work immediately; it takes time. The effort will not work the first time it is attempted. We know of one organization that accomplished the initial goal setting phase of this strategy in only six weeks (the fastest we know of), but more typically the process will last from six to eighteen months depending on the size, complexity, and level of technology used in the organization. A full implementation may take several years.

Fortunately, some almost immediate benefits come from this process.

Step 1 Set Individual Job Goals. The first step in goal setting is for the individual employee to set job goals which will ultimately service the goals of the organization. In order to do this two sources of augmenting information must be taken into account.

As a subsection of this first step of the strategy we have introduced a departure from the usual notation used in other strategy guides. These are the steps "A" and "B" which are collateral with Step One.

Step "A" concerns the goals of the organization. Some mechanism must be utilized which provides the employee with knowledge of organizational goals before the employee can do a competent job of setting individual goals which contribute to the organizational goals.

Step "B" concerns the area goals of the area within which the employee operates. These goals are also in the service of the organizational goals but are different in that they represent the efforts of a subset of the organization to contribute to the organizational goals. Since the employee operates within this subset (be it a work group or a division), the goals of the area also must be taken into account when the employee sets individual goals.

Given that sufficient and appropriate information about the overall organizational goals and the area goals is available to the employee the individual goals may be stated.

Step 2 Employee Formulates Objectives.   When the individual has set goals for the job, these goals must be translated into objectives. What is the difference between goals and objectives? Goals are states at which a person or organization wishes to arrive after effort while objectives are measurably defined benchmarks and attainments which will indicate that a goal has been reached.

An individual defines objectives in a measurable fashion so that both the employee and others (like the boss) will know that a portion of a goal has been attained.

Step 3 Employee Formulates Plans.   Now we have three terms: goals, objectives, and plans. How are plans different from objectives and goals? Plans are projected actions which should lead to predetermined objectives. In other words, plans are just what we usually call plans. When we want to achieve something, we plan what is necessary to attain that something. If we want to purchase a piece of real estate in an area where the norm is to provide a twenty percent down payment, then we estimate the cost of the real estate we may wish to obtain and plan in what ways and in what time period we will accumulate the capital necessary to provide the twenty percent figure plus certain estimable costs. When the plans are implemented and have come to a conclusion, we will have reached our objective. What is the objective? In this example it is the acquisition of the real estate while the accumulation of the necessary capital is the plan.

What, then, is the goal? The goal is the state that we will be in when we have acquired the real estate. It may be defined in several ways. It may be a part of our set of investments, it may be the acquisition of property for aesthetic reasons (we want to own the property around a lake because we like the lake), or it may be a combination of these things (the lake is both beautiful and valuable).

Step 4 Employee Implements Plans.   In a sense this step is simply a continuation of the previous step. However, things are rarely that simple. The implementation of plans is a curious mixture of mechanically carrying out plans and the subtle interaction of these plans with other plans of the individual and with the plans of others.

Step 5 Objectives Met?   Here is the first decision which must be made during the goal-setting process. If the objectives are not met an analysis of why this is so must be carried out.

If the objectives are met, we must go to Step Nine (Is the condition for which this action was initiated corrected?). Let us first consider what happens if the objectives are not met.

Step 6 Determine Reasons.   The first reason for objectives not being attained is time. Most people who are not accustomed to the setting of objectives which are simultaneously measurable and realistic is the failure to set reasonable time periods for the attainment of an objective.

The authors of your text conceived of the plan for this book nearly five years before the copyright date shown in the front of the book. The implementation of the concept, however, took considerably more time than was originally anticipated. Why was this the case? While an idea may be fully drawn out in its general scope in a very short time, the idea in its practical reality with all of the details worked out takes much, much longer.

Why is this so? Anything of value and of any complexity has innumerable subtleties which are not realized at first. Some of the implications of rather simple ideas are totally unforeseen by even the most experienced people. We note that complicated things simply stated take much more work than simple things complexly stated. We know of a college professor who makes term paper assignments to students in his classes with an upper limit on pages rather than a lower limit. Students are quite pleased when they learn that a term paper in a class with this professor may be no longer than seven pages. What a relief! No long papers. Much to their surprise the paper limited to seven pages is far more difficult to write than the required "at least twenty pages" in another class.

In summary, here are the reasons for which Objectives are not met:

1. Unrealistic
2. Lag time too long
3. Lack of cooperation

Step 9 Corrected?   Usually when objectives are met the situation will have been corrected. Sometimes, however, this will not be the case. If the objectives were well thought out and if the reason for the employee performance deficit was related to goals, then the situation will usually be corrected.

What happens when objectives are met but the situation is not corrected? This might happen because the objectives which were set were too easy, and, in addition, insufficient to produce the desired outcome.

If the situation appears to be corrected, you are successful for this employee at this time. Go to the last step which is to MONITOR FUTURE PERFORMANCE.

If the situation is not corrected, even though the objectives were met, then the objectives or the plans leading to the objectives, were insufficient to produce the desired effect. In this case go to Step Seven.

Step 7 Same Objectives?   Was the failure to resolve the employee productivity deficit due to the wrong objectives or to the method used to reach the objectives? If the objectives were not wrong, then the plans in the service of the objectives were the problem. Keep the same objectives and return to Step Three (Employee Formulates Plans).

If the problem seems to lie with the objectives originally stated then return to Step Two (Employee Formulates Objectives).

Step 11 Continue Action?   Why would one not want to continue? This all depends on the result of the analysis in Step Six. If it was determined that the goal setting effort was not the most appropriate technique for increasing employee productivity, then you should exit this step to SELECT ANOTHER STRATEGY. Do not be embarrassed by the fact that this strategy did not work. Some benefits still remain. The most important of these is that after a goal setting exercise, management will have a clearer idea of what other things may be done. Employees will have a better idea of what is expected of them on their jobs and most likely a better idea of how their jobs relate to the rest of the organization. These benefits alone are quite worthwhile as you will note in the following chapter on the redesign of jobs.

Let us suppose, however, that goal setting still appears to be the proper strategy. In this case you will decide to continue and go to Step Ten.

Step 10 Take Corrective Action.   There is not much to explain here since the corrective action to be taken will be dictated by the special circumstances of your organization and the specific issues with which you are dealing. The step is included as a reminder that if corrective action is to be taken it must take place before the next step.

Step 8 Same Objectives? The next Step is Eight and will not be separately discussed since it is identical to Step Seven which was covered above.

SUMMARY

In this chapter we have presented the strategy of setting employee goals as an approach to dealing with performance deficits. This approach is of general utility with positive consequences that reach beyond the productivity of individual employees. One popular version of the strategy presented here is called "Management By Objectives," or MBO.

The strategy requires that managers be able to give appropriate information to employees. In turn, the employees use this information to propose goals, specific objectives, and plans for reaching those objectives. Because of this, one of the least publicized benefits of this strategy is the clarification of the organization's goals. It is the effort which this goal clarification entails that we believe accounts for the less than universal use of the goal setting strategy and for much of the management resistance to it. Attempts to use goal setting without such goal clarification also appear to account for the failures reported in goal setting programs.

Goal setting is most successful when the following conditions are met:

1. Goals are specific
2. Goal attainment can be measured
3. Goals are hard, not impossible

It also appears to be beneficial if:

1. Commitment is obtained
2. Peers are involved
3. Rewards and incentives are used (see Chapter Eight)

The manager has much to gain personally from using goal setting. Use of this strategy serves to clarify both the organizational and area goals toward which the manager must work. It gives employees greater certainty about their roles within the organization. Because employees are likely to work in a more efficient manner, the manager's job is just as likely to become more enjoyable.

The delegation of functions which this strategy recommends reduces the manager's own supervisory responsibilities and at the same time encourages independence in employees. The effects are cumulative, too.

A successful implementation of this strategy can make a manager's own job performance look very good indeed. Since the employees are producing more and this is apparent to everyone, the manager receives a double bonus.

Within a goal setting program, performance appraisal is greatly simplified. Employees usually will know the results of any appraisal before it is done. There are no surprises. The friction caused by annual appraisals is reduced and the appraisals are more helpful because they deal with measurable attainment at timely intervals.

The major disadvantage of goal setting is that it can take a long time to establish and it requires a high level of initial effort.

RECOMMENDED READINGS

Arvey, R. D.; Dewhirst, H. D.; and Boling, J. C. "Relationships Between Goal Clarity, Participation in Goal Setting, and Personality Characteristics on Job Satisfaction in a Scientific Organization." *Journal of Applied Psychology* 61(1) (1976): 103-5.

Bassett, G. A. "A Study of the Effects of Task Goal and Schedule Choice on Work Performance." *Organizational Behavior and Human Performance* 24 (1979): 202-27.

Bavelas, J. and Lee, E. S. "Effects of Goal Level on Performance: A Trade-off of Quantity and Quality." *Canadian Journal of Psychology/Review of Canadian Psychology* 32(4) (1978): 219-40.

Becker, L. J. "Joint Effect of Feedback and Goal Setting on Performance: A Field Study of Residential Energy Conservation." *Journal of Applied Psychology* 63(4) (1978): 428-33.

Campbell, D. J. and Ilgen, D. R. "Additive Effects of Task Difficulty and Goal Setting on Subsequent Task Performance." *Journal of Applied Psychology* 61(3) (1976): 319-24.

Campbell, J. P. and Prichard, R. D. "Motivation Theory in Industrial and Organizational Psychology." From *Handbook of Industrial and Organizational Psychology*, edited by M. D. Dunnette Chicago: Rand McNally, 1976.

Carrol, S. J. and Tosi, H. L. "Goal Characteristics and Personality Factors in a Management By Objectives Program." *Administrative Science Quarterly* 15 (1970): 295-305.

Cummings, L. L.; Schwab, D. P.; and Rosen, M. "Performance and Knowledge of Results as Determinants of Goal Setting." *Journal of Applied Psychology* 55(6) (1971): 526-30.

Dachler, H. P. and Mobley, W. H. "Construct validity of an Instrumentality-Expectancy-Task-Goal Model of Work Motivation: Some Theoretical Boundry Conditions." *Journal of Applied Psychology Monograph* 58(3) (1973): 397-418.

Dossett, D. L.; Latham, G. P.; and Mitchell, T. R. "Effects of Assigned Versus Participatively Set Goals, Knowledge of Results, and Individual Differences on Employee Behavior When Goal Difficulty is Held Constant." *Journal of Applied Psychology* 64(3) (1979): 291-98.

Erez, M. "Feedback: A Necessary Condition for the Goal Setting-Performance Relationship." *Journal of Applied Psychology* 62(5) (1977): 624-27.

Hall, D. T. and Foster, L. W. "A Psychological Success Cycle and Goal Setting: Goals, Performance, and Attitudes." *Academy of Management Journal* 20(2) (1977): 282-90.

Ivancevich, J. M. "Different Goal Setting Treatments and Their Effects on Performance and Job Satisfaction." *Academy of Management Journal* 20(3) (1977):

Ivancevich, J. M. "Effects of Goal Setting on Performance and Job Satisfaction." *Journal of Applied Psychology* 61(5) (1976): 605-12.

Ivancevich, J. M. and McMahon, J. T. "A Study of Task-Goal Attributes, Higher Order Need Strength, and Performance." *Academy of Management Journal* 20(4) (1977): 552-63. (a)

Ivancevich, J. M. and McMahon, J. T. "Black-White Differences in a Goal-Setting Program." *Organizational Behavior and Human Performance* 20 (1977): 287-300. (b)

Kim, J. S. and Hamner, W. C. "Effect of Performance Feedback and Goal Setting on Productivity and Satisfaction in an Organizational Setting." *Journal of Applied Psychology* 61(1) (1976): 48-57.

Koch, J. L. "Effects of Goal Specificity and Performance Feedback to Work Groups on Peer Leadership, Performance, and Attitudes." *Human Relations* 32(10) (1979): 819-40.

Korman, A. K. "Toward an Hypothesis of Work Behavior." *Journal of Applied Psychology* 54(1) (1970): 31-41.

Latham, G. P. and Baldes, J. J. "The 'Practical Significance' of Locke's Theory of Goal Setting." *Journal of Applied Psychology* 60, (1975): 122-24.

Latham, G. P. and Kinne, S. B. "Improving Job Performance Through Training in Goal Setting." *Journal of Applied Psychology* 49 (1974): 187-91.

Latham, G. P.; Mitchell, T. R.; and Dossett, D. L. "Importance of Participative Goal Setting and Anticipated Rewards on Goal Difficulty and Job Performance." *Journal of Applied Psychology* 63(2) (1978): 163-71.

Latham, G. P. and Saari, L. M. "The Effects of Holding Goal Difficulty Constant on Assigned and Participatively Set Goals." *Academy of Management Journal* 22(1) (1979): 163-68.

Latham, G. P. and Yukl, G. A. "A Review of Research on the Application of Goal Setting in Organizations." *Academy of Management Journal* 18 (1975): 824-45. (a)

Latham, G. P. and Yukl, G. A. "Assigned Versus Participative Goal Setting with Educated and Uneducated Woods Workers." *Journal of Applied Psychology* 60 (1975): 299-302. (b)

Latham, G. P. and Yukl, G. A. "The Effects of Assigned and Participative Goal Setting on Performance and Job Satisfaction." *Journal of Applied Psychology* 61 (1976): 166-71.

Locke, E. A. "The Relationship of Intentions to Level of Performance." *Journal of Applied Psychology* 50 (1966): 60-66.

Locke, E. A. "Toward a Theory of Task Motivation and Incentives." *Organizational Behavior and Human Performance* 3 (1968): 157-89.

Locke, E. A. and Bryan, J. F. "Knowledge of Score and Goal Level as Determinants of Work Rate." *Journal of Applied Psychology* 53(1) (1969): 59-65.

Locke, E. A.; Cartledge, N.; and Knerr, C. S. "Studies of the Relationship Between Satisfaction, Goal Setting, and Performance." *Organizational Behavior and Human Performance* 5 (1970): 135-58.

Locke, E. A.; Cartledge, N.; and Koeppel, J. "Motivational Effects of Knowledge of Results: A goal-setting phenomenon?" *Psychological Bulletin* 70 (1968): 474-85.

Mossholder, K. W. "Effects of Externally Mediated Goal Setting on Intrinsic Motivation: A laboratory experiment." *Journal of Applied Psychology* 65(2) (1980): 202-10.

Motowidlo, S. J.; Loehr, V.; and Dunnette, M. D. "A Laboratory

Study of the Effects of the Relationship Between Probability of Success and Performance." *Journal of Applied Psychology* 63(2) (1978): 172-79.

Nadler, D. A. "The Effects of Feedback on Task Group Behavior: A review of the experimental research." *Organizational Behavior and Human Performance* 23 (1979): 309-338.

Nemeroff, W. F. and Cosentino, J. "Utilizing Feedback and Goal Setting to Increase Performance Appraisal Interviewer Skills of Managers." *Academy of Management Journal* 22(3) (1979): 566-76.

Organ, D. W. "Intentional Versus Arousal Effects of Goal-Getting." *Organizational Behavior and Human Performance* 18 (1977): 378-89.

Pritchard, R. D. and Curtis, M. I. "The Influence of Goal Setting and Financial Incentives on Task Performance." *Organizational Behavior and Human Performance* 10 (1973): 175-83.

Quick, J. C. "Dyadic Goal Setting and Role Stress: A field study." *Academy of Management Journal* 22(2) (1979): 241-52.

Ronan, W. W.; Latham, G. P.; and Kinne, S. B. "The Effects of Goal Setting and Supervision on Worker Behavior in an Industrial Situation." *Journal of Applied Psychology* 58 (1973): 302-7.

Steers, R. M. "Task-Goal Attributes, Achievement, and Supervisor Performance." *Organizational Behavior and Human Performance* 13 (1975): 392-403.

Steers, R. M. and Porter, L. W. "The Role of Task-Goal Attributes in Employee Performance." *Psychological Bulletin* 81 (1974): 434-52.

Terborg, J. R. "The Motivational Components of Goal Setting." *Journal of Applied Psychology* 61 (1976): 613-21.

Terborg, J. R. and Miller, H. E. "Motivation, Behavior, and Performance: A Closer Examination of Goal Setting and Monetary Incentives." *Journal of Applied Psychology* 63(1) (1978): 29-39.

Thota, V. "Managing By Objectives Through the Planning-Implementing-Evaluating (PIE) Approach to Individualized Instruction." *Educational Technology* September 1979, pp. 49-51.

Umstot, D. D.; Bell, C. H.,Jr.; and Mitchell, T. R. "Effects of Job Enrichment and Task Goals on Satisfaction and Productivity: Implications for Job Design." *Journal of Applied Psychology* 61(4) (1976): 379-94.

Vroom, V. H. *Work and Motivation.* New York: John Wiley, 1964.

Weed, S. E. and Mitchell, T. R. ''The Role of Environmental and Behavioral Uncertainty as a Mediator of Situation-Performance Relationships.'' *Academy of Management Journal* 23(1) (1980): 38-60.

White, S. E.; Mitchell, T. R.; and Bell, C. H., Jr. "Goal Setting, Evaluation Apprehension, and Social Cues as Determinants of Job Performance and Job Satisfaction in a Simulated Organization.'' *Journal of Applied Psychology* 62(6) (1977): 665-73.

7

Restructuring Jobs

INTRODUCTION

Bethlehem, Pennsylvania: Circa 1910[1]

One of the first pieces of work undertaken by us, when the writer started to introduce scientific management into the Bethlehem Steel Company, was to handle pig iron on task work. The opening of the Spanish War found some 80,000 tons of pig iron placed in small piles in an open field adjoining the works. Prices for pig iron had been so low that it could not be sold at a profit, and it therefore had been stored. With the opening of the Spanish War the price of pig iron rose, and this large accumulation of iron was sold. This gave us a good opportunity to show the workmen, as well as the owners and managers of the works, on a fairly large scale the advantages of task work over the old-fashioned day work and piece work, in doing a very elementary class of work.

The Bethlehem Steel Company had five blast furnaces, the product of which had been handled by a pig-iron gang for many years. This gang, at this time, consisted of about 75 men. They were good, average pig-iron handlers, were under an excellent foreman who himself had

[1]Abridged from pp. 41-47 in "The Principles of Scientific Management" from *Scientific Management* by Frederick Winslow Taylor. Copyright, 1911, by Frederick W. Taylor, 1939 by Louise M. S. Taylor. Reprinted by permission of Harper & Row, Publishers, Inc.

been a pig-iron handler, and the work was done, on the whole, about as fast and as cheaply as it was done anywhere else at that time.

A railroad switch was run out into the field, right along the edge of the piles of pig iron. An inclined plank was placed against th side of a car, and each picked up from his pile a pig of iron weighing about 92 pounds, walked up the inclined plank and dropped it on the end of the car.

We found that this gang were loading on the average about 12½ long tons per man per day. We were surprised to find, after studying the matter, that a first-class pig-iron handler ought to handle between 47 and 48 long tons per day, instead of 12½ tons. This task seemed to us so very large that we were obliged to go over our work several times before we were absolutely sure that we were right. Once we were sure, however, that 47 tons was a proper day's work for a first-class pig-iron handler, the task which faced us as managers under the modern scientific plan was clearly before us. It was our duty to see that the 80,000 tons of pig iron was loaded on to the cars at the rate of 47 tons per man per day, in place of 12½ tons, at which rate the work was then being done. And it was further our duty to see that this work was done without bringing on a strike among the men, without any quarrel with the men, and to see that the men were happier and better contented when loading at the new rate of 47 tons than they were when loading at the old rate of 12½ tons.,

Later, commenting on the outcome of the restructured job and one of the workers in particular, the author writes:

...he received 60 per cent higher wages than were paid to other men who were not working on task work. One man after another was picked out and trained to handle pig iron at the rate of 47½ tons per day until all of the pig iron was handled at this rate, and the men were receiving 60 per cent more wages than other workmen around them.''

Job enrichment is more than a currently fashionable technique taught in business and management schools. It is an attempt to change the experience of work in a very fundamental and important way. We have chosen the preceeding example to open this chapter for several reasons. First, Taylor and others have tried to redesign jobs before and so the idea is certainly not a new one. Second, the idea is not a radical one as may be demonstrated by the above quote. Although Taylor's work is not normally cited as an example of job redesign, it clearly exists as one classic example of such efforts. While the focus of job redesign in Taylor's time was to increase the efficiency of work processes, current practice uses a more comprehensive model concerned with producing greater worker concern for the outcomes of work. Some of the factors which may have contributed to a lack of worker concern for the outcomes of their work are discussed below.

Positions Versus People

Many organizations are hierarchically structured sets of jobs. Many jobs at the bottom of the pyramid are ultimately controlled by a single position at the top. Actual control is usually by positions below the top of the pyramid to which the control has been delegated. An organizational chart reflects this structure. What is frequently missed in this analysis is that the hierarchy which composes the organization is composed of jobs, not people.

If the structure is one of jobs, not people, then how is work done? By the people who fill the jobs, of course!

When we stop to realize that people are regarded and treated as replaceable disposable units which are useful only when they fill a position in the hierarchy, we get the first hints of what job enrichment is all about.

The last thing individuals want to be regarded as is a "plug-in" replacement part. Yet, in most corporations, we routinely treat employees in this way. There are good historical reasons for this condition which are founded in realistic historical conditions. It is because conditions and potential employees have changed that job enrichment is both possible and advisable.

In the automobile manufacturing industry it was once necessary to get large amounts of production using basically unskilled employees. This production was of a sort that demanded the skills of tool makers, machinists, and many other skilled craftsmen. The solution to the problem was to break down each job into a series of simple steps, each of which could be performed by an unskilled worker with minimal training and supervision.

It is the nature of jobs which permits their restructuring and which simultaneously makes it necessary to restructure them. The workers of today are not restricted to the labor category of production. There now also exists the knowledge workers: employees whose job it is to think, create, plan, and manage the work of others. This particular kind of employee was simply not available to the supervisor of yesteryear. A job which would be among the best available for the worker with few skills becomes less and less appealing as the worker obtains more experience and knowledge.

So, some will ask, why should we be interested in how our workers feel about their jobs; we pay them and don't people work for money?

There are several ways to answer that question. Do people work for money? Yes. Do they work for other things as well? Yes. Do they work in the absence of money? Yes, and to those readers who are entrepreneurs we must ask for the reason from their own introspection.

We will bet that most of the readers of this book actually enjoy their work. Clearly it is not just the money that produces this enjoyment. If you have ever started your own business you know the forty hour week is a joke; you probably put in closer to eighty hours. You probably could not hire somebody to work as hard as you do and even if you could afford to hire such a person there are probably protective labor laws to prevent it. Those of you who are in middle management work far harder than most people know. You are under more stress. Your overtime is not compensated, at least not in money. Now, down the road somewhere the owner or manager can see rewards which make the initial efforts worth the trouble. But it is so far down the road that the simple promise of future compensation (unsure at best) is not sufficient to account for why some people work as hard as they do.

The most basic reason why many managers work as hard as they do is that they like their work. They get a kick out of accomplishment. It is the work itself which provides the reward they experience.

Managers are not unique in their enjoyment of the use of their skills, their pleasure at accomplishment, the satisfaction that comes from seeing that something they have planned actually worked out the way they expected.

This is the key to job enrichment. Non-managerial personnel often react to jobs in the same way. The more skills they have, the greater their pleasure in using those skills and the greater their displeasure when only one or a few of their skills can be brought to bear on the job. The knowledge worker is particularly sensitive to these problems since he possesses more skills which are potentially not utilized by the job.

If you think about this particular problem it becomes quickly apparent that the manager considering job enrichment is in a truly enviable position. The low worker productivity which frequently accompanies job dissatisfaction can be caused by a job design which makes it actually difficult for the worker to increase productivity.

Sometimes it is those aspects of the manager's job that the manager most dislikes and wishes could be delegated which form the basis of the successful job enrichment effort. Worker dissatisfaction is typically not related to too much work but to too little work of the productive kind.

ACTION

Job redesign, as developed by Hackman et al. (1975) and Walters et al. (1975) consists of five separate interventions which will be discussed below. Before covering these elements of the job redesign action, however, we must begin with some practical warnings about the ways managers may be constrained from using some interventions due to internal factors in the organization.

Some Special Problems in Application

Unions.   In general, labor unions historically have been nonsupportive of efforts to redesign jobs. Several factors account for this union position. First, and for very good historical reasons, unions as well as workers will think of job enlargement when job redesign is first proposed. Early union experience with job redesign amounted to combining tasks so that the worker would have the perception that a "meaningful whole job" was being done. This was a good approach in theory, but in practice it amounted to placing the worker in a position where more work was expected for the same compensation. Unions, of course, responded to this overload of work with cries of "exploitation" and began to firmly resist any change in the content of jobs as a matter of continuing policy.

In a less obvious sense, it must be observed that some unions have a vested interest in opposing any move on the part of management which undercuts the adversary relationship between management and worker. Keep in mind that this adversary relationship provides some unions with their basis of power. This may be a harsh observation about the nature of unions but it is a subtle truth which functions to the ultimate detriment of all concerned except entrenched union leaders.

Given these observations, it is clear that any job redesign effort in a unionized environment must include union leadership, not simply representation, in its planning. The most potent lever managers have in this regard is that effective job redesign requires increased worker control over the conditions and structuring of work. This is nearly always a goal of union leadership and, if they participate in attaining it, not only are management goals met, but so are the goals of the union leaders as well.

Your Organizational Position. Not all managers are in a position of sufficient power to unilaterally plan and execute job redesign. In addition to union constraints, managers also must face constraints within the organizational hierarchy. First line supervisors, for example, frequently have relatively little authority or power to make organizational changes. Job redesign can be difficult. However, this does not preclude them from introducing some of the elements of job redesign. Scheduling, for example, is frequently the responsibility of a supervisor. This does not mean that it is the supervisor who must do the scheduling; it only means that the schedule must be approved by the supervisor and must be workable. Some work processes are open to discretionary scheduling and some are not. Where the first-line supervisor has discretion, a judicious injection of worker control may produce greater compliance and efficiency in operations.

A supervisor's superior must be involved in whatever changes are made in job redesign. There are many reasons for this, not the least of which is that most supervisors do not like surprises. They particularly dislike surprises where their own performance will be affected. Obviously, job redesign efforts without the support of one's direct supervisor are inadvisable, to put it mildly.

On the other hand, support from above is one of the most helpful resources one can obtain. This is particularly true if the necessary organizational power to institute change rests just a few levels higher in the organizational structure.

THE INTERVENTIONS

Keeping in mind the constraints given above, the five job redesign interventions mentioned previously will now be discussed.

Combining Tasks

It is possible to break almost any job into a sequence of smaller tasks. The building of an automobile can be thought of as a series of

INTERVENTION	LOCUS
1. Combining Tasks	workers
2. Forming Natural Work Units	workers
3. Vertical Loading	workers
4. Establishing Client Relationships	users
5. Opening Feedback Channels	users

"sub-assemblies" that produce a car when brought together in the final assembly operation. Each sub-assembly, in turn, may be broken down into still smaller pieces until a point is reached where parts so small are assembled that nobody would recognize that a car is being built. The archetypical case is the automobile assembly line. There are advantages to this approach, such as apparent efficiency, interchangeable parts, low levels of required skills, and presumed low costs. The disadvantages, however, stem from the human dissatisfaction and lower productivity which result from people doing work that is perceived as both trivial and meaningless.

A job which is too segmented, one that consists of too small a portion of the whole job, is always a good candidate for the combining of several such small tasks into a larger task. In the next few paragraphs we will explore the main principle to be used in combining tasks.

Forming Natural Work Units

Pride in workmanship may be the philosophical foundation of high productivity, but before a worker can be proud of his work there must be something to be proud of, something that can be identified.

The principle of forming natural work units serves as a guide for efforts to combine tasks. When we speak of "natural" work units this is to emphasize that the combined tasks should feel natural to the worker. The product of the work must be a meaningful product which both the worker and others are able to easily identify and which is perceived as having a meaningful function. Two guidelines must be kept in mind when forming natural work units. First, it is the perception of the worker that the combination of smaller tasks is "natural" which is important. Second, the social comparison process must be kept in mind. By this we mean that the resulting workloads after task combination must be accepted as approximately equal.

Paradoxically (and fortunately), those jobs which are most highly segmented are those which are most in need of task combination using the principle of natural work units. These jobs also are among the easiest to combine. This is because in creating natural work units one must first identify the basic elements of the work to be done. These elements are frequently well-approximated by the highly segmented job. After identifying the elements of the task to be performed these elements are combined into a larger integrated set of tasks which result in a manageable and identifiable piece of work with a product which meets the guidelines for forming natural work units.

Vertical Loading

In the management-worker hierarchy which characterizes the bureaucratic organization, planning, organizing, directing, and controlling functions are normally split among several levels of the hierarchy. When a job is vertically loaded it contains these elements within it. The term *vertical* may most easily be understood if the reader will visualize an organizational chart. The employee's boss is literally above him in such a chart and if the employee has subordinates they are represented below the employee's position on the chart. Above any position there is a supervisory position which normally holds the planning, controlling, and organizing functions for the job performed by the employee. Vertical loading simply means that the employee who performs the job also holds total or partial responsibility for these functions as a part of the job. Workers who have vertically loaded jobs may participate in deciding when to start and stop their work, when to take breaks, what the budget for the job is, and what work methods and schedules will be used. Such a worker has considerable discretion and authority with respect to the job. By contrast, when working on a job which is not vertically loaded employees typically only follow orders.

Opening Feedback Channels

This concept relates to the worker's level of job performance feedback and it contains two parts. First, the job itself may provide direct and immediate information about the quality of the work performed. The worker may receive direct visual or auditory information. A machinist at a lathe can feel the cut being made. An artist can review the finished product. Some of the information is inherent in the nature of the task itself and some is the result of sophisticated human factors design.

The second part of feedback comes from others, particularly the supervisor, who evaluate the job which is done. This type of information, while important, is necessarily less immediate and therefore responses to such information are slower and less precise.

Establishing Client Relationships

A client, as distinct from a supervisor, is one who uses the product which was produced by the worker. While the supervisor determines whether or not the work product meets relevant guidelines and gives or withholds approval of the work performed, the client actually uses the work product and is, in reality, the best source of information about whether or not the product is usable for the purposes intended. By opening channels of communication between the worker and the client, as well as between the worker and the supervisor, the worker is willing and able, at least in theory, to produce more acceptable output. Regardless of the validity of this theory, it is apparent that in the absence of such information the worker has no way to correct any deficiencies which may be found by either clients or the supervisor.

A Final Note

We have seen that the action of job redesign may be broken down into five interventions. In the chart which ends this section (Figure 7-1) you will see how each of the interventions is related to certain core job dimensions and hence to the ultimate aim of job redesign: the improvement of work outcomes.

Before we delve into the intricacies of the reasoning behind the job redesign action, we will present three examples of the use of this technique in applied settings.

EXAMPLES

The examples which follow concern job redesign efforts in the relatively recent past. We have chosen to omit the very recent examples (1978-1982) of job redesign since they have not been published long enough for the comments of both scholars and practitioners to emerge.

We begin with Robert Ford's work at AT&T (American Telephone and Telegraph) because it is relevant to our purposes and marks the beginning of present thinking about job redesign. The second example comes from Texas Instrument, one of the most successful organizations in the electronics field. Rather than relating job design to the mysteries of microprocessor design, we focus on routine building maintenance problems. The third example is a classic clerk-typist job redesign effort in what must be among the most traditional of American organizations: the stock transfer department of Bankers Trust Company of New York.

Shareholder Contact at AT&T

In the Shareholder Relations Department, the job of each correspondent was to deal appropriately with customer complaint letters or telephone calls. High employee turnover and poor work quality existed as problems in a context of excellent salary, security, and employee benefits. There was no indication of important employee dissatisfaction other than with the actual job performed. This led quite naturally to a job redesign effort.

Ford's report on this particular experiment in redesign is startling since the three major changes in work design were not major at all. The style of work remained virtually unchanged, yet the small changes made exibited major effects. The following changes were introduced:

1. Employees signed their own reply letters. Previously the supervisor signed replies.
2. Total supervisory checking of work was reduced to a 10% sampling.
3. Members of the peer group with special expertise were designated as consultants as opposed to using the supervisor as such.

You may recognize these changes as "establishing client relationships" (Number 1), and "vertical loading" (Numbers 2 and 3).

Now, it would seem that with the supervisor doing less and each of the employees doing more that further job dissatisfaction would result. The point is that what was added was also what was wanted by the employees. After the introduction of the above changes turnover came close to zero, already acceptable productivity increased slightly, and the formerly troublesome quality issue showed noticeable improvement.

Cleaning Up at Texas Instrument

In the tradition of companies that do what they do best and know their limits—subcontracting in areas outside of one's interest and expertise—the building cleaning services at Texas Instrument were contracted to four outside firms. When the cleaning services proved to be unacceptable, TI's own personnel took over the cleaning function in one main building on an experimental basis. Eight supervisors were selected from among the former employees of the cleaning subcontractor after a seven-day program which doubled as a training and selection mechanism. Each of the new supervisors was placed in charge of a team which was given responsibility for setting its own goals, objectives, and schedules. Further, each team was given responsibility for a well-defined area of work.

Prior to the one-building experiment, the cleaning subcontractor had been plagued with high turnover, reported as 100 percent per quarter! In contrast, the quality of job performance in the experimental building increased markedly (ratings were up by about twenty-five percent) and the turnover rate dropped from 100 percent per quarter to 9.8 percent per quarter. In addition, a waiting list had developed for jobs on these cleaning crews.

Typists at Bankers Trust

Typists constitute a favorite group for job redesign people to work with. There are few positions in which so critical a function is performed by people so bored. A recent study has indicated that something like sixty percent of all typists who quit their jobs do so because of boredom and lack of work, not overwork.

In one division of Bankers Trust, typically bored typists were engaged in processing more than typically critical work—stock transfers. The problems were severe because of the consequences. In addition to the expected high employee turnover and attendant absenteeism, both the quality and the quantity of work were low. After training of supervisors and about six months of gradually introduced change, the following set of changes from the established routine solidified:

1. Groups of customers were designated.
2. Individuals whose work was accurate and reliable were no longer required to have their work verified by checkers.

3. Other typists and checkers became teams and these teams were responsible for a particular group of customers.
4. Typists corrected their own mistakes and feedback from checkers for those whose work still required verification was immediate.

The results of this job redesign effort, as you might expect by now, were that errors were greatly reduced and for the group of typists as a whole, the processing time was decreased. The speed of typists who worked without checkers and verified their own work was slightly reduced, but not enough to compensate for the total lack of time spent by others in checking their work.

Things have progressed quite a bit since an idle employee told IBM's Thomas Watson that she was waiting for a setup man to do a job she could be doing herself. The improvements have been more in terms of systematically describing what works and what does not than in basic approach. Jobs are still enriched, expanded, or redesigned with the same goal in mind. Employees who want to work should be allowed to work. In the next section we will look at some of the reasoning which underlies the current effort to make the proper design of jobs more of a science and less of an art.

REASONS

Probably people have always tried to enrich their jobs. After all, so much of one's life is spent at work. Only in the recent history of humanity has this become a major issue. When our grandfathers worked their farms, they milked cows, repaired roofs, plowed fields, pruned trees, baled hay and alfalfa, did light blacksmith work, took harvested grain to the feed mill, dug irrigation ditches, and the other usual things a farmer does. Many workers today spend their time doing one or two things, usually very tiny pieces of a total job. An automobile worker may install left-front wheel nuts on Pintos, Mustangs, and Mavericks but never do anything as fulfilling or complex as foaling, training, driving, and cherishing a work horse. A typist may transcribe an entire manuscript yet never experience the rewards of being an author. Probably beginning with the Industrial Revolution, something very important has been lost from the experience of work. What is missing?

Herzberg's Two-Factor Theory

Herzberg and his associates (1959) published the results of one attempt to answer this question. After intensive interviewing with engineers and accountants, they claimed to have found two basic underlying factors which describe workers' satisfaction and motivation. These were:

1. Motivators: The work itself, including responsibility, advancement, feelings of achievement and recognition.
2. Hygienes: The physical and social aspects of work, including working conditions, supervision, policy, and interpersonal relations; outcomes including salary and fringe benefits.

Another way to look at motivators and hygienes is as intrinsic and extrinsic with respect to the job itself. That is, the factor called motivators contains things which are direct attributes of the job itself or direct outcomes of the job. Outcomes of work itself, things that relate to a job's content are called intrinsic to the job. Herzberg's "motivators" are intrinsic to the job. Hygiene factors relate to a job's content. They come from things external or extrinsic to the job. Herzberg found that the motivators and the hygienes were independent, that is, a person could be at any level from high to low on motivators and this would be unrelated to their standing on hygienes. The factors are said to be uncorrelated or orthogonal. In practice, this means that even if you know how a worker stands in terms of motivators there is no way you can predict where the worker will stand on hygienes, and vice versa.

Herzberg also found that while motivators seem to bring about job satisfaction, hygiene factors do not. Perhaps attracted in part by the finding that employees are not motivated by hygiene factors (like pay), many companies have explored job enrichment using the "two-factor" theory advanced by Herzberg as their rationale. According to the theory, increasing employee productivity does not require an increase in pay or other hygiene factors. Instead it results from high levels of motivators being present on the job.

We are not convinced that the "two-factor" theory is totally valid. One major reason for this is that when other investigators attempt to duplicate Herzberg's findings they nearly always fail unless they use exactly the same method! This state of affairs is called being "method bound." It is like saying to your physician, "But *my* bathroom scale at home doesn't say I'm overweight." The problem we see with this work is that while an excellent descriptive study was done, the interpretations of the patterns found are rather more shaky than the description.

We suspect that the "two-factor" theory will eventually be found to hold for a specific subpopulation of workers and that the variables which will define this subpopulation will be related to critical demand characteristics of the job as they interact with the personal values of the employee. Such variables which successfully define a subpopulation are called moderator variables and we predict that they will be found to consist of variable interactions rather than single variables.

Whatever the problems with the motivator-hygiene theory on the predictive level, on the descriptive level it has been and still is extremely enlightening. To note that it is the properties of the job itself which may produce both high job satisfaction and increased employee productivity gives us a very powerful conceptual tool for improving the effectiveness of an organization.

The Hackman-Oldham Model

One of the most recent and valuable advances in the restructuring of jobs (a more descriptive phrase than "job enrichment") is the concept of job diagnosis introduced by Hackman, Oldham, Jason, and Purdy (1975).

This model shows how five points of intervention (the "implementing concepts") can moderate five "job dimensions" to produce one or more of three "critical psychological states" which, in turn, have beneficial outcomes for both the employee and the work produced. (See Figure 7-1.)

The model suggests that most people whose jobs seem to them to have skill variety, task identity, task significance, autonomy, and feedback also experience meaningfulness and responsibility in their jobs and have a good knowledge of the results of their work. They also seem to be motivated and satisfied on the job. The motivation and satisfaction in turn have valuable consequences for the organization. Among these are high quality of work, low absenteeism, and low turnover.

The model does not work for all employees, but it corrects for this by incorporating the concept of "growth need strength"; employees with high growth need strength are the most likely to respond favorably to a restructured job while those low on this dimension are least likely to respond well. But the best thing about

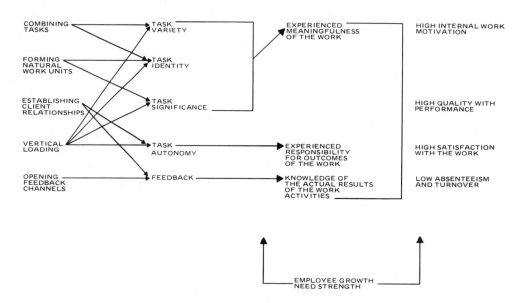

Figure 7-1. Job Redesign: The Hackman-Oldham Model

the model for the practitioner is that Hackman and Oldham have produced a measurement instrument called the "Job Diagnostic Survey" (JDS) which gives good estimates of where each employee who takes the survey stands on the core job dimensions, the critical psychological states, and on growth need strength.

Let us look into each of the components of this model and see how it can be made to work for you. Since we have previously described the "implementing concepts" in the Action section they will not be covered here. We will begin with the core job dimensions, then move on to the critical psychological states.

Core Job Dimensions

Skill Variety.   All workers have a variety of skills. There is a tendency for few of these to be used on the job. A worker may be a fine singer, an excellent pool player, a decent mechanic, and a mediocre draftsman. If this person is employed as a draftsman, the singing and pool playing are irrelevant to the employer. The mechanical skills, however, might be applied by assigning the worker to check out mechanical prototypes of drafting projects in which he was involved. When skill variety is high on a job the workers have a chance to use several of their skills, and to challenge their skills and abilities. Even as a mediocre draftsman, this skill may be challenged by the assignment of work of medium difficulty rather than just routine work.

Skill variety or the use of a challenging level of even a single skill contributes to a feeling that the job being done is meaningful.

Task Identity. If we had to limit ourselves to a single phrase which would best describe what is missing in assembly-line work it would definitely be task identity. More and more, task identity is achieved as the worker comes closer to producing an entire product. Just installing left-front wheel nuts does not make the worker feel like he is making a car, or a front end, or even a wheel assembly. Some workers do what is clearly a whole piece of work. The Volvo engine assembly team concept is now well known, both for the high task identity which the assembly team has and for the quality of the product.

Most jobs can be expanded to include enough elements of the total job so that at least an identifiable ''sub-assembly'' is produced by the worker. Suppose that a typist is given the task of typing a report. Traditionally, one starts from a written manuscript or from a dictation tape. The material is typed giving no thought to its contents—''in the eyes and out the fingers'' as one typing teacher said. The work can be so automatic that it is not difficult to find a secretary typing flawlessly while talking on the telephone and answering questions for someone in the office.

A secretary, if given a chance, may be able to take full responsibility for a report which might include rephrasing the original, typing the text, doing needed graphics, supervising the collating and binding, and the packaging and mailing. It should also be clear from the last whole report example that greater skill variety was an inevitable side effect of an increase in task identity.

Task identity is a powerful attribute of a job which, according to the theory, results in the worker feeling that the job is meaningful.

Task Significance. Task significance is the degree to which the job is seen by the worker as important and having meaningful impact. Just because a job is repetitive and boring does not mean that it must lack task significance. This was pointed out by some hospital laboratory technicians. One task of a medical technician in the laboratory is doing blood counts. This task consists of placing a blood smear on a special gridded microscope slide and then counting blood cells by specified type within the grid squares. Traditionally, this is done with a mechanical counter held in one hand, clicking the counter once for each appropriate blood cell found during a visual scan of the grid. While this task is almost unimaginably tedious and constitutes only a small part of the blood workup, it is literally a matter of life and death. The technician never knows when this will be so and therefore it is necessary to treat each count as critical.

The employees who reported on this particular task all stated that their jobs had the highest task significance. They also hated their jobs. All of them worked in the same hospital. Their supervisor had "read a book, and not very well" and believed that things would be more efficient if each worker specialized in an element of the blood workup. Other testing procedures were segmented in a similar way. Work soon became intolerable, particularly for two technicians, both former military medical corpsmen who had learned their trade under fire in combat.

Even the most significant task can have its contribution to perceived meaningfulness of the job offset by lacks in skill variety and task identity.

Autonomy.   "I was only following orders..."

We hear this phrase not only from the dock at war crimes trials but throughout the civil service of most nations today. Large and small organizations are not immune either. If supervision is close and the worker has no leeway in scheduling, decision-making, and work procedures, then the worker's success or failure may be easily seen by the worker as the responsibility of the supervisor and not that of the worker. While it may be a management prerogative to schedule, make decisions and set work procedures, it may be dysfunctional for a manager to do so, particularly if the worker is more competent in these areas. Frequently the worker is more competent since it is the worker, and not the manager, who has the practical day-to-day information necessary for these activities.

The major point of this section is that the worker who acts autonomously knows with great certainty where the responsibility lies if failure occurs. This helps insure that work will be done properly. The worker also knows where the responsibility lies when success occurs—and this is the essence of "pride in work"—the absence of which is decried by all those who want so desperately to improve employee productivity.

When work goes well for the worker on an autonomous job, the outcome is attributed (by the worker and by others) to the skill and initiative of the worker. This is an indispensable part of utilizing the intrinsic rewards available from the job itself to maintain high levels of quality and production.

Feedback.   On a firing range, shooting at targets 100 yards away, all serious marksmen use a spotting scope when practicing. Target practice is worthless if after each shot the position of the hit on the target is not known. People who drive automobiles need to see where they are going. This is not merely so they will be able to avoid obstructions in their path but so that when the car drifts slightly to the left or right they can make corrective movements and not run off the road. In both of the above instances, the key concept is feedback or knowledge of results.

Workers need feedback, the more immediate the better. In the ideal situation the work itself is structured so that the feedback comes directly from the work. A keypunch operator who punches Holerith cards for computer input hears a distinctive sound with each keystroke. This sound confirms that a key has been fully depressed and that a hole has been punched in the card. In the mid-1960s the key-tape machine was introduced. This was just like the card punching machine but the medium on which the key strokes were recorded was magnetic tape rather than cards. The designers of these machines decided that while converting to the new medium they would also eliminate the annoying noise made by the card punch and keyboard by designing a silent keyboard. This is technically no problem with microswitches and capacitance sensors. The operators of these new machines had outrageous error rates. The answer was simple. The feedback from the sound of the keyboard and the punching of the card gave feedback that a proper key stroke had been made. The silent keyboard cut out all such feedback and the operators' performance declined enormously. The problem was solved by adding an electronic beep which confirmed each keystroke. After this addition, operator error rates returned to normal.

We all need feedback to know how we are doing. The maintenance of productive results requires an ongoing knowledge of those results.

Critical Psychological States

We have examined both the implementing concepts and the core job dimensions used in this model. Now let us look at the critical psychological states which the model predicts will arise from the presence of the job dimensions.

Before beginning, think back to the last time you were enthusiastic about a job you were doing. What did it feel like to you?

Experienced Meaningfulness of Work. "The individual must perceive his work as worthwhile or important by some system of values he accepts."(Hackman, et al.,1975)

When we are involved in a job it occupies our interest. The structure and derivation of the word *interest* belies the fact that the word once indicated a more powerful involvement in something than is the case today. From the Latin, this word is evolved from both *inter* (within) and *esse* (I am). Thus, to be "interested" in something means almost exactly the same as the 1970s phrase, to "get into" a thing or activity.

People are valued for their skills; they develop much of their self-image based on what it is they do. People almost universally describe themselves in terms of their work. This is one of many reasons why a high level of skill variety on a job contributes to the personal experience of meaningfulness of that job. Since the very identity of many workers is a function of their skills and activities, the more of these skills used on the job the more of a worker's identity will be tied to the job and, hopefully, the more meaningful the job will be to them.

The job dimension of skill variety refers to how much of the worker is involved in his input to the job. Task identity, however, is a question of output. What does the worker get from doing the job itself? The key concept here is that the product of work must be identifiable, not only to the worker but to those with whom the worker associates.

"What do you do on your job, John?"

"I build tractors."

"Wow."

versus:

"What is your job like, Henry?"

"Well.. see that car?"

"Yes."

"You know, its got a turn-signal lever?"

"Sure."

"Inside the steering column it attaches with a little screw."

"I guess something holds it on."

"Well.. I put in the screw."

"Big deal."

As noted before, Henry probably does not use many of his skills, either, while installing the screw.

Since people frequently describe themselves to others in terms of what they do, if the job is trivial the person must either present themselves as trivial (unlikely) or refer to some other activity. If the employer, by the structure of the job, forces the employee to develop major areas of interest outside of the job, then the employee's interest and motivation will be somewhere other than on the job, even when they are working!

Not all small jobs are trivial in their impact on others. If Henry fails to install the turn-signal lever screw properly, what will happen? At worst, the driver of the car will be unable to make a proper turning signal—something most urban drivers, at least, seem not to do anyway. Suppose that Henry has a sister who works for Amalgamated Cardiac Implants Corporation, installing a screw in a cardiac pacemaker. The consequences of improper installation of a screw by Henry are trivial but for his sister the consequences are far from trivial.

Experienced Responsibility for Work Outcomes. Managers frequently believe that employees will do good work only if closely supervised. At the same time these same managers bemoan the fact that employees seem to be irresponsible—not necessarily malicious, but just that they seem to have no personal involvement or interest in doing a good job. Further, many managers feel that their personal productivity is diminished by the continual necessity for giving supervision, scheduling tasks, and directing how and when the work will be done. With the constant pressure to perform these tasks, too little time is left for the anticipation of problems before they occur and more comprehensive managerial planning. Far too often managers in this position find themselves doing crisis management, not the well planned activities of which they are capable.

One potential solution which a manager may use will go a long way toward resolving the problems cited in the previous paragraph. This action, which the model suggests, is difficult to take because it requires the delegation of control. Loss of control, even by intent, is rarely a comfortable experience for a manager or anyone else. The action is to allow the employee autonomy.

If we assume that people feel responsible only for those acts for which they are responsible, then we see that the necessary management action is to *give employees responsibility* which is a prerequisite before we can expect that *employees will feel responsibility*.

Let us look at the classic management cycle, Plan—Direct—Organize—Control, and examine which portions of each of these may be delegated in a way that will give employees the necessary autonomy for them to feel responsibility for the job.

Planning: This is an activity in which employees may participate effectively. However, the scope of their knowledge is likely to be too restricted for the generation of long-range plans which require cooperative efforts with other groups within the organization. Generally, with exceptions based on the competence of the particular employees and the nature of the organization, long-range planning is a managerial activity which cannot be easily delegated. Portions of even this activity as well as short-range planning can be effectively delegated on the level where the workers can plan their own work.

Directing: This management activity appears, at first, to be a core activity of management, an undisputed management prerogative, one that employees cannot and should not exercise. The wise manager, however, knows that highly involved team leaders are often the most capable of directing the work of members of their team. Employees seem to turn "instinctively" to members of their peer group for direction when it is recognized that an individual has particular expertise or experience with a particular task. Because of intimate daily contact with the work to be done, many employees are better suited to direct segments of work than the manager. When this condition occurs the manager who takes advantage of it not only has more time for other management activities but may get a noticeably better job done.

Organizing: This activity has many of the properties of the two previous ones. Manufacturing organizations in particular are aware, as a matter of established policy, that employee suggestions about work processes can save the organization significant amounts of money. The suggestion box has thus become a standard fixture in the automotive plant, for example, and employees know that they will receive a percentage of the dollar amount saved as a reward for any suggestion they submit which is implemented. On the level of the individual employee, the reorganization of work by an experienced worker or craftsman can be better suited to the individual working style and pace preferences than a process designed by someone else. This, as usual, is not always the case as Taylor (1911) noted in his discussion of Gilbreth's redesign of bricklaying. This activity had been carried out by highly skilled masons in a manner unchanged for at least three millennia (three thousand years) until Gilbreth's examination and redesign of the work process.

Control: This is where the problem lies more than any other area when attempting to establish employee autonomy. Close supervision and worker autonomy are logically incompatible. Lack of control and the manager's peace of mind are also incompatible, at least in the experience of most managers. The trick is to realize that deft and subtle control can coexist with worker autonomy. Close supervision is not the only kind of supervision. When a worker has relative independence on the job, and discretion (not token input) in the design and scheduling of work, the worker cannot escape the fact that responsibility for both success and failure lies with himself.

In summary, the fact that employees do not always feel a high degree of responsibility for their work is a very real problem and one that is a joint function of the style of management used and the design of the job. In order for employees to exhibit pride in their work, they need to feel responsible for that work. The prerequisite conditions for felt responsibility on the part of employees, in turn, simply amount to actual responsibility for work. It is logically contradictory for an employee to work at an autonomous job and to receive close supervision. These factors ultimately require that portions of the functions of the manager be delegated to the employee. This does not mean the total surrender of control; after all, the manager who delegates is still ultimately responsible, but it does entail both allowing and encouraging the employee to exercise initiative in the management of his own work.

Knowledge of Actual Results of Work.   The key to this final critical psychological state is feedback. As we mentioned earlier, there are at least two kinds of feedback. These are:

1. information from the job itself
2. information from those who use the products of the job.

The first type of information has been found to be the most powerful, because of its immediacy and direct relevance. The second type of information is also useful but is usually delayed and contains an overlay of personal preferences and perceptions.

"How am I doing?" is a normal question for anyone doing anything. As a manager you should realize that although employees may continually wonder about how their work is progressing, they may not come right out and ask you. There is a basic fear of feedback which coexists with a continual need for it. We are not sure where this fear comes from, but we realize it exists. Because of this fear of feedback, employees and managers alike become nervous when faced with evaluations of performance. The annual performance appraisal which is common in most organizations is a source of anxiety and yet is a very important feedback mechanism. Not all employees face the annual performance evaluation with fear, however. Perhaps a brief analysis of the differences between evaluations that arouse fear and those that do not will serve to clarify both the meaning and usefulness of feedback.

The major problem with an annual performance evaluation is that it is annual. It is not immediate. It consists of feedback from an agent (the boss) and it focuses, many times, on the employee's personality rather than work behavior. It centers on the supervisor's personal preferences rather than on objective standards. Some employees go into the annual performance evaluation without fear because they know just what the evaluation will be. There will be no surprises. How does this happen? Usually employees who either receive frequent interim feedback from the boss or who have a job that gives them feedback know where they stand in their job performance. Such employees (and their direct supervisors as well) treat an annual performance evaluation as a mere formality, an annual reporting of what they both already know.

Immediate feedback is better than delayed feedback because corrections cannot be made until the employee knows that a correction is required. With immediate feedback, corrective action can be applied when it is needed. Most delayed feedback makes corrective action possible only after it is needed, which is frequently too late.

The Hackman-Oldham Model: A Concluding Note

We have chosen to use the Hackman-Oldham model as the basis for the strategy guide for job restructuring (Figure 7-2) around which this chapter is centered. We have chosen this model because of its utility and because of the recent (1979) upsurge of interest in it. Those readers with theoretical interests will find many articles based on the model in major management, personnel, and psychological journals. Many of these are listed in the recommended readings at the end of this chapter. Those with primarily practical orientations will find reports of both successful and unsuccessful applications of some or all aspects of it. In our judgment this model represents the state of the art in job redesign. It also has the added advantage of being quantifiable so that fairly objective research within organizations using it is possible.

IMPLEMENTATION

Once you have decided to implement job redesign as a remedy for your employee work behavior problems, the strategy guide will be used for guidance (Figure 7-2). In the material which is to follow we will discuss each of the steps recommended in the job restructuring guide.

Step 1 Favorable Response Predicted? Remember that the approach advocated here does not presume that all employees will respond favorably to the restructuring of their jobs. There are several ways to determine which employees will respond favorably and which will not. Among the easiest is to ask the employee about the proposed restructuring. Another method, which is recommended, but not absolutely essential, is to make use of the Hackman & Oldham Job Diagnostic Survey (J.D.S.) which was mentioned above. The scores obtained from this instrument not only make it possible to estimate

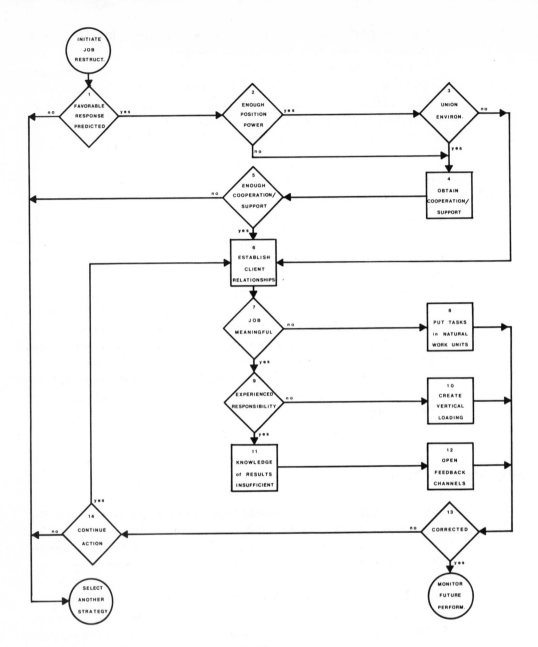

Figure 7-2. Restructuring Jobs: Strategy Guide

how likely it is that a given employee will respond favorably to job restructuring, but other scores allow a diagnosis of the employee's current job from the viewpoint of the employee. The patterns of these scores are invaluable in the actual redesign effort as will be seen below. We recommend strongly that the J.D.S. be utilized and in the material which follows we will assume that it is in use.

Step 2 Enough Position Power?   Is your own position power sufficient to carry out the intended plan or will you require the support of others in the organization, particularly the upper levels of management? If your answer was "yes" to the first part of this question, you are either the chief executive of your organization or you are misinformed about organizational realities. Always inform others who may be involved in the proposed restructuring effort of your plans and enlist their support. The support of superiors is normally required and the support of peers and subordinates is needed for successful implementation.

Step 3 Union Environment?   Are you working in a unionized environment? If so, as we discussed in the opening of the Action section, it will be necessary to obtain the cooperation of the union leaders.

Step 4 Obtain Cooperation/Support.   How does one go about obtaining the cooperation of union leadership in the restructuring of the jobs of the union membership? While we cannot give specific plans which will be applicable in all situations, it is possible to state certain principles which must be kept in mind in planning the method of approach to the union leaders. First, be aware that the proposed job restructuring is likely to be viewed with suspicion. Job enlargement, a euphemism for "piling on more work" will be expected because of the misapplication of job enrichment by others in the past. Second, a successful job restructuring effort has the potential for diminishing the union leaders' power base by lessening worker dissatisfaction. There must be an exchange which is seen as equitable by the union leaders in which they are seen as a major cause of the improvement in the quality of work life. Third, try to anticipate the reactions of the leaders before presenting plans for job restructuring. Many managers routinely utilize the informal communication network of the clerical personnel to gauge the reactions of workers to planned changes and to gain advance warning of current sources of worker dissatisfaction. A job restructuring plan which simultaneously heads off a grievance not yet formally filed and which appears (and may indeed be) an effort of the union leadership is an effort well begun.

Step 5 Enough Cooperation/Support?   As the above discussion should have made clear by now, the support and cooperation of those involved in the job restructuring effort, both internal and external to the organization, must be obtained. This is particularly true if all five of the implementing concepts are to be utilized. In fact, if you are unable to generate sufficient support and cooperation we recommend that you either forget the whole idea or reduce the scope of your redesign effort. Without support, a manager would be wise to select another action.

Step 6 Establish Client Relationships. The first objective in restructuring jobs is to make it possible for the employee to have personal client relationships. This single manipulation of the former job contributes to all three of the psychological states which need to be achieved in a successful job restructuring effort. We recommend this always be done.

Step 7 Job Meaningful? Does the employee perceive the job being done as meaningful? This question may be answered by inspecting the appropriate scores on the J.D.S. It may also, and should be, augmented by discussions with the employee in question. If the job is seen as meaningful then either Step Nine or Step Eleven are the best points of intervention. If the job lacks meaning in the eyes of the worker performing the job, then the two interventions in Step Eight are next.

Step 8 Put Tasks in Natural Work Units. The meaning of a job may be enhanced by combining tasks into natural work units. This requires a careful appraisal of what is actually being done on the job and on related jobs. Several hints about how to do this are given in the Action and Reasons sections above. Remember that what is important here is the employee's view of meaningfulness and the views of those significant others with whom the employee associates.

Step 9 Experienced Responsibility? Employees will not experience responsibility for work unless they are responsible. As hard as it may be to do, achieving a feeling of responsibility for work requires that control over the job be placed, as much as is practical, in the hands of the worker doing the job. Close supervision cannot coexist with a feeling of personal responsibility.

Step 10 Create Vertical Loading. Vertical loading of a job is a technique described previously which entails placing the supervisory functions for the job in the hands of the employee. Vertical loading also can contribute to job meaningfulness since the vertical loading is, in fact, a recombining of tasks into natural work units which consist of the planning, scheduling, execution, and checking of a job.

Step 11 Knowledge of Results Insufficient. If job restructuring is appropriate and neither Step Eight nor Step Ten were necessary or produced the desired result, then the intervention will consist of a remedy for insufficient knowledge of results.

Step 12 Open Feedback Channels. In order to increase knowledge of results it is necessary to open feedback channels so that the necessary information is available to the worker. You will recall from the previous discussion of feedback that both the job itself and the reactions of the immediate supervisor are the issues here. Be careful to check that the feedback is timely. It is entirely possible for there to be sufficient feedback from both sources but for that feedback to be so delayed that is of no use. While the fact that a truck is in a roadside ditch does provide information about the truck running off the road, it is really too late to do much about the problem.

Step 13 Corrected? Has the situation been corrected? If not, continue to Step Fourteen. If the level of job performance has changed for the better then proceed on to Monitor Future Performance. Remember that this is a complex strategy with effects that cannot reasonably be expected to be immediate. Wait long enough before you determine whether or not the situation has been, indeed, corrected.

Step 14 Continue? As noted above, improvement cannot be expected to be immediate. Does there seem to be some improvement? Talk to the employees involved and find out how they are reacting to the restructured jobs. In making changes in jobs you may have made things a bit more convenient for some employees. For others you may have made obsolete certain skills and activities which were quite central to their very self-concept and professional identities. Do not be hasty in determining whether or not to continue or to abandon the strategy for another. Changes as potentially fundamental as job restructuring may have their effects over an extended time period and in very subtle ways.

Some Final Notes

Job restructuring, like all the interventions we examine, takes some time to become workable. Before concluding that the desired result has not been obtained you should first decide if the action might not be profitably continued. If there is no reason to suspect that more time would contribute to success then you should consider selecting another strategy.

SUMMARY

In this chapter we have presented a set of methods for the restructuring of jobs. It is critical to obtain support for this effort whether or not you have position power sufficient to carry it out unilaterally. Union environments will require a special form of delicacy and diplomacy since the expected outcome of a successful job restructuring is increased worker job satisfaction. A list of five implementation strategies were presented which were designed to have positive effects on the critical psychological states which are precursors of enhanced job performance.

The use of this strategy has the potential to improve the quality of work life for both the employees and the manager. The delegation of what was formerly management functions and the incorporation of these functions into the job itself produces this effect.

This strategy is the only one the authors know of that gives the manager the opportunity to increase the intrinsic reward value of the job. Further, for those employees who have high needs to grow in the job this strategy is almost a necessity in order for the organization to keep the services of these employees over the long-term. The piecemeal introduction of job restructuring is quite possible and sometimes advisable so that organizational disruption will not occur. This strategy has a long term effect which allows you to retain your best employees. Better still, the reinforcing aspects of this strategy do not tend to adapt out.

While managing a person who wants and receives an enriched job is a rewarding experience for the manager, not all employees will respond favorably. Those who, by training or choice, have opted for the job which demands little and are not willing to change their position are not likely to respond to the enhanced job with enhanced job performance.

RECOMMENDED READINGS

Aldag, R.J. and Brief, A.P. "Examination of a Measure of Higher-order Need Strength." *Human Relations* 32(8) (1979): 705-18.

Clegg, C.W. "Process of Job Redesign: Signposts from a Theoretical Orphanage." *Human Relations* 32(12) (1979): 999-1022.

Evans, M.G.; Kiggundu, M.N.; and House, R.J. "Partial Test and Extension of the Job Characteristics Model of Motivation." *Organizational Behavior and Human Performance* 24(3) (1979): 354-81.

Ford, R.N. "Job Enrichment Lessons from AT&T." *Harvard Business Review* 51 (1973): 96-106.

Ford, R.N. *Motivation Through the Work Itself.* New York: American Management Association, 1969.

Green, S.B.; Armenak, A.A.; Marbert, L.D.; and Bedeian, A.G. "Evaluation of the Response Format and Scale Structure of the Job Diagnostic Survey." *Human Relations* 32(2) (1979): 181-88.

Hackman, J.R. "Is Job Enrichment Just a Fad?" *Harvard Business Review* 53 (1975): 129-38.

Hackman, J.R. and Oldham, G.R. "Development of the Job Diagnostic Survey." *Journal of Applied Psychology* 60 (1975): 159-70.

Hackman, J.R.; Oldham, G.R.; Jason, R.; and Purdy, K. "A New Strategy for Job Enrichment." *California Management Review* 17 (1975): 57-71.

Herzberg, F.; Mausner, B.; and Snyderman, B.B. *The Motivation to Work.* New York: John Wiley, 1959.

Herzberg, F. "The Wise Old Turk." *Harvard Business Review* 52 (1974): 770-80.

Ilgen, D.R.; Fisher, C.O.; and Taylor, M.S. "Consequences of Individual Feedback on Behavior in Organizations." *Journal of Applied Psychology* 64(4) (1979): 349-71.

Karasek, R.A. "Job Demands, Job Decision Latitude, and Mental Strain: Implications for Job Redesign." *Administrative Science Quarterly* 24(2) (1979): 285-308.

Katerberg, R.; Hom, P.W.; and Hulin, C.L. "Effects of Job Complexity on the Reactions of Part-time Employees." *Organizational Behavior and Human Performance* 24(3) (1979): 317-32.

Koch, J.L. and Rhodes, S.R. "Problems with Reactive Instruments in Field-research." *Journal of Applied Behavioral Science* 15(4) (1979): 485-506.

Orpen, C. "Effects of Job Enrichment on Employee Satisfaction, Motivation, Involvement, and Performance Field Experiment." *Human Relations* 32(3) (1979): 189-217.

Pierce, J.L.; Dunham, R.B.; and Blackburn, R.S. "Social-systems Structure, Job Design, and Growth Need Strength Test of a Congruency Model." *Academy of Management Journal* 22(2) (1979): 313-24.

Stone, E.F.; Ganster, D.C.; Woodman, R.W.; and Fusilier, M.R. "Relationships Between Growth Need Strength and Selected Individual-differences Measures Employed in Job Redesign Research." *Journal of Vocational Behavior* 14(3) (1979): 329-40.

Taylor, F.W. *The Principles of Scientific Management*. New York: W.W. Norton & Co., Inc., 1911.

Walsh, J.T.; Taber, T.D.; and Beehr, T.A. "An Integrated Model of Perceived Job Characteristics." *Organizational Behavior and Human Performance* 25 (1980): 252-67.

Weiss, H.M. and Shaw, J.B. "Social Influences on Judgments about Tasks." *Organizational Behavior and Human Performance* 24(1) (1979): 126-40.

Wimperas, B. R. and Farr, J. L. "Effects of Task Content and Reward Contingency upon Task-performance and Satisfaction." *Journal of Applied Social Psychology* 9(3) (1979): 229-49.

8

Basing
Rewards on
Job Performance

INTRODUCTION

One large Midwestern hospital developed what it thought to be a unique approach to motivating its new keypunch operators. The new approach involved the use of a two-tier financial compensation system. All employees were told that they were required to keypunch a minimum of 450 keypunch cards in an hour for which they would be paid $5.00. As an added incentive, employees were also told that if and when they were able to keypunch 600 cards per hour, they would receive a permanent pay raise to $6.00 per hour. After a period of several years, the hospital administrators found an interesting pattern of employee behavior emerging. New employees typically punched about 500 cards per week for the first week or two on the job. Within one month, however, all of them were exceeding the 600 level and hence were granted a permanent raise by the hospital. They were surprised to find, however, that during the next few months employees typically decreased their productivity gradually until it eventually stabilized between 450-500 cards per hour. In the meantime, the employees were being paid at the $6.00 per hour level.

Why should the hospital administrators have been surprised? Are you surprised?

ACTION

The incident cited above relates to the motivation strategy which is the subject of this chapter: basing rewards on employee job performance. Obviously, the key punch operators realized that if their job performance increased from 450 to 600 cards per hour they would receive a permanent raise. They wanted the raise and hence increased their productivity in order to receive it. However, they also realized that the raise was permanent and would not be retracted by the hospital if their job performance declined below 600 cards per hour. Therefore, they figured there was no reason for keeping their productivity at a high level. Indeed, there were many reasons not to do it. By producing at the lower rate, employees would have more time to socialize with each other and to take short breaks. In addition, they would be less tired at the end of the day.

Rewards for Performance

Now let us look at exactly what is meant by "basing rewards on job performance." It means that employees are rewarded differentially based on their on-the-job productivity. Those employees whose job productivity is relatively high will receive greater rewards than those whose job productivity is relatively low. It means an "excellent" job performer will receive greater rewards than a "good" employee; a "good" worker will receive greater organizational rewards than a "fair" job performer, and a "fair" employee will receive greater rewards than a "poor" worker. It means that a salesperson who sells fifty new cars will receive higher rewards than one who sells twenty new ones. It means a factory worker who produces fifteen widgets will receive greater organizational rewards than one who produces only five.

Typically the rewards given by organizations using this approach are monetary in nature, but this need not be the case. Organizations can differentially distribute to employees non-monetary rewards such as praise, recognition, promotions, office size and locations, and parking spaces.

It is important to observe that basing rewards on job performance necessitates that organizations reward results, not just a person's ability to perform a job or her motivation to perform it. In Chapter One, we stated that a person's job performance was a function of the product of her ability and her motivation. Workers can have a high level of ability, but if they are not motivated to apply that ability to the job, their overall job performance will be necessarily low. Conversely, a highly motivated person who has no job-related ability will most assuredly be a poor performer. Managers and others are occasionally known to base an employee's total rewards on one or the other of those two variables. For example, a relatively poor musician may be given a chance to play in a school band because she practices regularly and enthusiastically. Or, a coach may start a football player because she always attends practice and appears to be working hard even though she may not be as good as another player. Sometimes, people are rewarded on their presumed ability level. Teachers, for example, have been known to pass a failing student on occasion because of her reportedly high intelligence though her actual work was substandard.

It should be clear to the reader that managers and organizations which base an employee's total rewards only on her ability or on her motivation, are acting contrary to the rewards-for-performance strategy.

It is important to observe also that basing rewards on job performance also implies that rewards are not based strictly on an employee's seniority *per se* or strictly on her educational accomplishments *per se*. To repeat, the rewards for performance strategy emphasizes employee accomplishments on the job, not the causes of these accomplishments. If a new employee with an eighth grade education performs a job at the same performance level as one with twenty years experience and a Ph.D. degree, the two should be rewarded equally, according to the rewards-for-performance approach. A new field goal kicker who can kick the ball better than the old one should get a higher salary and be given the kicking job.

The reader undoubtedly realizes that in many situations either seniority or educational background or both are important determinants of an employee's job performance. A carpenter with many years' training and experience will undoubtedly have a higher performance level than will a new, inexperienced carpenter. The strategy of basing rewards on job performance does not deny the importance of either education or seniority. It simply argues that if they do not manifest themselves in the employee's job performance, they should not be rewarded.

What Is Meant By "Job Performance?"

The phrase *job performance* and the word *results* deserve further elaboration. If one is to base rewards on them, it is important to have a clear understanding of what they mean. Conceptually, at least, this is quite easy to do. However, in practice (that is, actual job situations) this is not always the case.

Conceptually, job performance means one's overall contribution to organizational or departmental goals, whatever those goals might be. If the goal of an organization is solely to raise money for charity, then job performance becomes synonymous with raising money for charity. If the goal of a department is to produce high quality metal castings, then the production of high quality metal castings constitutes results.

In some situations, however, it becomes quite difficult to define what is meant by job performance or results. For example, what constitutes results for a research chemist who is searching for a cure for cancer or for an architect who is working with a team of other architects and engineers to build a large bridge across the Ohio River? In many positions, particularly those in which the results of one employee's efforts are not readily apparent or easily measured, it becomes quite difficult to specify what is meant by effective job performance for that employee. We will be returning to this important question later in the chapter. At this point we simply want to raise the issue and make the reader aware of the difficulties involved.

Don't Organizations Typically
Base Rewards on Performance?

Earlier we stated that organizations do not always base rewards on job performance. Instead, they may reward employees based on other factors, even when these other factors are unrelated to job performance. Now it is time to address this question: On what basis are organizational rewards typically distributed? More specifically, to what extent do organizations actually base rewards on job performance versus other criteria?

A number of studies have been done on this issue. The results indicate that while most organizations base rewards on job performance between levels within the organization, for example, presidents receive greater rewards than do vice presidents, vice presidents receive greater rewards than plant managers, and so on, they do not typically do so within each level, that is, within a given rank, such as plant supervisor. A study by Lawler and Porter (1966) found that pay was related to job level, seniority, and other non-performance factors. Another study by Svetlik, Prien, and Barrett (1964) found a negative relationship between amount of salary and performance as evaluated by superiors. Several additional studies report the same basic results within managerial ranks. Interestingly, many of these studies were conducted in organizations which claimed that their pay systems were performance-based.

If organizations do not base their rewards within given levels on the criterion of job performance, what criteria do they use? Seniority is undoubtedly one of the major criteria used by many organizations. In many civil service jobs, for example, automatic raises are granted depending primarily on length of service. The pay of teachers in many school systems, too, is often determined by how long they have taught, even if their job performance has not improved since their first day on the job.

In addition to using seniority as a criterion, organizations often base rewards on the other criteria we suggested earlier: motivation or effort, innate ability, and educational level. The criterion of employee needs is another one which is occasionally used. During World War II, the military paid its employees based on the number of dependents each had. The Armed Forces still pay people who are married more than those who are single.

In recent years, the problems caused by inflation have resulted in organizations basing rewards on yet another criterion: labor market conditions. In many organizations, relatively less competent employees are now being hired at salaries higher than those of present highly competent employees. This occurs because organizations are finding that in order to hire new employees, they must pay the going rates. In many cases these rate are higher than those which they are paying their current employees! This situation is particularly prevalent for job categories in high demand such as computer professionals, engineers, and accountants. It also results in considerable felt inequity among established employees.

Lest we forget, rewards in some organizations are based on downright favoritism. An employee may be rewarded simply because she is well liked by the boss for whatever reason. Every reader is familiar with situations in which the president's daughter or son gets a salary higher than anyone else or an undeserved promotion. As one observer has humorously suggested, if you want to get to the top of an organization fast, "Select your parents wisely!"

The major point of this discussion is to make the reader aware of the fact that organizations use many criteria on which rewards are based, not just overall job performance. Unfortunately basing rewards on many of these criteria does more to reduce organizational effectiveness than to promote it.

Employee Attitudes
Toward Basing Their Rewards
on Performance

Before moving on to a description of how some organizations actually use the rewards-for-performance strategy, there is one further issue which deserves our attention: employee attitudes toward having their rewards based on results.

In general, studies conducted on this issue show that employees do not universally prefer to have their pay based on their work productivity. While many employees, particularly managers, have favorable attitudes toward the pay-for-performance approach, many blue collar workers do not. Two large-scale studies found that between sixty percent and sixty-five percent of the employees surveyed were opposed to a system of performance-based rewards (Opinion Research Corporation, 1949; Davis, 1948). Taken as a group these studies also show (Lawler, 1971) that employee attitudes toward this strategy are strongly influenced by the person's needs, prior experience, and job situation. Employees who have a strong need for security, or whose education is limited, or who do not trust the company to administer the incentive plan properly, can be expected to oppose a performance-based pay plan. On the other hand, employees who seek responsibilities or who have a relatively high education level or who have had favorable previous experiences with a pay-for-performance system are typically favorable to having such a system.

A manager who is considering a pay-for-performance strategy would be wise to consider what these studies have found. More than one organization has implemented a performance-based system only to have it fail because employees would not accept it.

EXAMPLES

Individual Financial Incentive
Systems

The most common application of the pay-for-performance strategy is the use of financial incentives. These typically take one of two forms: individual incentive systems and group incentive systems. In the former, an employee's financial rewards are based strictly on her own job performance, while in the latter, rewards are based on the job performance of the employee's total work group. We will look first at individual incentive systems.

There are many types of individual financial incentive systems used in industry today. Undoubtedly, the most well known of these is the piece rate plan. With this approach, an employee is paid a given amount for each item of work produced. Oyster shuckers, for example, are paid based on the number of gallons of oysters shucked per day. Truckers are often compensated based on the number of miles they drive to and from a delivery site. Auto mechanics are frequently paid based on the number and types of repairs they make. Factory workers, too, are frequently paid based on the number of widgets, or whatever, they produce.

Commissions are often thought of as the piece rate approach to paying salespeople. They represent yet another application of the pay-for-performance strategy. Car salespeople are almost always paid based on the number of cars they sell. In fact, almost all salespeople who sell expensive products (for example, television sets, appliances, encyclopedias, furniture) are paid on a commission basis. Stockbrokers and other financial advisers are frequently paid by commission as well.

The extent to which organizations use individual incentive plans is difficult to determine. Indeed, there is little information available in the literature which reveals what companies, which industries, or what types of plans are in use. It is reported (Patten, 1977) that sixty percent or more of the employees in textile and clothing manufacturing, cigar making, and the steel industry are paid using financial incentives. These industries appear to be the biggest users of these plans. On the other hand, very few office employees are paid based on performance, and in the automobile manufacturing industry only about one to two percent of all employees are reportedly covered.

How successful are individual incentive systems in improving employee productivity? Unfortunately, the answer to this question is unclear because no comprehensive study has been done. One could surmise, however, based on the large number of plans in use, that many organizations are having successful experiences with them. Otherwise, they would not continue to use incentives.

A number of conditions appear to be essential if an incentive plan is to be a success. Patten (1977) has suggested that if a system is to have "incentive pull," that is, to actually motivate an employee to increase her job performance, it should enable the employee to potentially earn thirty to thirty-five percent over her base pay. Thus, if employees have a guaranteed minimum of $5.00 per hour, then potentially they should be able to earn between $6.50 and $6.75 per hour. Keep in mind, of course, that the thirty-five percent rule only applies in situations which guarantee workers a minimum amount per hour.

Beech (1979) has suggested four other requirements of a successful plan. They are:

1. The output of employees must be measurable. A manager must be able to determine how many units of production were completed by each employee.

2. An employee's productivity must be directly related to his or her own skill or effort. As people's skill or effort increases so, too, must their productivity.

3. The work must be such that it can be counted and credited to the proper employee.

4. Employees must accept and support the wage incentive system.

The above prerequisites apply to group incentive systems as well. We will now examine the group incentive systems.

Group Incentive Systems

As we stated earlier, the major distinction between group incentive systems and individual systems is that with the former, each individual's compensation is based on the productivity of her own "group." Differences between group incentive systems often reflect differences in what constitutes the group. With some group plans, such as a group piece rate plan, the group constitutes an employee's immediate work unit. Other group incentive systems consider the group as the entire plant. The well-known Scanlon Plan and the Rucker share-of-production plan are two examples of this. Alternately, the group can be considered the entire organization. Profit-sharing plans are one example which typically falls into this category. Interested readers can find discussions of all of the different group incentive plans in most wage and salary administration books (for example, Patten, 1977; Henderson, 1979) and, hence, we will not elaborate on them. We should add that many of these plans are quite elaborate and require considerable study before one can fully understand the inner workings of them.

It is our contention that some group incentive plans fail to provide much real incentive for employees to increase their job performance. The bigger the group upon which the incentive system is based, the more this is likely to be true. The reason for this is that as groups increase in size, the less likely it is that an employee can see a direct relationship between her own job performance and her own compensation. To the extent that this relationship is not perceived by the employee, there will be no financial incentive for her to increase productivity. Consider, for example, that you participated in a profit-sharing plan along with 100,000 other workers. To what extent would you feel that your own productivity was directly tied to the amount you receive from the profit-sharing plan?

This leads us to our next point, which is that organizations often establish group incentive plans for non-motivational reasons. For example, some organizations institute group incentive plans to instill in employees a sense of partnership with management which ultimately may improve relationships between the two groups. In addition, other organizations may establish these plans to improve cooperation or reduce conflict among the workers themselves. Finally, some organizations establish incentive systems because such systems have the important attribute of allowing management flexibility in compensating employees. With some plans as company profits and productivity change, so, too, will the amount paid to employees. The funds distributed to each employee, for example, participating in a profit-sharing plan expand or contract depending on the organization's profits. Having a flexible compensation plan represents a significant advantage to companies since it permits them an opportunity to avoid being locked into high wage costs during recessionary periods. Thus, group incentive plans serve many purposes for an organization and one should realize that many are not designed strictly to improve employee productivity.

Merit Raises

The granting of raises to deserving employees is closely related to individual and group incentive systems. If, indeed, these raises are granted based on an employee's job performance, and not on some other factors, then they represent yet another application of the pay-for-performance strategy. One of the easiest, although perhaps not totally valid, ways to determine if an organization truly grants raises based on job performance is to look at the differences in raises given by the organization to various employees. True merit raises often result in radically different increases in compensation being given to employees. One university, for example, in 1980 granted its best faculty members raises exceeding 16 percent whereas others received no raise at all. Contrast this with an insurance company which granted its outstanding secretaries 5 percent raises, its average ones 4 percent, and those whose performance was barely acceptable, 3 percent raises. The important point is that genuine performance based merit raises will vary depending upon the relative job performance of employees. If employees differ significantly in terms of their job performance, so, too, will the raises they are given. On the other hand, if all of the employees within a department or organization are relatively equal in job performance (a rare occasion), their raises should be relatively equal.

Merit Based Praise: The Use of Complimentary Interviews

Praise is undoubtedly one of the most neglected motivational techniques available to managers. Yet, it is probably one of the most important, for employees like to feel appreciated, important, and proud of their accomplishments.

While praise is frequently given for improvements shown by employees on the job, such as when shaping is used, it can also be given for overall job performance. The rewards-for-performance strategy would suggest that those employees having the highest job performance deserve greater or more frequent praise than those displaying lower levels of job performance. Thus, the strategy suggests that praise to an employee be given in accordance with her accomplishments.

A rather novel approach to the administration of praise, and one that is fully consistent with the rewards-for-performance strategy, has been suggested by Cangemi and Claypool (1978). They recommend that managers conduct complimentary interviews with outstanding employees, the purpose of which is primarily to praise the employee for her job performance. They suggest that managers document the employee's behavior using a complimentary interview form. This form, of course, would be prepared prior to the interview itself, and, could be forwarded to upper management with the expectation that they too would congratulate and compliment the employee.

One of the major advantages of using complimentary interviews is that they focus attention on outstanding employees, a group often neglected in most organizations. By calling attention to this group of employees, organizations can demonstrate the importance it places on high productivity. Ultimately this may serve to encourage other employees to improve their performance.

Rewards-Based
Suggestion Systems

Another utilization of basing rewards on job performance is through rewards-based employee suggestion systems. This entails rewarding employees based on the quantity of suggestions submitted or the quality of these suggestions.

Honeywell Corporation's (Minneappolis, Minnesota) defense systems and avionics divisions reportedly (Zemke, 1980) has one of the most successful employee suggestion systems. In 1979, the company reportedly received over 18,000 suggestions (3.66 per employee) which resulted in a savings of over $1,300,000. The Honeywell Suggestion System is somewhat unique in that it rewards employees both in terms of recognition and financially, based on the quantity and quality of their suggestions.

With regard to financial rewards, Honeywell utilizes a combination of cash and merchandise awards. Cash gifts are granted employees for their suggestions on the basis of one sixth of the total first year's anticipated dollar savings. Thus, the more valuable the suggestion, the greater the reward given—a clear application of the pay-for-performance strategy. To encourage as many suggestions as possible, Honeywell grants employees merchandise awards for submitting three, six, ten, fifteen, or twenty-five suggestions. The larger the number of suggestions submitted by an employee, the more merchandise awards are given. Interestingly, basing merchandise awards on quantity of suggestions submitted does not seem to have resulted in employees submitting a rash of worthless suggestions. Reportedly, forty-nine percent of the suggestions submitted are accepted, a figure much higher than the national average.

With regard to giving recognition to employees for suggestions submitted, Honeywell also applies the rewards-for-performance strategy. It recognizes employees based on both the quantity and quality of suggestions submitted. Employees who submit three, six, ten, fifteen, or twenty-five suggestions have their pictures placed on "Super Star" charts in their department. Those who submit high quality suggestions are rewarded with recognition in yet other ways. Each week pictures of two employees, together with their cost-saving suggestion, are made into large posters and displayed on bulletin boards located in various company facilities. In addition, the company's newsletter carries articles about suggestion winners as do various departmental and division newsletters. Finally, each year three Honeywell divisions each single out one person for a special recognition award. This award is presented by the governor of the State of Minnesota to the employee in the presence of many other employees. Photos of the occasion are subsequently posted on various bulletin boards and appear in the company publications.

REASONS

The theoretical foundation of this strategy comes from the research done into "Expectancy Theory." In this section we will discuss expectancy theory, where it came from, its relationship to the need for achievement (nAch) and other learned social motives, and its basic similarity to other highly workable theories used in fields as diverse as animal learning and human economics.

Probabilities: Conditional and Subjective

The following is a very brief introduction to the notion of probability. It is inserted here because the expectancies to which we will refer from here on are normally expressed as conditional subjective probabilities.

A probability is a simple ratio formed from the number of things an observer is interested in for some reason, divided by the number of things that could have occurred. Thus, when flipping a coin, if one is interested in heads, the probability of heads is ½ or .5. This is because only two things can happen when flipping a coin (heads or tails) and heads were of interest. Using the definition then, the number one (the number of heads on the coin) is divided by the number two (the total number of different sides on the coin). The ratio ½ is the probability. It is customary, but not necessary, to express probabilities as the decimal equivalent of the probability ratio. Therefore, ½ is usually written as .5.

A conditional probability has a slightly different form than the simple probability described above. Instead of the "probability of heads" (a simple probability) we might be interested in "the probability of "a" given that "b" has happened." Think of "a" as a car starting in winter and think of "b" as getting a tune-up of the car engine. Those readers who have dealt with winter driving in a cold climate will immediately see the point of all this. In the winter some cars start only one-half the time. However, a car with the engine recently tuned may start 999 times out of 1000. We can think of two conditional probabilities which describe this situation. They might be stated as:

1. Probability of starting given no tune-up = .500
2. Probability of starting given a tune-up = .999

Just a bit of thought should convince the reader that, far from being a confusing abstraction, the conditional probability is one which reflects realistically how the world works. What we are interested in knowing is rarely a simple probability and frequently a conditional probability.

Subjective probabilities are just like what we have been discussing but are less precise. What they amount to is an educated guess about what a probability is without going through the mathematics and counting of alternatives which the non-subjective or objective probability entails.

When we run an experiment or survey employees and in the survey or experiment we ask "How likely do you think 'X' is?" what we are asking for is a subjective probability.

Expectancy

Two basic concepts are critical to the understanding of expectancy. These are normally called "Expectancy One" or E-I and "Expectancy Two" or E-II. E-I is a conditional probability, namely the likelihood that success will follow effort. E-II is also a conditional probability, this time the probability that reward will follow success.

Instead of thinking about the likelihood (probability) that a car will start in the winter if it has had a tune-up, let us simply insert different content into the same question.

How likely is it that I will successfully complete a job if I put forth the effort to do it? This may be stated as "the probability of success given effort." Because it is a guess, not a computed probability, it is a subjective probability.

In a similar manner we may describe E-II. How likely am I to receive a reward if I am successful? Or what is the probability of reward, given success?

An important advance in expectancy theory was the breaking of the effort-result-consequence sequence into two parts: E-I and E-II. What do these concepts mean in the practical sense? The likelihood that success will follow from effort is a major determining factor in whether or not the effort will be put forth, that is, will the employee try? Without effort few goals are reached. Once success has occurred, a second issue, separate from the first arises, namely, will a reward occur because of the success? If the task performed is not intrinsically satisfying enough to maintain the work behavior, then such work will diminish and eventually cease.

In the next section we will note that E-I has a lot to do with the employee's confidence in the work and in the employee's own abilities. Where abilities are lacking, E-I can be increased by training. Where only confidence is lacking, the manager can use encouragement and support.

Outcomes: L-1 and L-2

In addition to the two types of expectations that employees can have about the outcome of their job, the outcomes themselves may be classified into one of two types:

1. Level-1 Outcomes (L-1)
2. Level-2 Outcomes (L-2)

L-1 outcomes are the rewards which accrue to the employee for achieving success. They are the same rewards referred to in the E-II definition. L-2 outcomes are subsequent in time to the L-1 outcomes and are the needs the person has which may be satisfied by the rewards. Recognize that not all of an employee's needs will be served by the rewards coming from the job. In the Implementation section we will discuss further the consequence of offering a reward which does not satisfy needs.

Valence

This is another word for value. Outcomes have valence within the expectancy model. This makes sense because not all outcomes are equally valuable to an employee. While a good word from the boss is quite nice, a promotion is even better, and more highly valued. The more highly valued an outcome is the greater its valence.

The Basic Expectancy Model

If we know the values of two things we can estimate motivation of an employee to perform a task. This is the most abbreviated version of expectancy theory (Vroom, 1964):

$$M = f(V \times E)$$

The equation reads: Motivation is a function of the product of an (E)xpectancy and a (V)alence. Specifically, the value of E is the subjective probability that effort and performance will be followed by an outcome (a reward), and the value of V is the valence of the outcome (how valuable the reward is).

Note that a subtle extra concept has been included in this formulation. The values of E and V are *multiplied*. This means that if one or both values are zero the resultant motivation is also zero. Some scholars have debated whether the actual operation to be used should be multiplication or something more exotic. Some even have argued for simply adding the terms, but the general consensus is that both E and V must be greater than zero for motivation to perform the task in question to exist. Herein lies a practical dictum for the thoughtful reader. An employee who is certain to get something she does not want and an employee who is certain she will not get something she wants very much can be expected to perform in the same way, that is, they will not perform at all.

Expectancy Theory, Phase Two

Vroom (1964) has proposed a model which utilizes E-I, E-II, and Valence for L-2 outcomes to predict the level of motivation (he calls it *force*) to perform a specific task. We will state his formulation in our own way:

$$M = f((V(L-2) \times E-II) \times E-I)$$

Where:

M	= motivation to perform the task
V(L-2)	= value of Level 2 outcomes (pay, recognition, etc.)
E-II	= probability that performance will result in the Level 2 outcome.
E-I	= probability that effort will result in performance.

What Vroom has done here is to redefine Valence (V) in the simple formulation as E-II times the valence of the outcome, then, again to multiply the result by E-I.

This amounts to stating the following. Motivation is a function of the value to me of what I want, perhaps decreased by the percentage of the time I will not get it, and that estimate once again decreased by the percentage of the time I will not succeed if I try. (We apologize to the pure-minded among our readers for this interpretation; while it is not technically accurate, at least it is not misleading.)

The Need for Achievement, Atkinson Version

In his 1957 work on risk-taking John Atkinson treated both the need for achievement (nAch) and fear of failure (FF) in a manner quite similar to that used by expectancy theorists. He represented motivation in the following way:

$$M(t) = f(M \times P \times I)$$

Where:

$M(t)$ = total motivation

M = motive strength

P = probability of outcome

I = incentive value of outcome

If we interpret incentive value to mean the same as valence, and it does, then we see that Atkinson's model looks just like the simple expectancy model—but one extra term appears.

Now we shall make the little known distinction between motivation and motive. People have predispositions to act in certain ways. Most of these are learned. While motivation may be considered the existing force toward a particular goal, a motive (like a need for success) is the base-line state from which the motivation comes. All people have at least some need to succeed (it may be minimal or covered by a simultaneous fear of success, but it is there). When a person is exposed to a set of stimuli which arouse the motive, they are said to be motivated. Without arousal they still have the motive but it is not actualized. Civilized people with aggressive motives are not aggressive when with children (or they are not civilized) but given the cue of a football field the motive may become aroused.

Considering the above we can see that motivation simply is an aroused motive modified by the value of the goal and the probability of attaining it.

Expectancy in a Nutshell

Expectancy theory is a powerful and useful method of thinking about why an employee might be likely to perform a single task or even a large piece of work. In its various forms it states that two questions are asked internally by the employee (let us not worry about whether or not the employee is aware of asking these questions):

1. What is in it for me? = The valence of the outcome
2. Can I really get it? = Probability of success

And the more complex way of thinking about expectancy just divides question number two into two sequential questions:

1. Will I succeed if I try? ..... = E-I
2. Will I get rewarded if I succeed? .... = E-II

If you are able to provide answers to employees for these questions then, the model suggests, you will be able to secure their motivated effort on the task you desire.

Two additional notes need to be made. First, since the model multiplies its terms you must be careful that no value or probability approaches zero. If that happens you will get no results (that you want). Second, Atkinson raises another consideration, that if the motive involved is directed toward the goal you want, then the chances of your own success in using expectancy theory fruitfully are increased.

IMPLEMENTATION

This strategy guide (Figure 8-1) consists of eight steps and includes three conditions which managers may find existing together with solutions for each. If it is found that rewards offered to employees are not rewards which are desired (Step 5) the reader will be referred

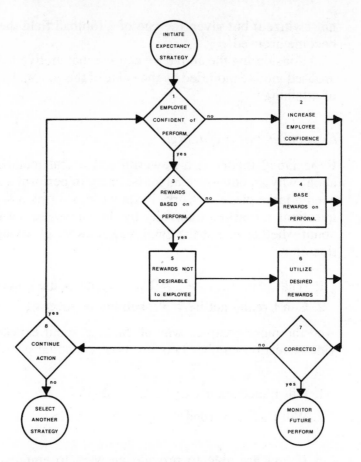

Figure 8-1. Basing rewards on Performance

back to Chapter Five on satisfying employee needs, for further coverage of the corresponding solution.

Step 1 Employee Confident of Performance? There are two reasons why an employee might not feel that the performance desired by the manager can be met. First, the employee may not possess the necessary skills to get the job done. This can occur for several reasons. The required work may be a new process or involve a new skill which the employee neither possessed when hired nor has acquired subsequent to hiring. With the rate of change in the technologies used by American business today this is a fairly common occurrence. There is an equally common solution to this problem: training.

The astute reader will point out that in the Chapter One strategy guide we specified (in Step 9) that one should "use training/

outplacement/counseling'' if no strategy for increasing employee productivity seemed advisable. This, however, does not rule out the use of employee training within any strategy. In fact, in the case under current discussion training is often the proper solution.

The second reason why an employee may not feel able to perform up to expectations is a unrealistically low evaluation of her own capabilities. This, also, can happen for a variety of reasons. The simplest reason may be that the employee has never tried to perform the work expected or never had occasion to perform that work at the level expected. Managers, themselves, encounter this frequently in their own work. New responsibilities in a new area or at a higher level in the organization are commonplace for management personnel. How would you handle a promotion to the next level in your own organization? Certainly you would not have prior experience in all facets of the new position. You would examine what was to be done, establish priorities, seek advice and information, and then proceed to figure out how to best perform your job. An employee faced with a parallel situation is in exactly the same position but with one important exception. You, as the manager, are in a position to provide information, suggestions, and most importantly, a great deal of support and encouragement. Remember, while managers are quite used to adapting to new demands and requirements, nonmanagement employees are not expected to do so very often. Prior managers may have encouraged dependence in the employee or the prior job requirements may have never demanded that the employee perform beyond the level of rote repetition of tasks.

An important consideration here is that employees with relatively greater tenure in jobs which made few growth demands may be quite resentful of new requirements. If you have a choice, it is usually better to place those employees who you know have a desire to ''move up'' and to use more of their skills in positions where you will increase performance expectations. We recommend that on this latter point the reader refer back to the previous chapter for a discussion of the implications of varying levels of ''growth need strength'' in the Hackman-Oldham Model.

Step 2 Increase Employee Confidence.   Let us first distinguish be tween the employee lacking in the necessary skills for the expected performance and the employee who has the necessary skills but lacks the confidence. In the previous step we described both of these extremes and they *are* extremes. Think of the two cases as lying at the opposite ends of a horizontal scale, like an attitude rating scale.

Sometimes this configuration is called a continuum, that is, employees can fall at any point on the horizontal line. It should be apparent that the continuum is one of skill level and for an employee at each point the manager should do two things. First, provide access to the necessary information or training. Second, and this holds for each point on the continuum, express to the employee that you have confidence that what must be learned can be learned, skills that must be acquired can be acquired. *By expressing your confidence in the employee you increase the employee's self-confidence.*

So, if an employee needs a higher level of skill, use training to provide for the necessary learning and increase the employee's confidence by providing support. If the employee already has the necessary skills but is just afraid to try the new skill or the new level of performance, provide support to the employee and increase self-confidence. Note that the above two steps correspond to the Expectancy One (E-I) concept presented above in the Reasons section.

Step 3 Rewards Based on Job Performance? "What is in it for me? Why should I work harder, I will be paid the same anyway." Have you heard these remarks from your subordinates?

If you have, then most likely the rewards you provide are not based on employee performance but on something else. Here is an analysis of pay from the worker's standpoint, and surprisingly few managers have thought about it.

Joe works in a factory. He is an hourly employee. His job is to assemble wheel-brake components on automobile wheels. What is Joe's day like? He gets up in the morning, drives to the plant parking lot, walks through the gate and into the shop. What is the first thing Joe does when he enters the shop? Does he inspect his work tools? Does he make sure the necessary parts are available for his day's work? Does he work out a new procedure which will improve his efficiency? No. Joe first punches in at the time clock. Why? Joe knows that if he does not punch in he will not get paid. The accountants in the plant office handle Joe's monetary compensation. They do this by looking at his time card, computing the time elapsed between the beginning and the end of Joe's time in the shop, and multiplying the hours by Joe's hourly rate of pay. *Joe is paid for his time, not his work.*

The pay policies of the plant, in effect, say to Joe, "What is wanted here is your time." All that is being asked of Joe is his time. If you were Joe, working under these conditions, what would you give the plant? We rest our case.

Unions

A question which is frequently raised at this point is: "What about the union contract?" Let us address this issue now.

There are two types of rewards which an employee may derive from working and we have spoken of both before. To review, there are intrinsic rewards, those that come from performing the job itself, and extrinsic rewards, those that are given to the employee for doing the job. Intrinsic rewards are given to the employee by the employee. They are self-administered rewards. The manager may influence intrinsic rewards by proper job design (see Chapter Seven) and work assignments. Extrinsic rewards are given to the employee by the organization; included among these is pay and benefits. Also included are such items as interpersonal consideration, reasonable use of policies, equitable assignment of overtime, vacation scheduling, and so on.

The union contract usually has little to say about intrinsic rewards and deals primarily with pay and benefits within the extrinsic rewards. Some contracts specify items like methods of vacation scheduling, for example, but few contracts cover interpersonal consideration and the reasonable administration of policy.

Union contracts are legal agreements and as such should include only those items which are enforceable. There is no practical way that a contract can say "All managers will treat employees with respect, administer company policy in a reasonable and humane manner, and respond to employees as mature, caring human beings." It would be unwise to include such language in a contract because there is no objective way to judge whether or not such a term of the contract is being met or not. An employee desiring to file a grievance concerning such an item could not produce convincing proof that this contract provision had been violated, nor could the organization convincingly show that it had been followed.

So, what can a manager do when a union is involved? Make a mental list of the intrinsic and extrinsic rewards your employees might want. Note which of these over which you have at least some control. Now cross out those which the union contract so rigidly defines that you can do nothing. The remaining list (hopefully it will not be too much shorter than your original list) consists of the rewards you can use as a manager in a unionized environment.

To summarize, you can assign work and structure jobs so that the possibility of greater job satisfaction and, hence, intrinsic reward is present. You can also choose to administer personal rewards such as praise and recognition. These things are possible even with a rigid union contract. Without a union you can add pay, benefits, and incentives to the set of rewards to be used, the only constraints being perceived equity and economic reality.

Step 4 Base Rewards on Job Performance. Here are some common methods of basing rewards on job performance. In each case, the definition of "performance" is entirely dependent upon what the manager can reasonably define as appropriate job performance in the particular applied setting.

Rate of Pay. "Piece rate" means that the total pay is determined by the number of pieces produced times the rate per piece. Piece rate is pure incentive. So that production will be predictable, this method of compensation is usually altered so that a minimum acceptable number must be produced. The minimum number is paid either at some hourly flat rate or at a minimum piece rate. Production above the minimum acceptable level is paid at an increased piece rate, sometimes called incentive pay. Here is an example:

Deborah sews seat covers for an auto company. She makes fifty bucket seat covers in an hour. For this level of production she is paid her regular hourly rate. Since she works seven hours per day (lunch and breaks considered) she should produce 350 seat covers per day. For the first fifty seat covers above the expected level she also receives an incentive payment, for the next fifty an even greater incentive payment, and so on.

Joe, in the example given earlier, receives the same pay as long as he comes to work and meets minimal production standards. If Joe works harder nothing happens. If Deborah works harder she gets more pay. Joe is paid for his time while Deborah is paid for her work. Deborah's rewards are based on performance while the only performance for which Joe is rewarded is showing up for work.

Vacation Pay. Both Joe and Deborah have fully paid vacation days specified in their union contracts. Also in the contract is the provision that to receive this pay they must work the day before the vacation day and the day after the vacation day. Here the performance which is rewarded is simply showing up for work. This is considered important because of the pattern of absenteeism which occurs near holidays like Thanksgiving, Christmas, and so on. The organization needs to maintain a sufficient workforce on the days before and after holidays so that work can go on. At the same time, employees usually want a somewhat longer vacation and are not likely to come to work on these days. In this situation the work performance which is critical is having the employee on the job. The organization is willing to pay extra if they come to work on these days and so the contract specifies the conditions for receiving vacation pay.

Step 5 Rewards Not Desirable to Employee.   Sometimes a manager is bewildered when an employee who is receiving a significant reward does not respond as expected. Susan, a particularly valued worker, was given a bottle of fine brandy by her supervisor for Christmas. She told the supervisor she did not want it and acted offended. Susan is a Jehovah's Witness. While some may drink, members of this religious group do not observe Christmas. In addition, neither Susan nor anyone in her family drinks alcoholic beverages. While your authors, and perhaps the reader, would respond to a bottle of fine brandy as a reward, clearly not all people will.

The reader is advised to check in Chapter Five for a further coverage of the differences which normally occur in worker's needs. A reward offered which is not desired by the employee will not function as a reward.

Step 6 Utilize Desired Rewards.   If you found in the previous step that an employee was not receiving a valued reward, then the reward offered must be changed. In Chapter Five there is a full discussion about how to determine what rewards an employee desires. In brief, what the manager does in this case is simple. To repeat the axiom: *If you want to know, ask!*

In addition to this simple and obvious principle, we will now discuss, once again, some of the most powerful rewards the manager can use. In keeping with our previous coverage of intrinsic and extrinsic rewards we will give some illustrative instances where nearly all employees will respond favorably.

Praise. Do not ignore the use of praise when an employee is doing well. Almost everyone likes praise. Some do not appear to know how to receive it gracefully, but it reliably acts as a reward anyway. We have performed this experiment many times. Ask a seminar of managers or management students how they know they are doing a good job where they work. Very, very few answer, "My boss tells me." What is heard instead is: "I don't know"; "When I don't get criticized"; or "If nobody says I did something wrong."

The preponderant pattern is one of the "negative definition," that is, the seminar members do not know that they have done a good job because they are *told* so. They know they have done a good job only if they have not been told the job was poor. Actually, the problem is worse than it appears at first. Upon further discussion it is apparent that these people never know for sure if their work is acceptable or not.

Why? Let us assume, for argument's sake, that there are only three levels of job performance: good, average, and poor.

Now, if an employee is not given feedback about anything but the poor job, then the absence of criticism for a poor job does not mean the performance level was good. It might also mean it was average. The employee cannot, on the basis of the manager's response, discriminate between a good and an average level of performance. Functionally this amounts to the three levels of performance being redefined as: not bad, and bad.

This strategy for rewarding employees is symptomatic of a manager who interacts with employees passively. Criticism for a job poorly done is a reaction to what the employee has done or not done. An active strategy is to intentionally compliment the employee for a job well done. This serves two purposes. First, it gives a reward which the employee will, more often than not, treat as a true and valued reward. Second, it is a part of the feedback which the employee gets from doing the job.

Release Time. As we pointed out in Chapter Five, employees satisfy their needs off the job as well as on the job. While the manager can only infrequently have a direct effect on needs satisfied off the job, it is possible to facilitate the meeting of needs by things which occur on the job. Suppose an employee is involved with a local Boy Scout group and needs time off to participate in certain activities. The manager can help to meet this employee's needs (and thereby provide highly valued rewards) by learning about the nature of the employee's activities. For example, in the summer, Boy Scouts have large gatherings (Scout-o-ramas, national camping activities, and so on) and awareness of this may benefit the manager. Since these activities do not always coincide with the vacation times preferred by other employees, being sure that time off is available for this employee at the desired times may provide a willing employee who will work at times when other employees want to take a vacation. In addition, the public service afforded by this employee's activities is an excellent source of favorable publicity about the organization in the local community.

Step 8 Continue Action?   The following are reasons for continuing the use of this strategy.

*Some Response By Employee, But Not Enough.*Employees may respond relatively well to the use of this strategy but the magnitude of the response may not be sufficient. In such a case, continued application of the strategy may produce the desired result. The idea that employees should be compensated based on actual performance has become so foreign an idea that the employees may take some time to become accustomed to it.

Confidence High Then Decreases Again. This eventuality may indicate that employees are not really certain that the manager can perform as advertised. This is a problem with E-II as cited above and should be treated as such.

Changing Conditions Change Reward Structure. Just because the employees formerly responded well to the rewards previously offered for excellent performance does not mean that this will last forever. The manager must continually check that the rewards offered are still appropriate to the current need of the employees.

SUMMARY

The strategy of basing rewards on job performance has several attributes which distinguish it from all of the other motivational strategies. One of the most important of these is that it impresses upon employees the meaning and worth of productivity to the organization. It reminds them that the success of the organization is tied to their productivity. Further, it reminds them that the organization's success is essential if employees are to receive high rewards. All too often employees lose sight of these fundamental facts. They delude themselves into believing that their productivity is somehow unrelated to organizational success and that the rewards an organization can give its employees are unrelated to success. The strategy of basing rewards on performance helps to shatter this delusion.

Using the reward-for-performance approach has a related advantage. It makes it clear to the deadwood or loafers within the organization that their behavior is definitely not acceptable. However, organizations use reward systems which inadvertently reward poor performers and lead them to believe that their job performance need not be improved. This happens, for example, in organizations which grant equal pay raises to both marginal and superior performers. By simultaneously rewarding the superior employees and not rewarding marginal ones, the latter know exactly where they stand.

And so do the superior performers. By not granting rewards such as pay raises to marginal employees, the organization may be able to reduce its costs.

Another attribute of the rewards-for-performance strategy is that its continued use may ultimately result in the development of a highly effective work force. Highly productive workers could be expected to be attracted to those organizations which use this approach. Unsatisfactory workers would be discouraged from joining or remaining at these organizations.

For managers who themselves are highly competent, supervising highly competent workers can be a very rewarding experience, both financially and otherwise. Thus, managers, too, can gain personally from the use of this approach.

RECOMMENDED READINGS

Cangemi, J.P. and Claypool, J.F. "Complimentary Interviews: A System for Rewarding Outstanding Employees." *Personnel Journal* February, 1980, pp. 87-90.

Davis, N.M. "Attitudes to Work Among Building Operatives." *Occupational Psychology* 22 (1948): 56-62.

Dunn, J.D. and Rachel, F.M. *Wage and Salary Administration: Total Compensation Systems*. New York: McGraw-Hill, 1971.

Henderson, R.I. *Compensation Management*. 2nd ed. Reston, VA: Reston Publishing Company, 1979.

Lawler, E.E. *Pay and Organizational Effectiveness*. New York: McGraw-Hill, 1971.

Lawler, E.E. and Porter, L.W. "Predicting Manager's Pay and Their Satisfaction With Their Pay." *Personnel Psychology* 19 (1966): 363-73.

Opinion Research Corporation. *Wage Incentives*. Princeton, N.J.: 1946.

Patten, Thomas H., Jr. *Employee Compensation and Incentive Plans*. New York: The Free Press, 1977.

Svetlik, B.; Prien, E.; and Barrett, G. "Relationships Between Job Difficulty, Employee's Attitude Toward His Job, and Supervisory Ratings of the Employee Effectiveness." *Journal of Applied Psychology* 48 (1964): 320-24.

Zemke, Ron. "Combine Recognition and Reward." *Training* July, 1980 pp. A12-A13.

9

Choosing the Strategy:
A Synthesis

INTRODUCTION

In the previous chapters we have described seven different strategies managers can use to enhance the productivity of employees. It is now time to describe how managers can choose between these alternative strategies. The following questions need to be addressed:

1. When is each of the seven motivational strategies most likely to be effective?
2. When is each of the strategies most likely to be unsuccessful?

Having read the preceding chapters, the reader is familiar with each strategy and will understand the importance of these questions.

Before addressing these issues, however, we will review the contingency approach to enhancing employee job performance which was first presented in Chapter One and referred to in some of the other chapters. This review will help the reader to place each of the preceding chapters into the proper perspective.

THE CONTINGENCY APPROACH: A REVIEW

The contingency approach to enhancing employee job performance is based on a set of three assumptions regarding motivational strategies. An organizational system which divides all motivational approaches available to managers into seven basic strategies has been presented. For each specific strategy an explicit set of strategic steps has also been presented to guide the manager in solving employee productivity problems.

The assumptions underlying the contingency approach are:

1. No single approach to increasing employee productivity will be effective under all conditions.
2. Most approaches currently available to improve employee productivity will be effective under certain conditions.
3. Under certain conditions two or more approaches to improving employee productivity will be just as effective.

When these principles or assumptions were first presented in Chapter One, the reader may have been skeptical about their validity. Now, however, having examined each of the seven core strategies, the reader can see that these assumptions have considerable practical utility.

There are undoubtedly thousands of different ways a manager can attempt to increase an employee's productivity. In order to make intelligent choices, however, it is helpful to organize and categorize the alternate courses of action. Choosing among alternatives within an organized structure is usually both easier and more economical than attempting to make choices within an unstructured body of knowledge. By dividing the possible actions into seven categories (Table 9-1), the contingency approach provides a structured framework for dealing with employee productivity issues.

The most important feature of the contingency approach is that it prescribes a framework or set of steps for improving employee productivity. Managers who are confronted with actual situations involving employee motivation often are at a loss as to where to begin and how to proceed. Employee job performance problems are often emotionally charged. This makes it quite difficult for managers to maintain the perspective which is needed to solve these problems.

Figure 9-1 shows the steps recommended by the contingency approach for dealing with employee job performance problems. The reader can now see that this diagram raises three questions which we have been addressing throughout the book. A review of these fundamental questions should help to refresh the reader's memory about these many strategies.

The first question is: "Has the manager communicated to the employee what he wants him to do?"

Table 9-1: Contingency Approach Strategies

---

1. POSITIVE REINFORCEMENT and SHAPING:
   With this strategy a manager uses shaping to enhance the employee's job performance. Intermittent reinforcement is then used to maintain the job performance at the desired level.

2. EFFECTIVE PUNISHMENT and DISCIPLINE:
   This approach utilizes disciplinary interviews with employees and, if necessary, penalties to improve the employee's job performance. The "Hot Stove Rules" of discipline are recommended as a way of successfully disciplining employees.

3. TREATING EMPLOYEES FAIRLY:
   This strategy involves the use of one of two separate actions depending upon the circumstances. Sometimes managers may want to attempt to convince disgruntled employees that they are, in fact, being fairly treated. On other occasions, managers may want to make those changes desired by an employee so that the basis for feelings of inequity is removed.

4. SATISFYING EMPLOYEE NEEDS:
   This strategy uses two sequential steps. First, the manager determines which employee needs are satisfied and which are not. Second, the manager attempts to satisfy, within the organizational constraints, those needs of the employees which are unsatisfied.

5. SETTING EMPLOYEE GOALS:
   Using this approach, the manager and/or subordinate set hard, realistic goals for the subordinate. Specific objectives to service these goals and plans to attain the objectives are then established. Using this strategy the manager is a teacher, facilitator, and evaluator.

6. RESTRUCTURING JOBS:
   Restructuring jobs involves changing the job content and the organization of work in ways that increase the employee's feelings of responsibility for the job, feelings that the job is meaningful, and knowledge of job results. This is accomplished by yielding control of the job to the employee, combining tasks into natural work units, and increasing feedback to the employee about the goods or services produced.

7. BASING REWARDS ON JOB PERFORMANCE:
   This strategy recommends that managers reward employees based solely on their job performance. Those employees whose job performance is clearly superior should receive significantly greater organizational rewards than those whose performance is not.

Often employee performance problems simply result from a lack of communication between the supervisor and the employee.

The second question asks: "Should any motivational strategy be attempted?"

Before trying to enhance an employee's job performance, a manager should decide whether an outplacement strategy, such as a transfer, demotion, discharge, or additional training, would be a more effective course of action.

Throughout this book we have been focusing solely on motivational strategies. This may have created the impression that all employees should be salvaged and will respond to some motivational strategy. Obviously this is not the case. There are many occasions in which the outplacement approach is the most appropriate one.

The third and final question (Step 5 in Figure 9-1) asks: "Which motivational strategy is most likely to enhance the employee's job performance?"

The reader will recognize this issue as one which was raised at the beginning of this chapter. Where the question of selecting a strategy fits within the contingency approach is now also apparent. We will now address this issue directly and in doing so, the contingency approach will be present in its full version.

Figure 9-1. The Contingency Approach: Strategy Guide

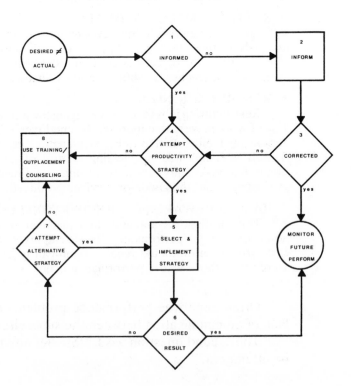

SELECTING A STRATEGY

The Manager as a Decision Maker

In 1978, for the first time in history, a management expert was granted the Nobel Prize. Herbert A. Simon, Richard King Mellon Professor of Computer Science and Psychology at Carnegie-Mellon had conducted research and written articles for several years about how decisions are made in organizations. It is well accepted that one of the primary functions of managers is decision-making. Simon challenged the previous ideas about how decisions are made and proposed an alternate view.

It was once believed that managers ought to make optimal decisions. To make an optimal decision the manager considers the costs and benefits of each possible course of action, then chooses the course of action which has the greatest benefits coupled with the lowest costs. Simon proposed that, rather than optimize, a manager must "satisfice," a word invented to indicate that managers make decisions which are satisfactory but probably not optimal.

Compromise: A Basic Leadership Function.   As it turns out, managers must compromise a great deal in the practical world. Returning to the ideas of Simon, there are very practical reasons why managers cannot often make optimal decisions.

First, considering all possible alternatives to a problem takes a very long time. Real managers rarely have all the time they need.

Second, even if there is plenty of time available, it is difficult, and perhaps impossible, to determine all possible alternatives to any but the most simple problems.

Third, even if all possible alternatives were known, to assemble the information necessary to judge the consequences of each possible action (benefits and costs) would be a remarkable if not impossible task. Real managers never have all the information they would like to have.

How does a manager compromise in decision making? The nature of management is that decisions must be made within a time limit and with information which is always incomplete.

Practicing managers assemble the information they can, then begin searching through the possible solutions to the problem at hand. Frequently, the first satisfactory solution encountered is chosen, although with enough time a manager may be able to pick what seems to be the best of two or three satisfactory solutions. This is "satisficing." This is also a compromise solution based on the realities of practical management.

Compromise in the Contingency Approach.   While the contingency approach may suggest an apparently ideal strategy for the manager to follow, the practical realities of the organization or the manager's skills or the employee's characteristics may prevent the use of the ideal strategy. A compromise strategy must be used instead. Here are just two examples.

A frequent problem with the use of job restructuring as a strategy is that the manager who can clearly see that this strategy is ideal may not have sufficient power within the organization to implement the strategy. A major restructuring of jobs may be impossible. The manager, in his organizational position, may be bound by the beliefs of superiors or by the terms of a union contract and be unable to restructure work flow, and job assignments and descriptions, in the most appropriate way. A compromise must be reached.

Actual inequity in the treatment of employees is another frequent situation in which the manager may not be able to take the most appropriate action. Suppose that a manager has just been assigned to a group of employees who feel unfairly treated and have felt that way for quite a long time. If the remedy for the problem is outside the manager's control (like a basic change in company policy) then the ideal strategy must be bypassed for a compromise solution.

Or, perhaps it may seem that there is some fundamental need deprivation being experienced by the employees about which the manager desires more information. The only way to find out is to ask. It may be, however, that the manager has not yet developed sufficient interviewing and communication skills to obtain the required information from the employees. A recently assigned manager may not yet be sufficiently trusted by the employees to obtain the required information. In such cases, once more, a compromise strategy will be used in place of the more ideal strategy.

FACTORS AFFECTING
THE SUCCESS OF A STRATEGY

Success in the implementation of any of the seven strategies depends on the specific nature of each strategy and on two distinct factors: the manager's attributes, and the employee's characteristics. Depending on these, keep in mind that a manager may need to compromise in selecting a strategy.

In chapters Two through Eight we discussed the unique qualities of each of the seven strategies. What remains is to discuss the manager's own attributes and those subordinate characteristics which must be considered before any of the contingency approach strategies are used.

Leader Power
and Choosing a Strategy

Amitas Etzioni (1961) made an important contribution to the field of leadership by pointing out the importance of a leader's power in taking managerial actions. If managers are to change the job performance of their subordinates, they must have sufficient power to do so. Etzioni observed that a manager can potentially have two somewhat different types of power: position power and personal power.

Figure 9-2. Factors in Selecting a Strategy

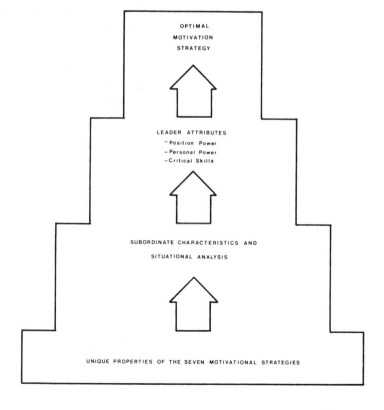

Position power refers to a manager's ability to motivate an employee as a result of the manager's own position within the organization. Almost all managers have been delegated some authority to administer organizational rewards or punishments to subordinates. To the extent that managers have this authority, they have position power. Authority *per se*, to administer organizational rewards and punishments is only a part of what constitutes position power. Clearly the amount and type of rewards, together with the severity of the penalties over which the manager has authority affects the amount of position power a manager has. Managers who have only a few insignificant rewards or penalties at their disposal will necessarily have little position power.

It is important to note that most managers do not have a stable or fixed amount of position power. Rather, this attribute changes over time. As managers demonstrate their ability to use their position power effectively, they are frequently delegated more power. By the same logic, an ineffective manager may lose some or all of the previously delegated position power.

Personal power is just as important and useful as position power but distinct from it. Personal power refers to a manager's ability to change an employee's behavior because the employee likes, trusts, or wants to be accepted by the manager. An employee's motivation to work hard is not always in direct proportion to the amount of organizational rewards received. It may be that he feels friendship or a sense of personal obligation toward the manager. He may desire to maintain the friendship and fulfill the sense of personal obligation. Statements like, "I am doing it because I want to help Bill (the manager) out," or "Mary (the manager) needs my help, so I am going to do it," reflect the concept and the actuality of personal power. Keep in mind that in your everyday relationships outside of work, you do many things for your friends. You do these things even though your friends will not reward you with pay raises, better vacation dates, and so on. Why do you do these things? You do them because you value your friendships with others. You enjoy your friends' company and companionship. A manager, of course, can be a friend too. Certainly there is nothing inconsistent between the role of a manager and that of being a friend. It is not uncommon, in some work settings, for an employee and manager to be extremely close friends.

It is not necessary, of course, that a friendship exist for personal power to exist. A relationship resulting in personal power may be based on respect and a reputation for fairness just as easily. A manager may be only "an acquaintance at work" and still command considerable personal power. Whether there is respect or personal friendship, personal power always rests upon some degree of personal relationship.

Since personal power is built upon a personal relationship, its magnitude is dependent upon the quality of the relationship between both the leader and the subordinate. If either party, for whatever reason, desires to terminate the relationship, either may do so. The magnitude of the leader's personal power depends on mutual consent and commitment. Hence, personal power is only as stable as the relationship between the manager and the subordinate.

The relationship between position power and personal power needs some elaboration. Observe that the amount of position power a manager has often affects the amount of personal power. The opposite, however, is only indirectly true. A manager who distributes lavish organizational rewards to subordinates and does not punish them is likely to be better liked than one who does the opposite. Since managers may be delegated more position power depending on their effectiveness, and effectiveness may be based in part on personal power, the manager who appropriately uses personal power may ultimately receive increased position power.

Observe further that a manager can have high personal power and low position power simultaneously, such as the well-liked supervisor at a shipyard. A manager can also have a high amount of position power but little personal power, for example, the disliked president of a large company. Thus, position power and personal power are really quite distinct even though one's position power may be used to accentuate personal power to some extent and effective use of personal power may lead to increased delegation of position power.

There remains one final observation. If managers are to increase employee productivity, they need either position power or personal power. Without either, a manager is helpless to deal with employees whose performance needs improvement. A manager can be somewhat effective with either position or personal power. To be maximally effective, as will become clear shortly, the manager needs both, and the more of each, the better.

The Leader's Critical Skills
and Choosing a Strategy

The leader's personal and position power affects the likelihood of success for each of the seven motivational strategies. A leader's power, of course, is not the only leadership attribute which determines whether a strategy will be successful. Power is a necessary, but not a sufficient, condition for success.

The success of a motivational strategy is also dependent on the leader's ability to effectively implement a given strategy. Keep in mind that even the best strategy will fail if it is ineptly implemented. Each of the seven strategies requires certain critical management skills if it is to be effective in enhancing employee job performance. While some skills, like communication, have utility across all strategies, some critical skills required differ significantly from one strategy to another. Before implementing any strategy every manager needs to assess his or her own skills and compare them to those required for each strategy. Only a remarkably naive individual would undertake to implement a strategy without the prerequisite skills.

Subordinate Characteristics in Choosing a Strategy

In the above discussion we have indicated three attributes of the manager which must be considered when choosing a strategy within the contingency approach. These are the manager's position power, the manager's personal power, and the manager's critical skills. Now let us look at those characteristics of subordinates which are relevant in choosing a strategy.

If there is one thing which can be unequivocally stated about human behavior, it is that people differ. They differ in terms of their personalities; they differ in terms of their values and goals; they differ in their innate abilities and their developed skills. They also differ in terms of how they respond to a leader's personal and position power. All of these factors, plus many others, affect an employee's behavior and the likelihood that a motivational strategy will be successful. Because people differ in so many ways, no approach to motivation (or to leadership, or to management) can possibly take into account for all or even most of the differences.

While people differ greatly, the types of situations which a manager will encounter are somewhat predictable. From the properties of the seven strategies within the contingency approach, it is possible to derive an approach to situational analysis. Such an analysis will give a structure to the manager's choice of an appropriate strategy. The approach we propose is based on a sequence of questions dealing with the nature of the problem to be solved and the employee characteristics involved in the problem.

We will first present a discussion of each of the strategies and their unique properties. Next, we will discuss some of the questions a manager should consider when choosing a strategy.

THE SEVEN MOTIVATIONAL STRATEGIES: LEADER ATTRIBUTES AND SUBORDINATE CHARACTERISTICS

In the following section we present each of the seven strategies separately. Within the discussion of each strategy the same format is followed:

1. The roles of position power and personal power in implementing the strategy are presented.
2. The critical skills which the manager must possess to be successful are discussed.
3. The characteristics of employees with whom the strategy will be most successful are given.
4. Those employee characteristics associated with a low probability of success are described.

An understanding of this information is essential in selecting an effective motivation strategy and makes clear the notion that a manager must often compromise when making this selection.

Positive Reinforcement and Shaping

This strategy typically requires both position power and personal power. The extent to which each of these is required depends on the reinforcement used. Praise, one of the most typical reinforcers, requires personal power if it is to be most effective. On the other hand, position power is needed if organizational rewards (for example, incentive pay, raises, promotions, recognition awards) are being utilized.

At least four skills are critical to the successful use of this strategy. Since praise is a low cost and often highly effective reinforcer, the manager must develop the competency necessary to give it effectively. More difficult, the manager must be able to detect when praiseworthy job behavior has occurred. To use shaping successfully, two additional skills are required. First, the manager must develop the skill of breaking down work behaviors into very small "pieces of behavior" so that each can be appropriately reinforced or extinguished. As a corollary, the manager must also be able to recognize progress when it occurs and reinforce it in a timely manner.

While almost all employees will respond favorably to receiving praise, it is exceedingly effective with employees who get little, if any, feedback from the job itself, and for those with a high need for recognition. The effectiveness of other rewards in improving an employee's productivity is dependent on the desirability of those rewards to the employee.

This strategy is most obviously not appropriate for workers whose job performance requires immediate change, such as for those who are fighting, stealing, or being insubordinate. In addition, praise is not effective for those few workers who have such a negative self-image that they feel unworthy of praise and, because of their psychopathology, resent it.

Effective Discipline and Punishment

While the manager may use personal power in conjunction with this strategy, it is specifically not recommended. We know of only one method of using personal power which is acceptable with this strategy. An expression of personal displeasure is both appropriate and effective, but *it must refer to the employee's behavior, not to the employee's personality*! Primary weight is given to the use of position power when using discipline and punishment. From the power of position alone, the manager can impersonally administer the negative organizational sanctions which this strategy may require.

In order to effectively use this strategy, managers must be skilled in conducting disciplinary interviews (following the "Hot Stove rules"), determining if a penalty is appropriate in each case, and knowing which penalties will work for a given employee.

Employees who value their jobs and their association with the organization are likely to respond better to discipline and punishment than those who are dissatisfied or nearly ready to terminate. Unhappily, these employees are more often in need of the controls discipline imposes. Personal needs and desires of employees must be threatened or punishment must be felt for the strategy to work well.

The use of punishment, particularly high levels, is specifically *NOT* recommended with violent employees. They may view the punishment as permission for reciprocal action.

Treating Employees Fairly

When an employee feels unfaily treated, the manager may deal effectively with this problem by using position power to eliminate actual inequities. If available position power is not sufficient to remedy the situation, managers may sometimes compensate for inequitable organizational actions by the use of personal power. When employees unjustifiably feel unfairly treated, personal power can be used by managers to clarify, explain, and reason with the employee.

Some personal qualities and skills of the manager are basic to deal successfully with an employee who feels unfairly treated. Chief among these are an empathetic ability to sense the nature and depth of the employee's felt inequity. The manager must be a good listener and able to understand why the employee feels the way he does. Sometimes it is necessary to persuade the employee that the perceived inequity does not exist or is not as great as the employee feels it to be. Here managers must make effective use of their persuasive skills. Instead of trying to force the employee's compliance with their view of the situation, managers need to use the art of persuasion to help the employee see the situation another way.

All employees want to be treated fairly, and their behavior is affected favorably when they are. This strategy is effective with employees who feel unfairly treated, who then request that changes be made by the organization or the manager, and who then see those changes made. It will also work when the employee is rational and amenable to legitimate persuasion. The strategy is not workable, however, with those employees who have an odd sense of what is fair, those employees who *always* feel unfairly treated no matter what, and those who cannot follow or accept a rational explanation.

Satisfying Employee Needs

Employee needs can rarely be satisfied by the organization alone or by the interpersonal skills of the manager alone. However, the combined position power and personal power of the manager are of substantial utility in this strategy. A manager needs position power to satisfy those employee needs which can only be satisfied using appropriate organizational resources. He needs personal power to satisfy other employee needs such as recognition, praise, respect, and approval from the leader.

Since this strategy, in its simplest sense, consists of identifying employee needs and then satisfying them, it follows that the ability to identify employee needs is the primary managerial skill involved. No substitute, in this context, exists for interpersonal sensitivity and the ability to both identify, and identify with, the needs of the employee.

This strategy works effectively whenever the needs of the employee and the need satisfiers which are available within the organization mesh together. Simply put, if rewards and other need satisfiers which an organization and manager can make available to an employee are those which the employee wants, this strategy will be effective. On the other hand, if what the organization and manager offer will not satisfy the employee's needs, this strategy will not be effective in enhancing the employee's job performance.

Some people are never satisfied. Due to pathogenic factors in their background they seem, upon close scrutiny, to be most happy when they are complaining. They seem to enjoy the game of "poor me," and attempts to satisfy the apparent needs of these employees will be both fruitless and frustrating.

Setting Employee Goals

For the goal-setting strategy to be successful, personal power and position power are both needed, but generally in different phases of the effort. Position power is needed for the definitive stating of area or departmental goals. The task of an employee, once area goals have been specified, is to either begin negotiating that portion of the goals which will be the responsibility of the employee (in MBO), or to begin the conversion of assigned goals into measurable objectives and the plan to service those objectives. Since employees are normally unfamiliar with these activities, the personal power of the manager can be helpful in educating employees in how to accomplish these tasks and in facilitating their efforts.

Managers must have the ability to clearly state area goals. They must be able to convert organizational and superordinate area goals into their own area goals. They must be able to facilitate integrative employee goal setting and the translation of these goals into objectives and plans. They need, further, to be skilled at facilitating the selection of acceptable hard goals by employees. A final attribute is the ability to evaluate employee progress toward goals and to facilitate remedial action when objectives are not met.

For the goal-setting strategy to be successful, employees must accept and be committed to the goals pursued. They must be able to learn to specify realistically difficult and measurable objectives. Some employee needs which goal-setting may help to satisfy are a need for less uncertainty, serviced by goal specificity, and a need for control over their own destinies, serviced by participation in goal-setting and the evaluation process. To the extent that employees have these needs, the strategy will succeed.

Those employees who refuse, or are unable, or unwilling to plan their own work are poor candidates for this strategy. This is also true for those who are unable or unwilling to see their jobs in the larger organizational context.

Restructuring Jobs

Successful implementation of this strategy requires sufficient position power to make meaningful changes in the structure of subordinates' jobs. The only exception to this occurs when a manager with insufficient position power is able to "borrow" sufficient position power from appropriate others (peers, superiors, union officials, and so on) in the form of support for the planned changes. While personal power is not absolutely essential to the success of this strategy, managers who lack personal power are likely to meet initial resistance when they suggest that jobs be redesigned. They will be suspected of expanding work, not enriching it.

The primary skill required for successfully implementing this strategy is the ability to creatively determine how a job can be restructured in a way that truly enriches it. Although much has been written to assist the manager in this regard, there is no substitute for this creative skill.

This strategy is usually effective when employees involved in the job restructuring effort have high needs for esteem and self-realization, meaning they want to grow in their jobs, accept greater and greater responsibility, and develop their potential to the fullest. Initial studies suggested that rural Protestants respond most favorably to restructured jobs, but subsequent research indicates that employees wanting enriched, meaningful, responsible jobs exist in all locations and come from all backgrounds.

Employees who like their present job as it is, who do not trust management, and who see the attempt at job enrichment as an attempt at job enlargement will respond least favorably to job restructuring. Where labor unions are involved, the union leadership often has a significant impact on employee attitudes toward job restructuring.

Basing Rewards on Job Performance

This strategy requires that a manager have sufficient position power to give institutional rewards to employees who perform well and to withhold rewards from employees whose job performance is unsatisfactory. Personal power is also involved here since it is the promise of reward (expectation), not the reward itself which precedes performance. The employee must trust that the system of rewards for performance will be implemented, and this trust is attached to the manager.

Three managerial skills are necessary for this strategy. First, the manager must be able to discriminate among poor, good, and excellent job performance. Second, the manager must be adept at giving rewards in a way that encourages all employees to improve their job performance or to maintain a high level of performance. Finally, the manager must have the ability to accomplish these tasks while preserving the feeling among employees that they are being treated fairly.

Clearly, the high achievers in the organization will profit most from this strategy and will respond most favorably to it. In addition, the strategy will be successful with those employees of medium and even low levels of skill who are capable of improving their performance and, in addition, want to attain the rewards given to high performers.

Those of low ability who are unable or unwilling to improve their job performance and those who do not desire the rewards offered by the organization for high performance will not respond well to this strategy. This is also true for those who persist in believing the strategy is inequitable. Poor management skills in implementation may make this latter response widespread.

SITUATIONAL ANALYSIS

Here are some practical questions which the manager should consider when choosing a strategy.

"How fast do you require results?"

This is a question concerned more with the nature and severity of the problem than with speed. When an employee is engaged in *behavior at work which is intolerable* and must be immediately dealt with, the discipline and punishment strategy should be considered first. Fortunately, most of the employee problems with which managers routinely deal do not demand immediate solutions. There is, unhappily, a class of employee behaviors which absolutely require the most prompt attention. We refer to theft, violence, sabotage, and other actions which endanger safety, health, continued operations, and sometimes lives.

If an employee working at a cash register is stealing from the till, this requires immediate remedial action. If habitual shortages occur, it may be a matter of ignorance or malice. If ignorance is the problem, inform the employee of what is required and its importance. This may be done during a disciplinary interview. If the problem stems from malice, consider discipline and punishment. As a practical matter, you should check out the possibility that the malicious behavior is due to a perception of gross inequity.

Financial damage to the organization is usually far easier to recover from than the damage to morale, personal loss, or public distrust engendered by gross negligence. When an employee engages in unsafe work practices, it may endanger the employee's life, the health of others, property, and sometimes the goodwill and trust of the public. Unsafe work practices rank alongside outright theft and sabotage as behaviors requiring immediate, decisive, and unambiguous response by the manager.

When the required managerial response need not be immediate for the reasons covered above, another question to consider is:

"Does the employee have the necessary skills?"

If you determine that needed skills are lacking, the solution is to provide for their acquisition. If the deficit is minimal, it may be sufficient to just inform the employee of what is expected and the correct procedure to be used. In more complex cases of skill deficit, those where the learning required cannot be covered in a simple discussion, a more structured approach will be indicated.

In such a case, the manager may engage in a systematic program of shaping or positive reinforcement or both. Shaping is appropriate when the skills of the employee are near to what is desired or when new behaviors must be "constructed" from elements of existing behaviors. Positive reinforcement is then used to maintain the appropriate work behaviors.

As an alternative to positive reinforcement and shaping, the manager should not ignore the opportunities for formal training of employees in the required skills. Many large organizations and, to a degree, many smaller companies offer such training internally or by arrangement with outside sources.

If long-term as opposed to immediate action is advisable and if the employee has the required skills for the expected level of performance, another question to consider is:

"Are the employee's feelings about the job the problem?"

This is a very subtle question which has far more to do with employee perception and feelings than with either objective or obvious reality.

We suggest that there are two basic loci of bad feelings about work. These are perceived inequity, and unmet employee needs.

Inequity, whether real, or perceived but not actual, is the more serious condition. This is because employees will always take steps to regain equity. Unfortunately, nearly all unilateral attempts to regain equity which are open to the employee (unaided by the manager) are dysfunctional for the organization. Among the most severe is sabotage. A highly simplistic explanation for this is that under extreme levels of felt inequity the employee feels so personally injured that the only "justice" is to just as seriously injure the organization. Hopefully, the manager will identify this condition before the extreme situation is reached. Dealing with inequity directly is a preventive rather than remedial action. Do not feel that you have failed as a manager just because you detect an employee who feels unfairly treated. Most of the time this employee is simply misinformed.

Needs which are felt to be unmet are closely allied to the question of inequity, yet not so immediately serious in their potential. Unmet needs typically result in a restriction of productivity in the worst case. An employee may feel a sense of deprivation whenever personal needs are salient but have not been met by the organization. Sometimes this is unrealistic because the unmet needs may be no legitimate affair of the organization. Among these may be conflict with the spouse or family. They may be needs which the organization cannot directly meet, such as feelings of respect and value. These latter needs may be met only through interpersonal exchange with peers and the manager within the organization, and a similar manner outside the organization. It is the role of the manager to meet as many of the reasonable and appropriate needs of the employee as is consistent with the good of the organization.

If the employee's problem at work is not based on the employee's feelings, then another question may arise:

"Does the employee understand the job's purpose?"

Why am I working? How does what I do fit in with what my coworkers are doing? If I do well, so what? If I do poorly, who will it affect and how?

This question deals with more than basic information about how to do the job and what is expected. It is remarkable that so few employees have a clear idea of what their jobs are all about in the organizational context. It is also remarkable that workers see so little of how what they do on the job affects others. It is not uncommon for employees to be uncertain about what is expected of them and why it is expected.

A frequently workable remedy for a lack of understanding about what is required for good performance is the strategy of setting employee goals. Only a part of the strategy consists of specifying clear goals for or with employees. The strategy continues beyond goals which are merely clear to suggest that challenging goals will still further enhance the level of performance by defining what is expected as requiring some improvement. Once clear, challenging goals are set, feedback about how the employee is progressing toward the goal should be added. This feedback allows the employee to assess progress toward the goal while still in the midst of working toward that goal. If it seems that the expected success is being achieved, then this confirmation itself reinforces the effective work behaviors. If the expected progress toward the goal is not being made, then there is the opportunity for remedial planning. Methods and procedures may be changed so that progress toward the goal may be resumed. Clearly absence of feedback or delay of feedback until the total amount of work is completed make interim corrections impossible. While the nature of some jobs is such that the work itself provides the needed feedback, this is not always the case. For jobs which do not innately supply feedback, the manager must arrange for the transmission of feedback information.

"Does the employee want more from the job?"

There are two ways employees can get rewards from a job. These are:

1. Intrinsically (satisfaction, accomplishment, and so on.)
2. Extrinsically (pay, benefits, and so on.)

A reward is said to be *intrinsic* if it comes from the job itself. A reward is said to be *extrinsic* if it comes from outside the job. There are two strategies in the contingency approach which are recommended for use when employees want to get more from the job.

To increase intrinsic rewards the strategy of restructuring jobs is not only the best, but to our knowledge, the only applied strategy designed to produce this effect.

To increase extrinsic rewards the strategy of basing rewards on job performance shows the manager how to supply desirable rewards to employees in addition to any intrinsic rewards the job itself may provide. Further, it demonstrates how the employee's receipt of the extrinsic rewards may be made contingent upon a high level of job performance.

SELECTING THE STRATEGY:
A SUMMARY

The contingency approach to improving employee productivity argues that a manager often needs to compromise in selecting a motivational strategy. The theoretically ideal approach may, in fact, be practically undesirable or impossible. More specifically, the approach states that the success of a strategy is contingent upon three major factors:

1. The particular properties of each of the seven motivational strategies.
2. The leader's power (position and personal) and critical skills.
3. The characteristics of the subordinates.

When choosing a motivational strategy, the manager will want to consider each of the above carefully.

There is an alternative to the selection of a single motivational strategy which has been mentioned in previous chapters, but which deserves to be stressed here. It is that a manager is often wise to use a combination of the seven strategies. Major aspects of many strategies can be combined quite easily and often quite effectively. To illustrate, parts of the strategy (treating employees fairly) can be readily combined with all of the other six approaches. In fact, doing so typically enhances the effectiveness of these other strategies. The strategy of using penalties and discipline is frequently used in combination with that of basing rewards on job performance. Some of the major aspects of positive reinforcement and shaping are frequently combined with the goal-setting approach. In sum, parts of each of the strategies can and should be used in combination with parts of all of the other strategies. This point cannot be stressed enough. Every manager should consider utilizing aspects of several, even all, of the seven approaches. This should be considered even though the resulting system may strike one as a hodgepodge approach, one quite dissimilar to the seven presented in this text. Keep in mind that most organizations already mix together parts of at least two of these seven strategies, and many times the result is quite effective.

CONCLUSION

All organizations are vitally concerned with productivity. Employee productivity is the necessary groundwork upon which all organizational productivity must rest. This book has focused exclusively on productivity. When we discuss a manager's power, we do so to examine the ways in which the manager's power may be used to enhance productivity. When we discuss a manager's personal skills, we do this because the productivity of the employees supervised by the manager is heavily influenced by those skills. When we speak of employees with differing characteristics, we are examining those characteristics which relate to the productivity of the employee. When we suggest that a strategy in the contingency approach might work for a manager, we always mean that it might work as judged by an increase in productivity after the implementation of the strategy.

Productivity is the only reason for the existence of a manager. Managers are usually nonproductive labor, at least in the sense of direct production of goods or services. Managers integrate the work of many employees into a total productivity effort that must result in a net productivity greater than the simple sum of the individual productivities. If this is not the case, if the work group produces no more with the manager than without a manager, the manager is only a dead weight being carried on the backs of the employees. Managers increase productivity only indirectly, by aiding employees to produce more.

If managers are to increase the productivity of employees, they need an approach to guide their actions. They need a way of thinking about employee motivation; they need a roadmap for solving problems. The contingency approach discussed in this book provides one such framework. What remains is for the reader to make use of it.

Index

Index

Monitoring future performance, 15, 39, 58, 64, 149 (*see also* Strategy guides)
Motivation, 202
    and job performance, 3
    motive vs., 202–3
    needs and, 114–19, 122
Motivators, 168–69
Music and employee need satisfaction, 113–14

N

Natural work units, 162–63, 182
Needs (*see* Satisfying employee needs)
Nepotism, 70–71, 91 (*see also* Fair treatment)
Nixon, Richard M., 57

O

Objectives (*see* Management by Objectives)
Office space, allocation of, 74–75
Oldham, G. R., 165 (*see also* Hackman-Oldham model)
Opinion Research Corporation, 192
Organizational goals, 143–47
Outcome/input in equity theory, 82–86
Outplacement, 15
Output, definition of, 2

P

Patten, Thomas, H., Jr., 193–94
Peace Corps, 122
Penalties (*see also* Discipline and punishment)
    definition of, 44, 46–47, 50–51
    "Hot Stove Rules" and, 52–55, 59–61, 63, 65–67
    progressive, 47–49
    Thorndike's "Law of Effect" and, 52–53, 66
Performance:
    ability-motivation equation and, 3
    actual vs. desired, 7–9, 12–13, 15, 24–25
    baseline, recording of, 30
    basing rewards on (*see* Rewards based on performance)
    feedback on, 21–22
    future (*see* Monitoring future performance)

Performance audit, 21
Personal power, 220–21
Phased retirement, 107–8
Physiological needs, 116–18
Pliny the Younger, 29
Porter, L. W., 190–91
Position power, 220–22
Positive reinforcement, 3–4, 17–42, 215, 223–24
    definition of, 19–20, 45
    Emery Air Freight studies on, 21–24
    examples of use of, 17–19, 21–24
    implementation of, 34–39
        strategy guide (chart), 35
    rationale of, 28–39
        ethical criticisms, 33
        Skinner's contributions, 28, 29–32
        survey of research results, 32–33
        Thorndike's "Law of Effect," 28–29
    schedules in (*see* Reinforcement schedules)
"Practical Significance of Locke's Theory of Goal Setting, The" (Latham and Baldes), 132–33
Praise, merit-based, 196
Prien, E., 191
Principles of Scientific Management, The (Taylor), 156–57
Probability, 198–99
Progressive penalty system, 47–49
Prudential Life Insurance, 106
Psychological Corporation, 102
Punishment (*see also* Discipline and punishment)
    definition of, 44–47, 50
    fear of, 56–58
Purdy, K. (*see* Hackman-Oldham model)

Q

Questionnaires, 102–4, 120–22

R

Reactive questions, 121
Redesigning jobs (*see* Restructuring jobs)
Reinforcement (*see* Positive reinforcement; Reinforcement schedules; Shaping)
Reinforcement schedules (*see also* Positive reinforcement)
    definition of, 19–21
    example of use of, 17–18, 23, 24